I WILL HOLD

I WILL HOLD

THE STORY OF USMC LEGEND CLIFTON B. CATES,
FROM BELLEAU WOOD TO VICTORY IN THE GREAT WAR

JAMES CARL NELSON

CALIBER

New York

CALIBER
Published by Berkley
An imprint of Penguin Random House LLC
375 Hudson Street, New York, New York 10014

Map by David Lindroth

Library of Congress Cataloging-in-Publication Data

Names: Nelson, James Carl, author.
Title: I will hold: the story of USMC Legend Clifton B. Cates, from Belleau Wood to victory
in the Great War/James Carl Nelson.
Other titles: USMC Legend Clifton B. Cates, from Belleau Wood to victory in the Great War
Description: New York, New York: New American Library, an imprint of Penguin Random
House LLC, [2016]
Identifiers: LCCN 2016012586 | ISBN 9780425281482 (hardback) | ISBN 9780698196735 (ebook)
Subjects: LCSH: Cates, Clifton B. (Clifton Bledsoe), 1893–1970. | Belleau Wood, Battle of,
France, 1918. | United States. Marine Corps. Marine Regiment, 6th—Biography. | United
States. Marine Corps—Officers—Biography. | Marines—United States—Biography. | United
States. Marine Corps—History—World War, 1914–1918. |
World War, 1914–1918—Campaigns—France.
Classification: LCC D545.B4 N45 2016 | DDC 940.4/34—dc23
LC record available at http://lccn.loc.gov/2016012586

First Edition: September 2016

Printed in the United States of America
1   3   5   7   9   10   8   6   4   2

Jacket art: Battlefield Explosion During World War One by Popperfoto/Getty Images;
Soldier by US Army Signal Corps/The LIFE Picture Collection/Getty Images
Jacket design by Steve Meditz

ACKNOWLEDGMENTS

By November 1918, four million American men were in uniform, with some two million of them in France when the armistice was declared. This is a book about just one of those men: an overlooked individual named Clifton Bledsoe Cates who made his mark on the battlefield again and again, and whose service, while renowned within the halls of the Marine Corps, has been mostly relegated to being a footnote in the larger picture of the war.

I Will Hold seeks at its base to illuminate the contributions Cates made toward "saving the world for democracy" in the violent latter half of 1918—and to some degree the further contributions he made at Guadalcanal, Tinian, and Iwo Jima during World War II, and as presiding Marine Corps commandant when the Korean War erupted in 1950.

It was in the Great War that he endured unending frontline combat, and it was in it that he gained the nickname Lucky Cates. It was a well-deserved moniker, as we shall see, and one Cates never minded, saying, "I'd rather be lucky than good-looking."

Many thanks are due to those who helped me in researching the life and times of this ultimate marine, first and foremost John Lyles and Gregory Cina at the Library of the Marine Corps, and Fred Allison and Kara Newcomer at the USMC History Division.

Thanks as well to Jay Hilbish, Clifton Cates's grandson, and Ann Prothro, Cates's grandniece, both of whom graciously provided reminiscences about their famous relative and, in Jay's case, permission to use his grandfather's account of his 1st Marine Regiment's time on Guadalcanal.

As well, Paul Grasmehr, reference coordinator at the Pritzker Military Museum and Library in Chicago, provided me access to several rare books needed for my enterprise. Jeffrey Kozak, archivist and assistant librarian at the George C. Marshall Foundation, was most helpful, as was Dr. Winifred Smith, former president of the Lake County Tennessee Historical Society.

I'd also like to thank Lori Berdak Miller for her help in obtaining documents from the National Personnel Records Center in St. Louis. As well, Rebecca Livingston of Archivespro was of great assistance in pulling needed records and photos from the U.S. National Archives in Washington, DC, and College Park, Maryland.

Thanks also to Lucy Chubb at the Army Heritage Center Foundation, and Kathy Nichols, senior library specialist in the Archives and Special Collections at Western Illinois University.

And of course, last but far from least, I want to thank my agent, James D. Hornfischer, for inspiring the idea for *I Will Hold*, and my editor at Penguin, Thomas Colgan, for his great skills and encouragement.

James Carl Nelson
April 2016

CONTENTS

OCTOBER 3, 1918   1

LUCKY   4

WHAT IS A MARINE, PART ONE   14

PRISON ISLAND   23

SWACKED   37

A NEW DANCE   44

"LA GUERRE EST FINIE"   58

"DO YOU WANT TO LIVE FOREVER?"   69

BOCHES   77

INTO THE WOOD   84

BOURESCHES   92

BESIEGED   103

HELLWOOD   114

"MY COMPANY IS DEFUNCT"   123

"VIVE LES MARINES!"   135

A BON FIGHT   144

A BAD DREAM   159

DEAD MEN   175

WELL AND SANE   188

MOSELLE   192

NO MAN'S LAND   203

THE HILL   216

"RAUS MITTEN!"   228

ZOMBIES   241

THE VALLEY OF DEATH   252

BEGINNING OF THE END   260

TO THE RIVER   269

ELEVENTH DAY   277

PRETTY WELL SHOT   288

WHAT IS A MARINE, PART TWO   299

HE LIKED THE WORK   307

JULY 29, 1943   318

Bibliography   321

Sources   325

Index   333

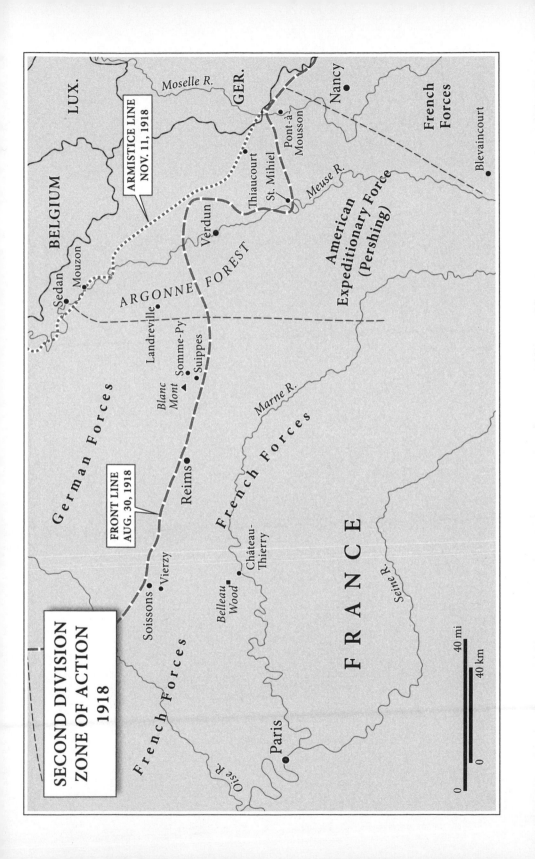

SECOND DIVISION
ZONE OF ACTION
1918

ARMISTICE LINE
NOV. 11, 1918

FRONT LINE
AUG. 30, 1918

LUX.

BELGIUM

GER.

Moselle R.

Nancy

French
Forces

Pont-à-
Mousson

Thiaucourt

St. Mihiel

Blevaincourt

Meuse R.

Verdun

American
Expeditionary Force
(Pershing)

Sedan

Mouzon

ARGONNE FOREST

Landreville

Somme-Py

Suippes

Blanc
Mont

German Forces

Marne R.

Reims

French Forces

Vierzy

Château-
Thierry

Soissons

Belleau
Wood

FRANCE

Seine R.

French Forces

Oise R.

Paris

40 mi

40 km

0

0

I WILL HOLD

OCTOBER 3, 1918

HE HAS ALREADY spent one night sleeping almost atop the bodies of dead men, French and German, dead for days and weeks and thankfully unseen now in the blackness, though there was no mistaking their odious, putrid smell. And so, when the whistles shrilly pierce the early-morning air, it is something of a relief to be up and off, even in the first rays of daylight, at least until he and his men are greeted rudely by the whistling of Minenwerfers and the *zip-zip-zip* of machine-gun bullets and, soon enough, the familiar, dull slapping sound of metal encountering flesh and bone, the accordant screams of the wounded, and the muffled coughing of those already dying.

Quickly out of the trench and up the hill, he pushes past blasted dugouts and through and over the wire, red with rust after four long years of war but still a prickly impediment to reaching the crest. Before too long he is almost to the top, almost there, through the wafting gray smoke and the squeezing *pup-pup-pup* of the machine guns and through the long brown grass and the shell holes pocking the hill like vacant black eyes and past the blue-green bodies of the dead, marine and German, and still he pushes on, almost laughing, almost floating from the sheer bloody wonder of it all; keep going, keep going, keep going. . . .

Artillery rounds plop at random here and there, sending black geysers of soil high into the air, and more men fall; keep going, keep going past deep redoubts and blasted, crumbling trench lines in which dead men lie splayed in their deathly innocence, and through the wafting acrid black smoke that stings the eyes; keep going.

Men scream; men die. He finds himself almost laughing. It is not so horrible to him, not so bad; he has done something like this before, at Belleau Wood and Soissons, and he knows it is something he will do yet again before this war is done.

His right hand oozes sweat, coursing slippery and wet down the handle of his .45, and more streams from his brow under his deeply dented helmet; a shadow at his side tumbles forward and lies still; keep going, keep going.

Almost at the top, he sees one of them racing away. He follows instinctively at a run and fires, almost laughing. Marines all along the line now reach the main trench and begin the work of the bayonet, or swing their rifles like baseball bats, or fall on the enemy with fists and knives, even, if that is what it takes.

A German officer suddenly appears from the dank recesses of a dugout. They eye each other, just for a split moment and pistol to pistol, as if they were gunslingers on the streets of old Laredo, each waiting for the other to draw. Suddenly, the German fires; he fires back. The German tumbles into his hole, a look of surprised horror on his face and a deep red stain spreading over his heart.

Keep going.

And as he does, he takes it all in, the chaos and the shouts and the shots and the smoke and the chattering guns and the wails of the wounded. He feels somehow impervious, almost immortal, as he moves now along the hilltop trench, tossing grenades and shooting until the brow of the massif is finally taken, and long lines of the enemy slouch down the hill even as ever more marines come up.

It is almost comical sometimes, he thinks; this war-making, these bloody, glorious, horrible, life-taking battles sometimes almost make him laugh.

God, he loves this war.

God, he loves this awful, tragic, soul-grinding, terrible, wasting, wonderful war.

LUCKY

FASTER, GODDAMNIT, FASTER!

Bleak figures bundled against the snow and leaning forward into the sleety wind, blanketed horses pulling the wagons of street vendors, gnarled immigrants wrapped in blankets and shoveling ice-clogged sidewalks, gaggles of truants heaving snowballs from tenement rooftops crisscrossed with a cat's cradle of wires; his taxi passed all of these things on the morning of January 22, 1918, speeding from Herald Square for the harbor, where the transport, the USS *Henderson*, either was, or was not, waiting at anchor.

And as the taxi raced on, twenty-four-year-old Clifton Bledsoe Cates fretted in the back, chain-smoking furiously and ignoring all of these varied sights of Lower Manhattan, his mind spinning gloomily as it obsessed on one overriding concern: that his career in the United States Marine Corps had died even as it was aborning, and he was finished.

His ship had been slated to leave port more than an hour beforehand, and he knew if he wasn't on board when it sailed, he'd be court-martialed for desertion.

"There is no question about it," he would recall with a comfortable laugh years later.

The old *Henderson*, carrying the 2nd Battalion of the 6th Regiment of marines, had sailed from Philadelphia on January 20. The next day it heaved to in New York Harbor, and the officers on board were allowed shore leave—with the understanding they would be back on board by eight a.m. So Cates headed to shore with his mates for the bright lights of the city. After some hours of carousing, he decided at two a.m. he'd had enough.

A heavy snow caressed the dark night in rippling currents, blanketing the streets, and there wasn't a taxi in sight. So he took a room at the grand McAlpin Hotel at Broadway and West Thirty-fourth Street instead, and left instructions with the night clerk to awaken him at six a.m.

He crawled into bed, not even bothering to take off his uniform.

When he awoke, it was well past nine a.m.

"I was frantic," he would recall.

He raced downstairs to the lobby and paused only long enough to colorfully tell the hapless clerk some of what he thought of him, and then hurried out of the hotel, quickly hailed a cab, and was soon speeding toward the docks, hoping against hope that the *Henderson* would be there, hoping against hope that this new life he was learning to love hadn't ended abruptly on the streets of New York on this cold and miserable morning, hoping that he could rejoin his men before they sailed into a world war and endure with them whatever was to come in the trenches that split France like a heaving sidewalk crack.

Faster, he told the hack. *Faster . . .*

Certainly more veterans would come out of World War I more famous than Clifton Bledsoe Cates, some of them becoming heroes for great exploits performed over the course of a minute, ten minutes, or a few hours. Some of their names would spill from the history pages in perpetuity: Alvin C. York, Cates's fellow Tennessean, was of course the most famous of these, and Sam Woodfill would have his measure of fame, as would Michael "Mad Dog" Ellis, wildcat marine John Joseph Kelly, Charles Whittlesey of "Lost Battalion" notoriety, and many others.

Clifton Bledsoe Cates was not destined to share as bright a spot-light. His acclaim, such as it was, came not for one single act—single-handedly capturing one hundred prisoners, bravely knocking out twelve machine guns with but a bayonet and a hand grenade—but for his body of work in World War I.

He would be knocked out, knocked down, gassed, nicked, pinged and dinged numerous times, and still rise to lead men; he would by force of example show men what they could do, what they needed to do; his bravery, his pluck, his sheer bursts of illuminating optimism would shine daily in the worst of circumstances during the second half of 1918, from Belleau Wood to Soissons to Blanc Mont and, finally, to the last days in the Meuse-Argonne; and it would be no coincidence that his unit—the 96th Company, 6th Marine Regiment—would suf-fer more casualties than any other American company in the Great War.

Cates did his work quietly, with almost unearthly confidence and a dash of derring-do; ordered forward over and over again, he would lead his company into the thickest of battles, and against all odds, and though his men fell dead and wounded all around him, he would emerge safe and alive and sometimes even laughing, as if protected by some divine providence.

Other marines could only shake their heads in wonder at him.

Cliff Cates, they all said. *The luckiest man in the Great War.*

He would become one of the most famous of United States ma-rines, a Corps legend, and, on his way to becoming the nineteenth commandant of the Marine Corps in 1948, he would lead a platoon, then a company, then a regiment, and, finally, a division, into battle.

It was a somewhat unlikely destiny, perhaps, considering his origins were pastoral rather than martial to much degree. It had been expected that young Cliff Cates, born to some wealth at a long-held family cot-ton farm known as Cates Landing, Tennessee, at a spot where the broad Mississippi River dips south and then violently north again as it meanders toward the onetime earthquake epicenter at New Madrid,

Missouri, would someday become a yeoman farmer and businessman like his father and grandfather, or an attorney, handling civil cases instead of ammunition boxes, under a shingle to be hung in Memphis, Knoxville, or maybe Nashville.

But as with some of the nation's other notable military commanders who came from the soil—Clarence Huebner comes to mind, as do Dwight Eisenhower and Ulysses S. Grant—Cates would find his calling as a lifer in the United States military. A world war that had not even been a shadow as Cliff gamboled among the fields and along the riverbanks of the Mississippi as a boy would provide the setting for a permanent career change, and provide as well the battlefields on which he would display the utter fearlessness and coolheadedness that would make him a Marine Corps legend.

Anderson Cates, his grandfather, had been born in North Carolina, but, like many restless souls of the time, meandered west, arriving in northwest Tennessee in 1836 with but two dollars to his name. He went to work as an overseer on a local plantation, and, by the late 1840s, had saved enough to purchase the riverfront acreage that would come to be known as Cates Landing.

There, the pioneer Anderson Cates finally put down roots, taking a wife, Alice Jane Emily Peacock, in August 1848; she soon died, and he remarried, this time to Susan Box, and together they farmed and produced nine children between 1851 and 1868.

A biography would note that while Mr. Cates was a Methodist, he was also "a Democrat"—among whose ranks were, as the historian James McPherson would put it, "yeoman farmers in the upcountry or backcountry who disliked city slickers, merchants, banks, Yankees, or anybody who might interfere with their freedom to live as they pleased."

Anderson Cates's fifth child, Willis Jones Cates, was born in 1860. He would spend his life improving on and prospering from his father's hard work, operating three cotton gins, farming the land, overseeing a general store at the landing, and also serving on the board of directors of the Farmers & Merchants Bank in Tiptonville, ten miles south.

Willis took as his wife a local girl from a prominent family—Martha "Mattie" Darnall Bledsoe, whose maternal grandfather, Henry McKinney Darnall, at the age of thirty in 1838, had been made captain of the local militia. From then on he was known in accordance with peculiar Southern tradition as "the General," despite declining a commission with the Rebs, and despite being just one of only two men in Obion County to vote against Secession.

With one hand on the plow and another on a ledger, Willis was regarded as one of Lake County's most stolid citizens. "While not hasty in reaching a conclusion, his mind when once made up was unchangeable," his obituary in the local paper would read. "Modest and retiring of disposition and slow to put himself forward, nevertheless he possessed that force of character and strength of purpose that enabled him to face every situation squarely and to do 'justice though the heavens fall.'"

The first of two children born to Willis and Mattie Cates—a daughter, Katherine, would arrive in 1896—Clifton Bledsoe Cates was born at the family's riverbank home on August 31, 1893. As he grew, his cherubic face and soft features belied an inner strength developed through a childhood that rivaled that of Tom Sawyer, as his parents allowed young Cliff Cates plenty of room to roam, and plenty of time to explore the woods and the waters of the Mississippi, in which six-foot-long catfish still lolled at the bottom, and where the canebrakes and old-growth forests spreading east and south were still rife with targets.

Davy Crockett years before had hunted the same land, and on one single day, it was said, had killed twenty-five black bears within the borders of Obion County. Wild hogs, leftovers from Hernando de Soto's early explorations of the area, still posed a threat to a young boy, and water moccasins and the remaining bears and other fauna also taught any youngster wandering the woods to keep his wits about him at all times—or suffer the consequences.

Cliff Cates roved, he hunted, he trapped, he fished the river like a latter-day Huck Finn, and he learned how to work a shotgun—with dubious early results. On one occasion, he nearly blew his head off when he placed his weapon on a bottom fence post and it discharged upward, singeing his very eyebrows. On another, he endured a whipping at the hand of Willis Cates after shooting the prized family hog that he may have mistaken for the wild variety.

Attending first a country schoolhouse, he was bright but not particularly studious. His mind and body often roamed from his reading and recitations and mathematics to the lures of the nearby wilderness and Reelfoot Lake, a favorite of his uncles Council and Reuben. Though they farmed nearby, each year they spent a month drifting the lake's shallow waters, trapping and hunting and fishing. They also consorted with a rough-and-ready brand of outdoorsmen who were "a law unto themselves," as a newspaper story from 1893 would have it.

The lure of the wilderness and his testing of himself within it would remain constant themes in Cliff Cates's life. Combat, at heart, is a test of one's courage, will, and stamina—and the battlefield itself is a wilderness of dangers known and unseen, a place where heightened senses, learned responses, and sometimes plain old instinct could be the difference between life and death.

The wilderness and its tests imbued in the young Cliff Cates a lifelong self-confidence, and an independent streak that on a few occasions was rubbed raw against the strict discipline of the military. But his carefree ramblings, his life among the Indians, as it were, also imbued in him a certain cocksureness, while his family's modest wealth, and his parents' preaching, instilled in him a generosity of spirit and—perhaps oxymoronically for a Corps lifer—a compassion that would help him quickly endear himself to the men who followed him into hell on many a battlefield.

While the roving and exploring only hardened his body for the grueling ordeals that a war would shortly bring him as a young man, Cliff's parents no doubt fretted over other traits he would exhibit through his life. He loved a prank, he loved a joke, he loved to swear and gamble, and eventually he would learn to love a drink, not to mention a smoke. He displayed a certain laconic, devil-may-care approach to the world that would confound his professors and betters.

Though not rebellious, from an early age he displayed a certain savoir faire that was a tad out of step with the more staid and—yes—aristocratic conceits of his parents. Willis and Mattie would try to wash some of the Huckleberry Finn out of the once and future heir to Cates Landing by sending him at the age of twelve to far-off Nashville to attend the Branham & Hughes School for Boys, and thence to the Missouri Military Academy across the Mississippi River in Mexico, Missouri.

There, his instructors furthered the task of, in effect, trying to wipe that silly smirk off Cliff's face, and instilling into his studies some needed discipline. The medicine eventually took, at least to some degree, as Cliff finally applied himself in the classroom, and on the parade ground.

"Up to then I had never done much studying and work," Cates would later concede. "I went up there with my mind made up to settle down and work hard. I went in for everything, and I did make good."

After graduating from the academy, Cates in 1912 enrolled at the University of Tennessee in Knoxville. Having learned some discipline of mind as well as body, he indulged the latter with baseball, basketball, and football, taking the underappreciated position of guard on the Volunteers' team—long before helmets were de rigueur.

Playing football brought his love for the test of battle quickly to the fore. "Cliff was the lightest of the guards, but by all odds the most enthusiastic and hardest-fighting lineman on the squad," one of his teammates would remember. "I do not believe he started a single game, but he played a lot. While playing and practicing, his face was always lit up like that of a small boy with his first football."

But it remained difficult for Cliff Cates to sit still in a classroom.

Classmates would recall that "Clifton Cates loved his fun, and it some-times appeared he didn't want his studies to interfere," as one newspaper would recount years later; in fact, he cut so many classes at Tennessee that one of his instructors once gave him a sweeping mock reintroduc-tion to the class when he reappeared after a long absence.

A newfound appreciation for the fair sex may have run interference with his schoolwork; the still easygoing, laconic Cates had developed an easy way with *les femmes*, and his letters from the time are peppered with the names of numerous belles—among them Elizabeth Rose, Helen Petway, Ruth Stiles, Mildred Sisson, Joan Rayner, Margaret Devareaux, and Phoebe Walker.

While on summer breaks from the university, he worked the land and docks around Cates Landing, and also tended to the beacon that at night guided riverboats through the perilous New Madrid bend of the Mississippi. During the course of one summer, he invited a good friend, his fellow Vols' athlete and future Philadelphia Phillies man-ager, Tommy "Doc" Prothro, to stop by Cates Landing while Thomp-son was working as a purser on one of his own grandfather's riverboats. Prothro stayed in one of the Cates guesthouses, and it wasn't long before Prothro and Cliff's eighteen-year-old sister, Katherine, became an item; they would wed in October 1917.

Despite his ways with and interest in the ladies, no such matrimo-nial urges pestered Cliff. When his schooling at Tennessee ended in the spring of 1916, he instead returned home with a law degree to help his mother, Martha, tend the farm and cotton gins, his father having passed from cancer at the age of just fifty-two on June 20, 1912.

He would pine on occasion for his father and fret over his mother's being left alone on the homestead after his sister married, but he had a life to live, too, and was making plans for a career in law—at exactly the same time as the United States was stumbling toward war.

A world war had been playing out in bloody fashion since August 1914, but there's little evidence that Cates had paid much heed. Like many in the United States, he was content to keep the war Over There, to let decrepit nations slug it out with one another while millions bled and died.

Given his training at the military academy, he may have had the odd military interest in the conflict, strategy-wise; certainly he'd read of Washington's struggles at Valley Forge and victory at Saratoga, Lee's brilliance and Jackson's daring at Chancellorsville, of the Greeks at Thermopylae and Wellington at Waterloo. But if Cliff Cates had any military ambitions at that point, he left no record, and it wasn't until early 1917, when events began spiraling toward a U.S. declaration, that he, like many other young men of the time, seemed to even sit up and take notice.

That February, Germany, the natural enemy should the Anglophile United States enter the fray, increased its campaign of submarine warfare, and began sending U.S. ships carrying materiel for the Allies to the bottom of the Atlantic. Then it was revealed that Germany, too, had inveigled to have Mexico stir things up on the U.S. border should the United States declare war, promising to Mexico the return of California, New Mexico, Arizona, and Texas should the Germans come out victorious.

The insidious nature of the latter revelation stunned and angered a nation that prior to this had regarded the European conflict with little more than passing interest. It was then that men such as Cliff Cates took the world more seriously, and began to think about the eventuality of their country entering the conflict, and what their part, if any, might be in that.

And when war was finally declared on Germany by the U.S. Congress on April 6, 1917, the world came to the doorstep of men like Cliff Cates, men who had until then led a certain sheltered life, and were certainly privileged in his case, considering that at the time just one in thirty U.S. men aged eighteen to twenty-four was enrolled in the nation's colleges and universities.

When the United States entered the world war, Cliff was back in leafy, genteel Knoxville studying to take the state bar exam and preparing to begin a quiet and prosperous life as a lawyer. He had by then accepted that his fate was to lead his clients through the maze of the courts; but the world outside Cates Landing and Knoxville had finally piqued his interest, and he had begun to consider entering the service—which one, he did not yet know.

He felt an urge to test himself now as a man, as the woods and fields around Cates Landing had tested him as a boy; and like thousands and thousands of young American men, he felt the need to do the right thing and be a part of history—no matter how terrible the history that was playing itself out in the grimy and bloody trenches of the western front.

Still undecided over what to do, one afternoon in April 1917 he ran into John Ayers, whose father, Brown Ayers, was the university president. Cates asked him whether his father had had any calls from the military about students entering the service. His friend said he had not. Cliff told him, "Put my name down if things change."

Two weeks later, he again ran into Ayers, who told him his father had been contacted by the United States Marine Corps, which was seeking candidates to fill eight second lieutenancies in the Marine Reserve.

"Do you want to apply?" Ayers asked.

Cliff looked at him blankly.

The Marine Corps? he asked. *What's that?*

WHAT IS A MARINE, PART ONE

THE FIRST TAXI blew a wheel rounding a corner on that barren and cold New York morning as the future commandant of the U.S. Marine Corps raced to see what his future might hold—a world war or a navy brig—and so he leaped out, paid the hack, and flagged another.

Fog had crept in and buried the streets and obscured the city's buildings, making driving hazardous, dangerous. But he didn't care.

To the docks! he told the driver.

Faster!

Finally, the hack slammed to a stop at the harbor's edge, and a lone figure in uniform jumped out and raced to the edge of the pier. The harbor was a miasma of mist and sleet, and he couldn't tell if the USS *Henderson* was still at anchor.

Crestfallen, Cliff Cates tried to resign himself to his fate, which did not look to be pleasant.

Here's one bird who will be held as a deserter, he thought.

At last, a British ship went by, and he asked for a lift out beyond the soup. After plying the waters for some time, he looked up and saw "the old *Henderson.*"

Clifton Bledsoe Cates managed to somehow slip aboard unnoticed, and he did not reveal his close brush until many years later. "I would have been court-martialed for desertion if the *Henderson* had sailed on time," he would say. "There is no question about it."

It would be several more days, in fact, before the ship would exit the harbor. Cates found his quarters, heaved himself into a bunk, and reflected on his close call—an event he would never forget.

That evening, officers were again offered overnight leave, but Cliff Cates wasn't about to try his luck one more time:

"No, sir," he replied. "Not me! I'm not going."

Clifton Bledsoe Cates had taken up the challenge of enlisting in the United States Marine Corps, and then took and passed a rigorous test aimed at officer candidates. When the word came that he had been accepted, he was in the middle of the state bar examination; he stood up, walked out of the hall, and never looked back.

He quickly discovered, to his own surprise, that he had been born not to be a lawyer, but a marine; he had been born to lead men into desperate battle across wide, open killing grounds, up hillsides strewn with machine guns and barbed wire and the dead and the dying, and through acrid, thick air singed by war.

But, standing on that shady sidewalk in Knoxville, Tennessee, on that spring day in 1917, the flatlander Cliff Cates could have little knowledge of the Corps, what it was or who they were or what deeds marines had performed in relative obscurity in the far corners of the world.

The Marine Corps? he had wondered aloud. *What's that?*

Prior to Belleau Wood, prior to Blanc Mont, the Corps had operated almost as a secret society, a sparsely populated fraternity that sent its members to exotic places of which many had never even heard; the men who went to these places were two-fisted, hard-living salts who considered themselves married to and subject to the Corps, and little else.

They were tough, profane, proud—and lifers, most of them.

But they were more than just that.

One *Washington Times* writer would in 1919 describe a marine as "a trained athlete, a picked man, a he creature with muscles and a jaw, whose motto is 'kill or be killed,' and who believes with all his soul that no man on earth can lick him. And it comes pretty near to being so."

The United States Marine Corps was created in 1775 as a branch of the navy, and over the years its men had served on ships and at lonely outposts almost worldwide. Marines were men "who have done about all the fighting under the American flag since the Civil War," another writer would say.

"Under all skies and climates, they are always at the point where they are needed; the skirmish line, the police patrol of our Government, the guardians of National dignity and American citizens wherever there may be the threat of trouble.

"The young American with an ambition for real adventure, with [the] wish to see and learn the art of war, has in recent years been commended to the Marines. If there is trouble, it means marines to the front, first to get orders, first in motion, first ashore, first to fire. There is no finer body of fighting men in all the world, none more thoroughly seasoned or widely experienced."

In other words, a marine "is a baby they send for when some country gets fresh and tries to go Republican," the marine Winslow Belton Marshall would say. "There never is any trouble. The revolutionists are buried in lots of a thousand each.

"Once a marine got wounded. He stumbled over the Porto Bananas army on the way back to the ship."

Porto Bananas. Indeed, the Marines had deployed in dribs and drabs in many a so-called banana republic, and had always worked with handfuls of men, not by regiment or even company.

When "national dignity" or the interests of the nation's turn-of-the-last-century capitalists were threatened, marines were sent for, and pitched into the Moros in the Philippines, the Cacos in Haiti, the

Spanish in Cuba, various rebels in Nicaragua, and the Boxers in China, among others.

In the spring of 1917, much of the Corps was spread around the world, doing what its members always had done from Guam to Nicaragua to Haiti to China and a hundred other stations where one or two or half a dozen lonely marines were stationed to watch out for American interests.

Salty, tough, worldly, and cocksure, some of them should have become legends as much as for their deeds as for their fantastical, musical names—Smedley Darlington Butler, Littleton Waller Tazewell Waller, Johnny "the Hard" Hughes, "Hiking Hiram" Bearss, Albertus Wright Catlin, John Twiggs Myers, Presley Neville O'Bannon, Joseph Henderson Pendleton, John Archer Lejeune. . . .

"And there were also a number of diverse people who ran curiously to type, with drilled shoulders and a bone-deep suntan, and a tolerant scorn of nearly everything on earth," the marine John W. Thomason would write. "Their speech was flavored with navy words, and words culled from all the folk who live on the seas and the ports where our war-ships go.

"In easy hours their talk ran from the Tartar Wall beyond Pekin to the Southern Islands, down under Manila; from Portsmouth Navy Yard—New Hampshire and very cold—to obscure bushwhackings in the West Indies, where Cacao chiefs, whimsically sanguinary, barefoot generals with names like Charlemagne and Christophe, waged war according to the precepts of the French Revolution and the Cult of the Snake. They drank the *eau de vie* of Haute-Marne, and reminisced on saki, and vino, and Bacardi Rum—strange drinks in strange *cantinas* at the far ends of the earth; and they spoke fondly of Milwaukee beer."

All could fight, however obscurely, "protecting Americans from their own worst enemies—usually themselves," as the marine historian George B. Clark would have it.

"Missionaries were saved in China and large banking houses in New York didn't lose their investments in Haiti or Santo Domingo. Second-rate Latin governments that had recently overthrown third-rate governments were helped out of office with assistance from U.S. Marines. . . .

"Their enemy was usually an illiterate peasant with, most likely, just a machete as the weapon of choice—choice because it was the only weapon available."

Marines, Clark would add, "were the chosen instrument of the United States State Department for a reign of terror in the Caribbean" in the early years of the last century. "Until quite recently, Nicaraguan mothers obtained their children's obedience by threatening them with being taken by 'Major Butler.'"

That would be Smedley Butler, who would have concurred with Clark's assessment of the marine role—but who had had a sort of epiphany after retiring from a glorious career that saw him earn two Medals of Honor while fighting from Tientsin, China, to Vera Cruz. He went on to write a book titled *War Is a Racket*, and in one 1933 speech noted:

"I helped make Mexico, especially Tampico, safe for American oil interests in 1914. I helped make Haiti and Cuba a decent place for the National City Bank boys to collect revenues in.

"I helped in the raping of half a dozen Central American republics for the benefit of Wall Street. . . . I brought light to the Dominican Republic for American sugar interests in 1916. In China I helped to see to it that Standard Oil went its way unmolested."

Be that as it may, theirs, once in the Corps, was not to question why, but to do or die, and marines, if nothing else, were doers and performers of deeds heroic and spectacular in their lonely and godforsaken outposts.

Witness no farther than Gunnery Sergeant Dan Daly, whom Butler called "the fightin'est marine I ever knew," manning that lonely solo outpost on a wall in Beijing and killing scores of Boxer attackers through the course of one long night. Witness as well his heroic action in retrieving a much-needed machine gun from a dead mule while under fire in a deep, black Haitian swamp, each deed garnering him a Medal of Honor.

Witness as well John Quick, who braved the fire of Spanish *and* Americans during a landing at Cuba's Guantanamo Bay and calmly directed a U.S. gunship's fire, thus earning the first of two Medals of Honor.

Despite such heroics, the Marine Corps labored and fought in comparative obscurity for much of its history, operating not en masse but in small units. The Corps numbered just eighteen hundred men at the outbreak of the Spanish-American War, "and the forces which so often brought order out of chaos in turbulent lands and put to rout armies of rapacious revolutionaries were few in numbers though mighty, like a squad of New York policemen quelling a riot," the 6th Regiment's first commander, Albertus W. Catlin, would write proudly after World War I.

"Americans have come to take it as a matter of course that a marine should be able to do the work of ten ordinary men, and the Marines have come to that belief, too."

Such hubris did not endear the Corps—which by March 1917 had been enlarged to eighteen thousand men—to the larger regular army. After war was declared in April 1917, the Marines' effort to send a regiment immediately to France was contested by the army general staff, who saw no need for a "second army" and whose motto quickly became "No Marines in France."

George Barnett, Marine Corps commandant, was told to go talk to the navy.

But the Corps had itself adopted a motto: "First to Fight." Determined to prove those words were more than mere rhetoric, the politically connected Barnett went above heads and behind backs not only to win approval for a regiment of marines to sail for France, but also to get President Woodrow Wilson to approve the raising of *another* 4,250-man regiment of marines, and Congress in May 1917 increased the size of the wartime Corps to more than 31,000.

From its scattered forces across the world, the Marine Corps cobbled together a regiment, the 5th, consisting mainly of veteran fighters but also a contingent of eager young Americans who'd been lured into volunteering with the promise of a quick trip to France and *action*.

By mid-June 1917, the 5th Marine Regiment was already on its way to France, accompanied by the army's new 1st Division, put together from elements of the 16th, 18th, 26th, and 28th Regiments.

Once in France, the 1st moved to a training area around Gondrecourt, while the marines, left to grumble and labor as guards and stevedores at Brest, St. Nazaire, and other ports, wondered whether they would ever see action.

The undersized army, meanwhile, faced the herculean task of growing its numbers toward one million men through volunteers and a draft, which was to be held on June 5, 1917. The recruits and draftees would need housing, training, and outfitting, tasks that would take months and months to accomplish.

To that end, sixteen training camps were set up around the country to handle draftees and those who had enlisted in their local national guards. Still, by the end of 1917, elements of just four American divisions—each of which would be double the size of an Allied division at twenty-eight thousand men, and consist of four regiments, two to each of two brigades—would be in France.

Even as the gears were set in motion to build a huge army almost from scratch, and the desperate and pleading French begged the United States to send men, men, and more men, the Marines had already set to work recruiting the best and the brightest to fill out the ranks of the 5th Regiment as well as create a new regiment—the 6th.

Promising a quick trip Over There to whip the Hun, the Marines were inundated with eager applicants. The Corps opened recruiting stations across the country, and, seeking top candidates, flooded the nation's college campuses—including the University of Minnesota, where some five hundred students enlisted as one on a single day; half would go to the 6th Regiment's 78th Company, the other half to the 5th Regiment's 20th Company.

They came, as well, from the Ivy League; Harvard football great Eddie Mahon, the original "triple threat" in running, kicking, and passing the ball, now lent his talents to the Corps. Harvard's rival Yale added baseball and football star Harry Le Gore, the hockey star Holcomb York, the track star Johnny Overton, and the swimmer Louis Ferguson.

But the volunteers-only Marines were picky. Applicants had to be between five feet five and six feet two in height, and weigh more than 130 pounds. They also had to be at least eighteen years old, but not older than thirty-six; the Corps required that they be U.S. citizens, proficient in reading and writing English, unmarried and without dependents, and "of good health, strong constitutions, well formed, sound as to senses and limbs, and not addicted to the use of intoxicants or drugs."

Some eighty percent of applicants overall were turned away for various reasons, physical or mental, and Catlin would one day boast that sixty percent of the 6th Regiment's men were "college men," many of whom were quality physical specimens standing more than six feet tall.

"The American colleges doubtless supposed that they were turning men into scholars," Catlin would write with great mirth. "When the test came, they found they had been training soldiers."

The Marines also sought quality officers to lead this mostly educated mob, and Barnett had ingeniously sent letters of inquiry to colleges and universities around the country, offering quick lieutenant commissions in the Marine Corps Reserve to top candidates—candidates such as Cliff Cates, who applied, was accepted, and soon found himself on a life journey he could never have imagined or dreamed while growing up at bucolic Cates Landing, Tennessee.

PRISON ISLAND

MARINE CORPS OFFICER trainee Clifton Bledsoe Cates's first test of battle came not against some steel-jawed Hun operating a machine gun on some blood-drenched battlefield in France, but against a clench-jawed marine tyrant wielding his arbitrary pen in an office in Washington, DC.

Upon his acceptance as an officer candidate for the Marine Corps Reserve, the first order of business for Cates and other potential officers had been to take a physical. And it was while preparing for that seemingly routine procedure that Cates displayed his innate ability for leadership—an ability that would in the coming months bond him to his men, who would one day profess their willingness to follow him to the gates of hell, if that was where he might be headed.

Told to report to the Marine Barracks in Washington, DC, for a physical examination, he and some two hundred other young officer candidates from all over the East Coast crowded the designated office at nine a.m. on May 21, 1917, only to be told to come back at one p.m. But when they returned, they were rebuffed and told to return the next morning.

"They said, 'Come back this afternoon at one; come back tomorrow morning at nine o'clock; come back in the afternoon at one o'clock,'"

Cates would recall. "That kept up for three days and we were all running out of money."

Finally, pockets empty, the fed-up would-be marines decided to appoint a three-man committee to go see the terrifying, intimidating, and very loud commanding officer, Major Dick "Terrible Terry" Williams.

Cates was not only one of the three designated but was quickly made the small group's spokesman, and when he appeared in Terrible Terry's office, he told the major in no uncertain terms that the whole lot of the boys were almost out of dough and would leave Washington—and the Corps—behind if they weren't examined that very day.

Terrible Terry, of course, was almost apoplectic at Cates's college-boy gall.

"He pounded the desk and said, 'What the hell is this? Insubordination before you get into the Marine Corps? Get out of here!'" Cates would recall.

Cates left—but as he went through the doorway, he turned and told Terrible Terry, "If we're not examined this afternoon, we're going back."

The physicals were held that same afternoon.

Cliff Cates had faced down Terrible Terry—and lived.

Cates passed his physical with flying colors, he would say later, though he had secretly quaked at the thought that the doctors would find something wrong with him as they poked and prodded and pummeled and thumped chests and backs, and then turned the recruits into human pincushions with a variety of inoculations.

Marine recruit Lemuel Shepherd, newly graduated from the Virginia Military Institute, was examined by naval captain "Bobo" Dessez, "a rough, gruff old seagoing bull surgeon."

Shepherd, like Cates, worried he wouldn't pass. He weighed just 123 pounds, as he "ran on the track team and was pretty thin in those days."

Dessez looked him over, took his blood pressure, and then told Shepherd, "Get down over there and stick up your ass. Have you ever had a dose of the clap?"

"No sir," Shepherd replied.

"Have you ever had piles?"

"No sir!"

"You pass," Dessez told him.

"They certainly were rough with us," Cates would later write, "but I did not mind as long as we passed."

Cates and the others who passed were sworn in as second lieutenants in the Marine Corps Reserve, and Cliff then returned to his suddenly empty frat house in Knoxville, from which the boys had all fled into one branch or another of the service.

"It sure is sad to think that I may not ever get to see some of my frat brothers again," he would write. "It was real pathetic telling them goodbye."

He awaited further orders, and in the meantime struggled to fulfill orders to "procure" certain property, including one suit of "undress" blue, four summer suits, a winter field coat, trousers and breeches, six pairs of white gloves, one pair of tan leather gloves, a belt, a watch, a compass, two or more flannel shirts, an overcoat, a scarf, a raincoat, one "sword," its length, quality, and appearance not delineated. There were also shoes and leggings and caps and bedding rolls to be ordered from the Depot of Supplies in Philadelphia—"a thousand and one things," Cates would write.

The final tally for his outfitting ran to $296; his monthly pay for the coming year would be $141.50. Well, he was in the army now, or rather the Marines, and what was to come would come—and he told himself he would bear it no matter what. He hoped soon enough to end the suspense as to exactly what that might be as he cooled his heels in Knoxville.

The suspense ended when his orders arrived. He was to report with his baggage to Port Royal, South Carolina. "I do not know whether I am glad to go or not," he would write on June 11, the eve of his departure from Knoxville.

"I have made a lot of friends here, and of course I hate to bid them goodbye. It is awful hard to tell anyone goodbye; I would rather just leave.

"I know that I can make good," he would add in a letter to his mother. "And someday you will be proud to call me your son."

Cates arrived at Port Royal on June 13. There, a ferry—just a scow, really—waited to transport him and a group of just-arrived recruits to a place called Parris Island, which, in the spring of 1917, housed a marine detention center.

With the coming of the Great War to America, the eight-thousand-square-acre spit of land became the primary recruit depot and training ground for those who had enlisted from places east of the Mississippi River—among them Cliff Cates. He had known the southern summer sun, but this was something else, something venal and insidious and vengeful. There was no way and nowhere to hide from its venomous rays, no escape from its baking sting, no respite from its exacting toll until nightfall.

He had also known insects on the bottomlands along the Mississippi at Cates Landing, stinging, flying nightmare squads of flies and mosquitos, and even contracted malaria as a youngster. But even those perfidies were no match for what he found at Parris Island.

"This is an awful place," Cliff Cates would write upon arrival. "Just a dock and some houses. It is on a bay, but it is fifteen miles from the coast. It is awful hot, and the mosquitos and flies are awful."

Parris Island was a vile, hot, level piece of land that the French had tried to settle way back in the 1500s, building a doomed and short-lived settlement known as Charlesfort. Between the heat and the insects and the intrusions of the local Indians, the settlement had quickly gone kaput. In later years, it served as a naval base, as home to a hand-ful of plantations run by hardier settlers than the French had been able to find, and then as a training ground for marine officers.

It would see thousands of newly minted marines pass through in 1917 and 1918, and some of those who survived the training, and then the ordeals of battle in France, would later in life look back in misery and wonderment at what one recruit would refer to as his "prison island."

In 1917, it was almost a wilderness, with just a few isolated planta-tion homes but no roads, no barracks, no latrines capable of handling thousands of men at a time, and no truly fresh drinking water. It was hell on earth, and it was intended to be just that—a place where under the sadistic watch of veteran noncoms, boys became men, and then, with any luck, marines.

Recruits who would mostly fill the 6th Regiment were greeted at the island's dock by a jeering crowd of those who had come before—some just the day before, but after twenty-four hours in the place, one already considered oneself a veteran.

Get your silk pajamas over here, this way for your ice cream, get your white sheets over here, the cynical, heat-crazed bastards would sing, and then the neophytes would be hustled through a gauntlet of sadists who thumped them with rolled-up newspapers, rubber hoses, and "other handy tools of torture," as one would remember.

The next day, the fun would begin. They drilled; they built bar-racks; they dug an extensive latrine system; they drilled, they drilled, and drilled some more under the blazing and unforgiving sun. They ate foul-smelling eggs, potatoes boiled in brackish water, rancid fried fatback and hair-raising salty black coffee—fare they called hen fruit, spuds, punk, piss, and sow belly.

They endured as well as they could. As one recruit remembered, "The first day I was at camp, I was afraid I was going to die. My next two weeks, my sole fear was that I wasn't going to die."

They were also introduced to colorful characters, long-serving marines sent to the new regiment to imbue them in the marine traditions. One "old-timer" marine, drunk as a skunk, lurched into Private Levi Hemrick's fifty-man tent on Hemrick's first night on the island, pulled a "whopping big pistol" out of his belt, and pointed it, slowly, at each recruit. Satisfied he had the men's attention, he reeled to a table and faced his audience.

"Suddenly, he banged on the table with the butt of the pistol and began to harangue us on the virtue and history of the Marine Corps, boasting of his own exploits and acts of heroism," Hemrick wrote.

"We couldn't tell for sure whether he was actually drunk, acting out a wild-west barroom scene, or just showing his true nature under the influence of alcohol."

Hemrick, a former principal in a rural school in Panthersville, Georgia, was shocked, and wondered what he'd gotten himself into.

"Was this drunken slouch the real marine?" he would write. "Was the poster in Atlanta and the recruiting officer's talk just window dressing to lure fellows like me into the Corps? Was this just another phase of our initiation to boot camp?

"These and other painful thoughts plagued me as the old fellow ended his thick-tongued lecture and lurched out of the tent."

In the coming weeks, the recruits drilled under the hot sun, went on long hikes with full packs, hauled arm-busting oyster shells from the beach to pave new camp roads, and did their laundry daily in buckets. Their wash was then inspected—and even if clean was sometimes thrown into the muddy street by their superiors, who told them their clothes were not clean enough and instructed them to wash them again.

After a month of such labors and indignities, they moved to the rifle range and learned to become marksmen, the marines especially prizing their abilities on the rifle range. They continued to kvetch and complain and wonder if they'd made the worst mistake of their lives—

but lo and behold, at the end of ten weeks, the hard work "melted the fat from the over-large belt lines and replaced lumps of fat with bulging muscles," Hemrick wrote.

By the third week, many of the men noticed they were being physically transformed, hardened; their city-feller white skins were turning golden, what was flab had turned to sinuous muscle, their once-soft college-boy brains had somehow endured the petty tortures of their vengeful Svengali sergeants, and they learned they could take it.

"I knew I would never die because I had become so hard that nothing could kill me," one recruit would conclude.

"The lanky and underweight, as I, took on from fifteen to twenty-five pounds, most of it going into broadening of the shoulders, hardening the arm and leg muscles," Levi Hemrick would write.

In the end, each recruit underwent a change "that indicated development of physical power, firmness, determination and boldness; a fighting man's image."

They were marines—almost.

Cliff Cates did not dwell on the privations of "prison island"—he simply noted that he had been issued a small tent, and "had to run around and get blankets, gun, buckets, chair and etc."

He would remember his time there as consisting mainly of work on the rifle range—a luxury afforded those with commissions, but not the average recruit.

In any event, while the enlisted men went through their ten weeks of torture, Cates and the other trainee officers in early July were moved off the island, and after receiving leave were sent to a new destination: a six-thousand-acre camp being built adjacent to Quantico, Virginia, up the Atlantic coast, another brand-new, sprawling training ground where the recruits would eventually be formed into companies, battalions, and finally a regiment—the 6th.

The town of Quantico "looked just like pictures of mining towns I had seen," Second Lieutenant James McBrayer Sellers, a Missourian whose father was president of the Wentworth Military Academy in Lexington, Missouri, would remember.

"There was one small street which constituted the original town. This street led right up from the pier. . . . Then there were rows and rows of unpainted wooden shacks, sprung up almost literally overnight.

"Down town [sic] there were little restaurants where we could get an egg sandwich for 50 cents. And there was also a dance hall where they charged 20 cents for a dance with one of the painted ladies brought to town for the purpose."

They had other purposes as well, among them servicing the thousands of construction workers who were busy throwing up barracks and other buildings. Anticipating the arrival of thousands of recruits and the manly temptations they would bring with them, base commander John A. Lejeune ordered the "painted ladies" to hit the bricks.

Second Lieutenant William A. Worton drew the job of rounding up the ladies and sending them packing, and dutifully arrived at ten a.m. on a quiet Tuesday morning to do the job. After having the one hundred or so women line up in the town's dirty street, he handed out train fares to Washington, DC.

But as they were about to board the train, one old-time sergeant whispered in the ear of one of the prostitutes. Then, "About six of them came over and kissed me goodbye," Worton recalled. "And they all waved, and so forth to me. God!"

The mortified young officer marched his detail back to Lejeune's adjutant, William T. Hoadley, who'd heard all about the overly friendly send-off. "Somebody told me they were kissing you right and left," he told Worton. "You been running down there and looking these girls over every night?"

Worton remained quiet; inside, he was "furious" at the insinuation.

As at Parris Island, where his so-called officer training mainly consisted of time on the rifle range, Cates pooh-poohed the value of the regimen, and would later say he "spent at least half of [his] time in trying to learn the semaphore and the Morse code, and what good was that for a second lieutenant?

"And, of course, we had lots of close-order drill. We had some extended order drill and we dug trenches and we threw dummy grenades and some of the training was good but a lot of it wasn't worth much. I would say that at least half of it wasn't worth a hoorah."

Officer training began on July 30 and was supposed to last three months. Rising at five forty-five a.m., the men did physical drills at six—usually consisting of little more than racing for half a mile through the rough streets of Quantico—breakfasted at six thirty a.m., drilled from seven thirty a.m. to nine a.m., and then drilled and studied until ten p.m., when they turned in.

There was some time for some fun, too; James Sellers would remember Cates's being "quite a craps player," one time taking three thousand dollars from one colonel's "cowardly translator" Sydney Colford, "the camp clown whose main job was to find liquor for the old colonel."

When Colford offered Cates an IOU for the sum, Cliff tried to sell the note to others for three cents on the dollar, with no luck. "However, after the war, Colford married a wealthy Vanderbilt divorcee, so the IOU was good!" Sellers remembered. "I wish I had bought it from Clif [sic] when I had the chance."

Lucky Cliff Cates . . .

The laconic Cates was popular with the other officers, but he did not immediately endear himself to his future battalion commander, Major Thomas Holcomb, a seventeen-year veteran of the Corps, during their time at Quantico.

The thirty-eight-year-old Holcomb had spent years in China with the Corps, and was renowned as a crack shot with a rifle. He had been married to the Corps only until the previous year, when he wed twenty-year-old Washington debutante Beatrice Clover. He was now faced with his first combat command, and he and Cates would become close during the coming trials—but first Holcomb would have to learn something of Cliff Cates's sense of humor.

During a session on field engineering, Holcomb looked at Cates and asked, "How many entrances should a dugout have?"

Cates, who typically had not read the engineering manual as instructed, slowly drawled, "Well, at least one."

Unamused, Holcomb said, "Well that's a hell of a bright answer!"

Just a few weeks into the routine, the students became teachers, as the Corps, short on junior officers, cut short their training and began the earnest work of assembling the 6th Regiment. The first of the recruits, fresh from their ordeals on Parris Island, began arriving at Quantico, and were assigned to one of twelve new companies.

The marines were in a hurry, a war was on, and within weeks the three battalions that would make up the 6th Regiment were being formed, four companies to each battalion. By mid-August, the regiment was at three-quarters' strength; reaching full strength depended on how fast the remaining barracks needed to house three more companies could be built.

Whereas the army lettered each company in each regiment from A to M (excluding J), the Marine Corps held fast to a numbering system. The 1st Battalion consisted of the 74th, 75th, 76th, and 95th Companies; the 2nd carried the 78th, 79th, 80th, and 96th; and the 3rd Battalion was made up of the 82nd, 83rd, 84th, and 97th Companies.

Three companies—the 95th, 96th, and 97th—weren't formed until late August, each becoming the last company assigned to each battalion. Cates on August 28 was assigned to the 96th Company, part of the regiment's 2nd Battalion, and was placed in charge of the 4th Platoon.

Despite their weeks on Parris Island, Cates was unimpressed with the state of his men, militarily at least. He found them to be "as green as grass. We have to start and build the company from the ground up; it sure is hard work; we haven't a non-commission [sic] officer in the company, and that makes it hard on us lieutenants."

Complicating matters was the fact many of the men assigned to the 96th were heading right out on leaves—as were two of the company's new lieutenants. For weeks, what was supposed to be a 250-man company remained understrength, with ninety men being absent well into September.

Cates, meanwhile, struggled to equip all, drawing what materiel he could from stingy marine quartermasters. "It would not be so hard if they could supply the clothing, but you can only get it by little dabs," he complained.

"There is so much red tape to it, and you have to do a lot of desk work, and you have to check up on every little article, and have it correct to a cent."

If there was any consolation—and there most certainly was—Cates eventually had put at his disposal one of the Corps's old stalwarts, a marine named Fred Stockham, a veteran of service in the Philippines, Nicaragua, the Canal Zone, and with Thomas Holcomb in the Legation Guard in Beijing.

A native of Detroit, Stockham had been orphaned as a young boy and joined the U.S. Marines at the age of twenty-two in July 1903. He served one four-year hitch before leaving the Corps to become a firefighter in Newark, New Jersey. He reenlisted in May 1912 and was working as a recruiter in St. Louis when he decided he'd rather see a war. He transferred to Quantico, and into the 96th Company, taking with him a "temporary warrant" as a gunnery sergeant. The thirty-six-year-old Stockham would prove invaluable to his young platoon leader as they worked together to whip it into shape.

Joining Cates in the work of forming and equipping the 96th was its captain, Donald Francis Duncan, who'd been appointed a second lieutenant way back in January 1909.

Originally from St. Joseph, Missouri, Duncan attended the Culver Military Academy in Indiana, where he was nicknamed "Napoleon" for his success as a boy military strategist. After receiving his commission, he saw action in Nicaragua and also served stints at Vera Cruz, in the Canal Zone, and, shortly before being sent to the 6th Regiment, on Guam, where he was promoted to captain.

The thirty-year-old Duncan was the scion of a "distinguished" local family; his grandfather, Frederick Smith, "was associated with Joseph Robidoux in fashioning the primitive outlines" of St. Joseph, a newspaper would report, adding that Duncan himself was "a particularly high type of man—earnest, modest, brave and chivalrous."

Duncan was, in other words, a marine's marine—as was his executive officer, James F. Robertson, a profane, tough, ass-kicking South African and son of a bitch to boot. Robertson was a "big rough and ready man," Cates would say, "a fine soldier, fine marine, but the men hated his guts. He was a hard-boiled rascal."

Others were more refined: Twenty-four-year-old Evans Spalding, "prepared" at the Noble & Greenough School in Boston and a 1914 graduate of Harvard, had already served in a volunteer ambulance unit Over There and "made sure his comrades knew all about it," Worton, destined for the 79th Company, would recall.

Spalding had a certain above-it-all savoir faire; it made many hate him and would result in his transfer out of the 2nd Battalion. Holcomb would quickly grow to hate him.

Thomas Reed Brailsford also joined the company as it was formed. The twenty-three-year-old, a newly married recent graduate of Texas A&M University, took over the 2nd Platoon. Like Cates, he would be considered, as one of his men said, "one of the most popular officers in the company," while John Dominic Bowling, a twenty-two-year-old from a prosperous farming family and recent graduate of the Maryland State College of Agriculture, took over the third. George B. Lockhart, fresh from the Virginia Military Institute, got the 1st Platoon.

Among the privates and other noncoms, there were these in the 96th Company: Corporal Herbert Dillard Dunlavy, a Houston, Texas, high school sports hero who at the age of just nineteen became Cates's orderly and would, naturally, become known as "Tex" within the company; twenty-seven-year-old Sergeant Aloysius Patrick Sheridan, a friend of Captain Duncan's from back in St. Joseph who was working as a shoe salesman for the Regal Shoe Company in Kansas City before hearing the call and enlisting on June 21, 1917; and twenty-seven-year-old Julius Steinberg of Omaha. Nicknamed "the Count," Steinberg was the son, so it was said, of a former bodyguard to the former Crown Prince Kaiser Frederick, and was married and working as a salesman when duty called and he enlisted on June 21.

Also sent to the 96th Company were brothers Leslie and Robert Cunningham, twenty-four and twenty-two years old, respectively, who were working as a farmhand and laborer, also respectively, in their native Door County, Wisconsin, and who enlisted together on June 23. There was also the Chicagoan Gus Andrew Turngren, twenty-three, whom one fellow marine would describe as "a fine, husky, hardworking boy," and who would quickly acquire the moniker "Bullet Head" after enlisting on June 20, 1917.

Despite the Marines' call for the best and the brightest and purest of heart, a few had less than sterling backgrounds. Among them was Corporal Harrison Cale, a twenty-seven-year-old Indianapolis attorney who had blown through an inheritance left him by his prominent attorney father and survived several scandals and brushes with the law before trying his luck with the Marines and enlisting on May 24, 1917. Another was Charles V. Iotte, twenty-four, who had been sent to a Minnesota reformatory in 1914 after being caught breaking into a home in Duluth. He served some unknown term in prison despite begging for leniency, claiming "some unexplainable and uncontrollable influence" had made him do the deed.

Some of these became Cliff Cates's charges that fall of 1917. Most had enlisted in the spring or summer and been rushed to Parris Island and then Quantico, but there were some veteran noncoms also brought in, men such as Sergeant Alcide St. John, who had been a marine almost since February 1902, the aforementioned Fred Stockham, and Sergeant Joseph Sissler, aka Steele, who'd been a marine since September 1914, and Sergeant Irby F. Langston, who'd also enlisted in 1914.

James Sellers, assigned to the 1st Platoon of the 2nd Battalion's 78th Company, would write that the gunnies "really ran the platoon. When the platoon was given an assignment, the platoon leader delegated responsibilities, but the sergeant made certain the enlisted men carried out their duties."

Men such as these would show Cliff Cates and his college-boy lieutenant friends how to drill men, how to punish men, how to lead men, and how to mold men into the rock-hard killing machines they would need to become on the deadly western front to which they were headed—someday.

SWACKED

THE WAITING TO leave dragged on and on, but finally came hope that all
would, indeed, someday march out of Quantico and head for France.
On September 16, Johnny "the Hard" Hughes, his leg still oozing from
a gunshot wound he'd taken in the shin the previous December while
hunting *insurrectos* in the Dominican Republic (he cut off the protrud-
ing bone himself with a pair of wire cutters and continued fighting, in
the process earning his moniker), led his 1st Battalion of the 6th Regiment out of the camp, to the cheers of the remaining two battalions
and the ringing endorsement of the post's band.

Johnny the Hard and Co. were indeed bound for France, by way of
Philadelphia and New York. Cates and the men of the 2nd and 3rd
Battalions could only watch and cheer as the 1st Battalion marched off
to glory—or whatever awaited it in France.

Though they'd read the news of the war's progress—or lack thereof—
for the past three years, few Americans, civilian or military, seemed to
truly understand the challenges facing them.

American Expeditionary Force commander General John J. Pershing, convinced that the Americans' larger division could work as a single battering ram, exhibited a divine intuition that American troops,

properly trained, would hit the ground running once there and break the stasis of the trenches.

While marines and regular army soldiers paid lip service to the reality of trench warfare, taking instruction in trench-digging and the building of fortifications, Pershing believed in the concept of open warfare—in getting out of the foul, sloppy trenches in which the war had been bogged down for more than three years and advancing quickly over open country, carrying enemy trenches en masse, and not looking back until Berlin was in sight.

Open warfare was more than just a theory to Pershing—it was his doctrine. But he and his army would find it more difficult to budge the Germans from their fixed and well-fortified positions than seemed likely on paper, and thousands of soldiers who attacked willy-nilly across the French countryside and toward the German lines would find that a rifle, or even one hundred rifles massed together, proved a poor match against machine guns spewing six hundred rounds per minute, and ground-shaking artillery barrages that made quick work of heads, arms, legs, and torsos.

The Allies and Germans had already learned this lesson, and so had hunkered down in their trenches chopped from limestone and muck since the fall of 1914, attacking only after days- or even weeks-long bombardments of the enemy lines. The Marine Corps in 1917 still clung to an overriding and ill-advised belief in the value of massed rifle power, a theory that by then had been shot down along with the rows and rows of Tommy boys and French *poilus* and Germans who had tried such tactics against machine-gun emplacements earlier in the war.

By 1917 the machine gun was king, artillery the queen, and the only viable antidote to breaking the enemy's fortifications was massive artillery barrages followed by fast-closing infantry, or infiltration by picked bodies of storm troopers. And even those had had limited success; hence, the almost permanent stalemate that existed on the western front.

But at Quantico, the order of the day in the fall of 1917 was not training in the tactics that might lead to individual survival and eventual victory, but the stale and disproved concept of massed attack by sharp-shooting riflemen. So as Johnny the Hard and the 1st Battalion sailed off to reality, Cliff Cates led his men of the 96th Company in close-order drill and bayonet theory.

"We have four hours of drill in the morning, and two in the afternoon," Cates wrote to his family on September 19. "We put in the first hour by giving the men the new English bayonet exercise; the next hour is taken up with close order drill; each platoon separate; the next hour is taken up with skirmishing, signaling, and bomb throwing; then we have one hour of battalion parade or (other) battalion drill.

"The afternoon is taken up with close order mostly, but anything they choose to give. Next week, the men will go to the woods two days a week, and commence digging trenches, and building barb wire entanglements. We have to dig a complete set of trenches, and put in all the revetments, and everything, just like it was for use."

It was almost like it was real.

Almost.

Berton Sibley's 3rd Battalion left Quantico and sailed for France on October 24, and every day hence brought new rumors of impending departure to the 6th Regiment's 2nd Battalion. But the wait had gone on for almost three months, eliciting a new rumor that the departure schedule had been altered so battalion commander Major Thomas Holcomb could attend at the birth of a son. The boy, named Frank, was born a week after Sibley's battalion had sailed, and still the men would wait for their turn to go Over There.

As the weather turned colder, Cates and the men of the 2nd Battalion continued to train. Allied officers—British, French, Scots, even Italian—who had seen action were brought in to lecture on "modern" trench warfare, and the men continued in the not-so-modern art of close-order and massed drill.

The 2nd Battalion, the regiment's history says, "became very proficient in drill, maneuvers, and general combat"—and in the new "wave" formation of attacking entrenched positions.

"The crack of the rifles and the sputter of machine guns afforded an idea, somewhat vague, of the conditions of battle which were to be met in France. Vague, because there was no friendly artillery to help nor hostile artillery to hinder the advance upon the assigned objective."

Well, you get the idea. . . .

And there was talk for the first time of something with which Cates and his men would become very well acquainted: gas.

"They scared us to death, particularly on the gas question," Cates would remember. "If you get one sniff of mustard gas, you'll die," the marines of the 2nd Battalion were ominously told.

As Christmas approached, leaves were freely given to enlisted men and officers alike, and many were able to return home for the holidays with still no voyage to France in sight. Cates managed to get back home to spend Christmas with his mother and sister, and then spent a leisurely few days in Knoxville on the way back to Quantico.

A veritable social butterfly and man about town, and a man deprived of female company for much of the past six months, he managed to make up for lost time.

"I had a wonderful time in Knoxville," he would write of his short stay. "I saw most of my old friends. I was with Helen most of the time, but I had one date each with Ellen, Marion, and Elizabeth Rose."

Then it was back to the manly company of the marines, where the rumor of an imminent departure had grown stronger by the day. "We have not received any orders, but something is in the air," Cates wrote.

"I am really and truly ready to go now, this suspense gets on my nerves. The men are as restless as a wild tiger. . . . We are all packed up and ready to go. The men are all tickled to death to think that we are leaving sometime soon."

Cates had prepared himself, and his family, for the day when his ship would finally sail. He could have no real idea of what he would be facing but was realistic about the chances that he might not come back.

While trying not to alarm his family, he carefully wrote what amounted to a will, in which he divided property that had been bequeathed to him by his father between his mother and sister.

"I want you and Katherine to enjoy the benefits of the rents jointly all of your life," he wrote. "If one should die, I want the other to enjoy all of it. Provided that Katherine should have an heir, and that she would die, and if you are still living, I want you to have a lifetime interest in this property, and I do not want it to go to Katherine's heir until after your death.

"Of course," he would add, "it is awful to even think of these things, but we must look forward to the unexpected, altho it is disagreeable."

He was excited and eager to go, but knew his mother, like all mothers, would fret over sending her boy overseas and into a calamitous world war.

"I am going to take the best care of myself and it will just be a question of time until I will be back home again," he wrote Mattie Cates with perhaps some feigned optimism. "Just think of the honor of getting to go, and think of how I can always look back upon this trip. It will be wonderful."

The word finally came that the battalion would leave Quantico on January 18. A farewell was deemed appropriate, and so Cates and a covey of the battalion's officers—among them the bachelor captains Donald Duncan and Robert Messersmith of the 78th Company—gathered in the officers' quarters to drink a few dozen toasts to their impending journey.

"They decided they were going to raise hell down in the officers' quarters," William Worton, the commander of the guard on that epic evening, would recall.

As the cheeks grew rosier and the laughter louder and the jokes funnier, one of the officers decided he wanted to see what would happen when he threw a .45-caliber round into the hot cast-iron stove.

Blam! was what happened.

More rounds followed, as did more maniacal laughter. The sergeant of the guard, hearing the commotion, went to Worton.

"The officers are shooting themselves down there in the officers' quarters," he told the young lieutenant.

Worton and the sergeant raced to the quarters. He told the sergeant to stay outside. "I didn't know what the hell I'd find in there—they were all hollering and singing," Worton remembered. "I knew they were all drunk."

He entered the quarters and found each of the officers "swacked to the gills." He told them, "Gentlemen, this must stop." In response, one of the officers grabbed Worton from behind, tied his hands, and poured liquor down his throat.

"God damn it, they were going to get me in on the party, whether I liked it or not," Worton would say.

The fun ended when the sergeant, an old marine and a tough cookie, entered. "They got kind of scared of him," Worton said.

The party ended; not so its effects. At five a.m. Worton had the great pleasure of awakening the hungover revelers. "They said, 'Oh, for God's sake, use your head, let's delay it, what the hell do we care?'" Worton recalled.

"Well, you had better get going," Worton told the men, and, heads pounding, all complied. "They got up and got out," Worton would say, adding, "So the boys used to play in those days."

Soon enough, the men of the 2nd Battalion were marching to the train that would deliver them to the *Henderson*, waiting at anchor in Philadelphia.

"It was bitter cold, but even that could not dampen the spirits of the men," a sobered Cates would write that evening. "They marched out of Quantico like they were going home instead of to the most horrible thing ever.

"Our band led the way and they played patriotic pieces, and the men would all sing and yell and they are all happy. I wish every mother could have seen it. They would be proud and glad to have them go instead of sorry. It was very impressive, but still it was very sad."

A NEW DANCE

THE SHELLS CAME in thick and fast and with grim indifference as the men huddled in the bottom of their holes. The first one killed was Grober, Edward Adolph Grober, twenty-two years old.

Grober of Kalkaska, Michigan, and Keokuk, Iowa, and finally Peoria, Illinois, would be the first man of many to be killed within the ranks of the 96th Company; Grober would be, the newspapers would later decide (somewhat dubiously), "the First Marine to Die Over There." Grober, whose mother, Rose, was born in Germany, and whose draft-registration card from June 5, 1917, noted that he had "Enlisted in the Marines," died from shrapnel, and not, as the Marines always liked to delineate, as a "result of his own misconduct," on April 5, 1918.

James Hartford Metcalfe, also twenty-two years old, was the second of the company to buy it. The Jeffersonville, Indiana, native was next to Grober when the first shell came down; he died of his shrapnel wounds on April 6.

"Your son died from wounds received in action; he gave his life to his country and for those ideals for which the civilized world is striving," Captain Donald Duncan would write consolingly to Metcalfe's mother, Eva. "You have the sincere and heartfelt sympathy of every man in your son's company."

Four more in the 96th Company were wounded in what turned into a rain of shells—more than three hundred on that single day. But the first one did the damage, and the first one taught all in that front line that day an important lesson.

"After that, the men would make for their dugout whenever they heard a shell coming thru the air," Cliff Cates would write of his 4th Platoon.

After five months of playing at war, months of, as Cates would put it in his postwar history of the company, "close order drill, manual of arms, extended order, machine gun instruction, bayonet drill, dummy hand grenades, rifle range practice, trench digging, trench warfare, combat drills and the basic principles and fundamentals of modern warfare," somebody had forgotten to impart to Grober and Metcalfe another important art of modern warfare: When you hear a shell coming at you that just might have your name on it, run for the goddamn dugout.

There was still much to learn. And with spring ripening, and the German army on the move, there was not much time for anything more than an on-the-job education.

They were here, in a frontline area near Verdun known as Camp Bon Champ, to get that education. Cates and the 96th Company had come far in just the two-plus months since the *Henderson* had finally weighed anchor in New York Harbor and, at last, sailed into the treacherous waters where in every American marine's imagination a wolf pack of German submarines lurked.

The *Henderson* had set sail at one thirty a.m. on January 24, and was attached to a convoy of four transports and one battleship, which would add a complement of a squad of destroyers in the "submarine zone" once it neared the French coast.

The ship carried the entire 2nd Battalion of the 6th Marine Regiment, the men of which endured cramped quarters, long boring days, occasional lifeboat drills, and watches on deck in the freezing, dark Atlantic nights.

Cates's hardest duty was inspecting the ship (lifeboats, etc.), standing watch and censoring his men's mail—"an awful job," he would write.

The seas were rough—rough enough that the marines, many of whom, despite being part of the U.S. Navy, had never ventured farther off-land than a dip in a Wisconsin lake or Texas river, added seasickness to their list of woes. This despite Thomas Holcomb's stern, if bizarre, orders that no marine become sick.

One of Cates's men was so seasick, he joked about staying in France, should they arrive safely, until a bridge was built across the Atlantic on which he could return. Another said he would prefer to return to the United States via the North Pole; another said he'd drink the ocean and walk home before he'd get on a ship again.

The good news: No submarines were sighted, and the *Henderson* had taken a more southerly route than other convoys of transports that preceded them in a successful effort to stay afloat.

"Our trip across was uneventful save for raids on the kitchen," the 96th Company's Corporal Harrison Cale would write. "While one man regaled the cook with stories, nimble fingers searched the larder for dainties."

"Very few of us were sick and not one seemed to lose his appetite," twenty-two-year-old Corporal Harold D. Powell would add. "I guess the 'subs' didn't like our looks for they left us strictly alone, for which lack of attention we were sincerely thankful."

"Taken as a whole, the men have stood it very nicely and the morale is fine," Cates would add.

On February 5, the *Henderson* followed the Loire River to the port city of St. Nazaire. Given officers' leave on the next day, Cates and his coterie encountered their first experience of the war's toll.

Children in wooden shoes prowled the docks, begging for money and cigarettes, and there were no young men in town. "Pathetic," Cates would say of the sad state of affairs in France.

He walked the dirty town, trying mightily to communicate in his best University of Tennessee–learned pidgin French. It was of little use, and so he bought three French-instruction books.

Without knowing the language, "It is like trying to talk to a deaf and dumb person," he would write; of course the French could have said the same about trying to communicate with him.

The enlisted men of the 2nd Battalion remained on ship until February 8, when all debarked and immediately boarded rail cars—the famous "forty and eights," meaning each car had room for eight horses or forty men—and headed for the Vosges region of France.

Unlike their counterparts in the 1st and 2nd Battalions, who had arrived the previous fall, there would be no duty unloading ships or guarding ports from Nantes to Brest to Le Havre, or patrolling the streets of Tours or Marcheprime, and Cates and the 2nd Battalion were carried instead straight to the village of Blevaincourt, which sat about 150 miles east-southeast of Paris in the Vosges Mountains.

The trip took three days and three nights. "Fortunately, it was warm and we escaped some of the hardships others had undergone who preceded us," Harrison Cale would write.

"Men stood until they became so exhausted they were able to lie down and sleep despite that the others occasionally walked upon them. The floors were alive with 'cooties,' and while we didn't see the front for some days, we never spent another idle hour.

"But after all it was quite endurable and we enjoyed the trip in a way. It was a beautiful ride across the heart of France, and the way the villagers shouted 'Americans,' warmed our hearts and made us happy to feel we were there to help them."

On arrival, the men piled out of their lice-infested cars and looked around. One of the 96th Company's men quickly discovered the cheap cost of wine—just twelve cents a gallon—and "almost caused a stampede" when he raced through the streets shouting to other marines about his amazing find.

"This is some town," one of the company's sergeants muttered.

But the wine, the men discovered, was cheap for a reason. "One swallow was enough," Cale wrote. "It tasted like varnish."

Drinking was tolerated. "If they wanted brandy, let them have it," Second Lieutenant William A. Worton would say years later. "Nobody gave a damn.

"When you take a man to war, and you say this boy's going to be killed, you teach him to become a killer. That's his principal job. If he's old enough to understand that, he's old enough, if he wants liquor . . . in France, it was available. And you couldn't have stopped it if you had wanted to."

But there was plenty of work to do, and Cliff Cates, for one, was happy to bid the idle hours and the traveling adieu.

"It is going to be real hard work from now on," he wrote from his quarters in Blevaincourt on February 13, 1918. "Nothing can suit me better, as I am getting tired of loafing; I am getting as fat as a pig."

The village was not exactly Paris. The Americans gawked at and were disgusted by the piles of manure in front of each home, and were appalled—especially those who'd grown up with a pitchfork in their hands—at the way farm animals of all types were free to roam the streets.

The marines derisively called the area the "Manure Sector."

"You do not have to look out for street cars or automobiles in this town," Cates would write, "you just have to look out for the swine and cattle and see that they don't butt your brains out."

While the 6th Regiment assembled in and around Blevaincourt, some fifty miles west of the front line, Cates and his crew set up shop, the men sleeping mostly in haylofts and the officers finding quarters in the local homes—often sharing living space with the French—and other—occupants.

"The barn, the house and the chicken house are all in the same building!" small-town Kansan Corporal Harold D. Powell would write in wonder, as did many a young American getting his first taste of the animal-friendly French accommodations.

"The barn has the place of honor on the first floor. The kitchen is right off the stable. Upstairs is the haymow and sleeping room. The front room of the second floor is reserved for the abode of a flock of pigeons."

By February 20, a routine had been established: "Up at 6 a.m. and stand reveille," Cates would write, "breakfast at 7, inspection at 7:45, drill at 8, recall at 11:30, dinner at 12, drill at 12:45, recall at 3:20, officers school from 3:45 'til 4:15, inspect feet at 4:30, supper at 5, then after that, I have to censor a lot of letters and read a lot of work that is assigned."

He found his orderly, Private Herbert Dunlavy, to be a godsend. The nights and mornings were cold, but Dunlavy managed to scrape up a stove, which he set up in Cates's room and tended, "and it sure feels good," Cates wrote.

"Dunlavy is a fine orderly; he keeps everything in fine shape and gets everything in sight. He likes the job, as he gets out of drill and I pay him five francs a week, besides always giving him something."

It wasn't until late February that the previously orphaned and unwanted marines were assigned to a division—the 2nd. The 5th and 6th Regiments would make up the all-marine 4th Brigade, the only marine brigade to see action in the war, while the 9th and 23rd Regiments of the regular army formed the division's 3rd Brigade.

Marine and regular soldier would fight together, die together, and endure many a hardship and scrape together—but there would never be any love lost between the marines, who would come to be called "Devil Dogs," and their dog-faced counterparts.

On February 15, Cates's battalion was sent on a nine-mile, arduous hike to some practice trenches, where it remained through the bitterly cold night. They carried symbols with them that indicated just how far they had come from the rolling and placid hills at Quantico.

Their soft campaign hats were replaced with steel helmets, and each man was given a gas mask and would be expected to accomplish everything from throwing hand grenades to wielding a bayonet to shooting a rifle and close-order drilling while wearing the accursed, blinding, suffocating appendages.

"It sure was one hard hike, as the men were all soft from their oversea trip and everyone was just about played out by the time we got there," Cates wrote.

"We entered the trenches just about dark and stayed until dawn; it was one awful night, as everyone was just about dead from the hike and then we had to work most of the night."

The work consisted of digging, digging, and more digging as well as stringing and fixing the long, never-ending seas of wire that one day would be all that stood between them and Germany. By the time dawn glimmered to the east beyond that wire, the men were exhausted—from the hike, from their new burdens, and from the sleepless, activity-filled night.

"It was the first time that we had worn the steel helmets, gas masks and had carried one hundred rounds of ammunition besides the other full equipment," Cates would write. "Everyone stood the trip fairly well and besides a few blistered feet and sore muscles, the men are all right."

Cates would become intimately familiar with his men's feet, the condition of which would be put at risk once the men took their turns in the slimy, sloshy, and hard-to-drain trenches, where they stood at times in water up to their knees.

"I have to inspect every man's feet in my platoon every day," he would write. "They have to wash them daily and keep dry socks on. A lieutenant is given a court martial if there is a case of trench feet in his platoon, and I am going to be sure that there is none in mine."

The regiment spent several weeks training around Blevaincourt, often going on forced marches through sleet and snow and freezing temperatures to the play trenches, or on night patrols through the same.

"The training went forward every day, and manoeuvres were executed in snowstorms," regimental commander Colonel Albertus Catlin would write. "I can't say the boys liked it. Who would? But they learned their lessons with surprising aptitude and became hard as nails."

So hard and well-trained, in fact, that Catlin would claim that after inspecting the marine brigade, General John Pershing—the same who had once balked at accepting the marines into his army—exclaimed, "I only wish I had 500,000 of these marines!"

With the initiation at Blevaincourt finished, the 6th Regiment on March 15 began moving by foot and trains sixty miles north-northwest to the Verdun sector, the site of a brutal slaughter of German and French troops during the previous three years, but at that late date a "quiet" sector—"quiet" meaning no constant, ringing artillery duels, no smothering bombardments of gas, and no insane massed infantry attacks.

The closer they got to the front, the more the marines became cognizant that they were, indeed, heading to war.

"As one nears the front he sure sees things of interest as the towns are all shell-riddled and one mass of ruins," the 96th Company's James W. Carter would write to his sister back in New Jersey.

"Some places just a statue of some sort is left. In one place the only thing that is left of a once-peaceful little city is a statue of the Virgin Mary. You cannot realize what one of these big guns, miles behind the lines, can do until you have seen these places."

On March 18, the marines detrained at Fort Dugny, one of a ring of forts surrounding Verdun. Apparently having been spotted upon arrival, they were welcomed by a barrage of shells from German artillery emplacements. They quickly hightailed out, marching thirty miles into the relative safety of the heights above the Meuse River.

Soon after, the marines began their initiation into real trench warfare. Taking turns by battalion, they occupied the front line, men from each of the two regiments being sandwiched between two French units. In time, the two marine regiments, placed next to each other, held an all-American piece of the western front.

Cates and his men, meanwhile, found their places in the shacks and aboveground barracks in a reserve position. Though several miles from the front line, Cates here got his first taste of shell fire, as the Germans were happy to share their artillery power with the back-liners as well as those holding the frontline trenches and the support trenches to their rear.

"It is far from a rest billet, as they keep us busy dodging shells," Cates wrote. "It sure is comical to see us make for a dugout or hole when we hear a shell coming. We run a little piece, and if we can not make any cover, we drop flat on our face and trust that it will go over or to one side.

"I am learning to do a lot of new dances; mostly the side steps and the dips, and they are executed in double time; anything to get away from the shrapnel."

A nearby French antiaircraft battery attracted the enmity of the Germans, and the sounds of war rang deeper than ever.

"The roar of the guns on the front rolled up about us and vibrated through the valleys," the 96th Company's Corporal Harrison Cale wrote. "An occasional shell fell near enough to make us uneasy."

On the evening of March 28, the 2nd Battalion was sent to relieve the regiment's 3rd Battalion in the front line. The 96th Company's 1st, 2nd, and 3rd Platoons were put into the front line, which snaked through the ruined, ghostly village of Mont-sous-les-Côtes, while Cates and his 4th Platoon were placed in the support position some two hundred yards behind them.

The frontline companies found their dugouts cramped, and two men slept together through the long day on a single bunk just two feet wide. At night, the men slithered from their deep holes to improve their slice of the trench and wait for whatever the Germans might throw at them—be it a raid or an artillery barrage.

The trenches had been occupied by French colonial troops long before their arrival. "They were in a very bad condition and there was plenty of work to do in repairing them," Cale wrote. "The dugouts swarmed with vermin; huge rats ran across the men as they slept, and wrought havoc with the emergency rations."

For the most part, though, the rats and cooties remained the marines' worst enemy. "'Heinie' did not worry me so much, but the rats, which we called 'war babies,' insisted on sleeping in my arms," Private John T. Miller of the 96th Company would add.

"And as we were in a position where the slightest noise would send us to the hospital or perhaps 'west,' the 'war babies' had everything their own way. And the 'cooties' would keep us company every night. They would parade up and down my back, and of course I had to stand for it."

Cates occupied a dugout "covered with heavy iron, then four feet of logs and then rock and earth about six feet deep, so you see that it was just about bomb proof," he would write reassuringly to his mother and sister.

"A person sure feels good when he knows that his covering is good and strong and I had a few times when the dugout came in very handy."

His dugout came in handy on one day when more than 300 shells—127 in just one eleven-minute span—landed around or on the 4th Platoon's position, thankfully killing or wounding none.

On April 5, the platoon's luck changed, the first shell of many to follow killing Grober and fatally wounding Metcalfe, and also wounding Privates Earl Anderson and Lambert Hehl. The barrage was followed by a raid-in-force, giving the 96th Company's men a first good look at their foes.

"I was in a daze when I saw my first 'Heinie,' and he looked about as big as the Woolworth's Building," Private Miller would say.

"But I woke up in time to realize I had a rifle and hadn't forgotten to use it. 'Heinie' stopped in our wire and stayed there. Our visitors were given a royal reception. Six of our boys went to the hospital but we left over a hundred of the Kaiser's boys in front of, and in, the trench, and had the trouble of burying them."

Despite the company's first deaths, "all of the men are in fine spirits," Cates would write on April 10. "It is a wonderful life, although it [lacks] a lot of being as nice as home. . . . It is a grand and glorious feeling to hear the shells whizzing over, that is, if you are in a bomb-proof dugout.

"You know the marines—the best ever! I have a good bunch and I am proud of them."

The war turned more serious when on April 12 a deluge of high-explosive and gas shells inundated the portion of reserve trench held by the regiment's 74th Company, down the line from the 96th.

The bulk of the 74th's 250 men were in their billets when the shells came in, and, trapped in their holes, they suffered badly from the gas. More than 200 enlisted men were affected by the gas, and 40 of them later died. Every officer in the company was evacuated "in a serious condition," the regiment's history says.

Later that month, the 96th Company moved back to the front line. Though the "tacit agreement" between French and Germans within the sector had been, as Harrison Cale would write, "if you don't shoot at me, I won't shoot at you," the marines couldn't help themselves when they espied some real, live Germans within range one morning in the third week of April.

"They didn't know the Marines," Cale wrote proudly. "When the dawn came our men climbed onto the parapets and when they saw some Germans down by the creek washing their clothing they promptly opened fire on them.

"This not only brought down the wrath of the French but a raid by the Germans." Their ire up and the peaceful standoff ended by these boob Americans, the Germans laid down a barrage preparatory to an assault.

But when the attacking force reached the barbed-wire entanglements in front of the 96th Company, "we opened up such a heavy rifle and machine gun fire that we held them in the wire until the American artillery, which had only moved in an hour before, got into action, and the barrage they poured upon them sent them back with a heavy loss of life," Cale wrote.

Amid the fury and carnage of the fight, Private Charles D. Graham was shot and killed—by one of his own buddies. Private Roy M. Miller, while giving the German attackers what-for with his rifle, "accidentally" shot poor Graham.

C'est la guerre.

Cale would crow about the men's success: "A wave of such pride and enthusiasm swept over the line that it silenced all criticism and dispelled any doubt in the minds of the French that we could fight."

But if the Germans had not known it before, they now knew they were squaring off against the Americans, of whom they knew little. Patrols after that little squabble turned more serious, resistance on both sides more stubborn.

The marines of the 96th Company, for good or ill, had brought the war to this sector of the lines. "The Germans, infuriated at the appearance of this new foe, bombarded our positions and resorted to every device to make our stay in the trenches as uncomfortable as possible," Cale wrote.

"Every trick known to trench warfare was resorted to and sleep soon became impossible. There they first conferred upon us the name of 'Devil Dogs,' and as there had been only two other units named by the Germans during the war: the Scottish Troops, called 'the Ladies from Hell,' and the Alpine Chausseurs, the 'Blue Devils,' we felt that we had been very highly complimented."

Cates would confirm Cale's account of little sleep. "Up until this morning, I had two hours of sleep out of sixty-two hours," he wrote on April 25. On the same day, Cates would write in almost real time of a typical daily encounter that occurred just after mail call:

"Just as my Gunnery Sgt. handed me the packages, the Boche commenced bombarding my part of the trenches. I grabbed my pistol belt and gas masks and beat it up to my post thru a bunch of bursting shell[s].

"They sure did come fast and furious and I thought I would never get to my post, but I finally did cover the two hundred yards and I found my men all standing to and they had commenced a slow rate of fire with the machine guns.

"We thought [for] sure the Boche were going to try a raid, but if they ever did have such an idea, they changed their minds after they saw what they had to come thru. Our artillery opened up and they had a perfect barrage on. Between our artillery and the Boche artillery, the machine guns, my automatic rifles and the rest of the works, we had hell for about one half an hour.

"The Boche always start a raid by heavy artillery concentrated on the post to be raided. They expect to drive our men into their dugouts and then the infantry come into the trenches just as their artillery barrage raises and before our men can come out of their dugouts."

The marines were actively patrolling as well, slithering out into the black night into No Man's Land to listen for German movements, or to block enemy patrols from sneaking up on the marine line.

"I was scared to death every time I went out on patrol," the 96th's Corporal Meyer J. Lapine, the son of a Russian immigrant who had formerly sold dry goods in Chicago, would say. "The cold sweat would pour off me and my whole body would shake with chills, but I'd have died before I let one of my pals know it. . . .

"But once you were out in 'no man's land,' creeping around in the dark, trying to keep in touch with the rest of your own men and not fall over a Hun before you saw him, sneaking through the enemy wire to listen up against his parapet, you were sitting in on a man's game where the sky was the limit."

Cliff Cates was pleased with men such as Corporal Lapine, and exultant over how his company was handling its first tastes of combat.

"It sure is wonderful to look down a line of trenches during such a mix up [sic] as we had. All kinds of flares were shot up and the big shells exploding put a good touch to the whole scene. Not a man in our company was hurt in the whole bombardment."

Such luck would not last—except for Lucky Cliff Cates.

"LA GUERRE EST FINIE"

THERE WERE CHEERS, at first. Grizzled old men, sad-eyed women with lined faces, and marveling, beaming children lined the road for miles, waving flags and throwing flowers to *les Américains*, the marines, as they slowly trucked east along the Paris–Metz highway, unsure of where exactly they were headed but certain it was to a fight.

French colonial drivers—"yellow Tonquinese and Anamites, and men from Madagascar, small weary heathen in Khaki uniforms and crested helmets," one marine would write—drooped long, foul-smelling cigarettes from their tobacco-stained lips while they ground gears to speed up and then slammed on the brakes, jostling the men in back and making the long trek a spine-jamming ordeal.

Then slowly, gradually, as the long caravan inched past the Paris suburbs farther to the east, the happy crowds were displaced by signs of war, and they could hear now the muffled booming of big guns to the northeast, like the sound of fence posts being pounded into hard earth, and then a wave of epic human misery and desperation flooded west toward them on both sides of the highway, peasants and soldiers and small-town bourgeoisie alike fleeing the steadily advancing Boches.

"There were no smiles on their faces, no waving of their hands; instead their faces were pale and showed signs of fear and despair," the 6th

Regiment's Private Levi Hemrick would write. "All that could, stayed on the move, only stopping when their tired limbs could no longer move in the line of traffic."

Here were old men bearing their old women in wheelbarrows, household possessions of every sort lashed to the frames of old bicycles; here fear-faced women dragging ragged children two at a time, there a sobbing mother stopping to grieve over a baby that had died in her arms.

Chickens, ducks, rabbits in crates and birds in their cages were tied willy-nilly to every kind of conveyance, while burly oxen and horses, so worn out the French army had no use for them, trudged along under the hot sun. Meanwhile, French soldiers, faces smeared with black powder and uniforms stained with dirt and blood, lay exhausted on the swale while the bizarre procession passed by.

"The Boche are coming!" they called to the marines. *"La guerre est finie!"*

"We're here," a few Americans pointed out.

"Ah, *oui*," came the reply. "But the Boche, he is *still* coming."

The marines, shocked, quit their horseplay at the sight, which none had ever seen or even imagined before. Here was the detritus of war, the real war, their war, which up to now had been little more than a vague idea. Here were real people suffering and being displaced by strange world events, by history.

Their carefree lives were over.

"There were no more shouts or laughter coming from the men in our trucks," Hemrick wrote. "This was different. There was no jubilee for our men in this kind of war or fun to move along this kind of trail. . . . It was as if the emotional strain of witnessing so much misery had suddenly turned carefree youths into mature men. We rode along in silence."

"We got a chance to see what war is this time for fair," wrote Private Thomas L. Stewart of the 96th Company. "The road we came on was simply lined with civilians going to the rear. It is certainly pitiful to see them—mostly old people with all their possessions on wagons, carts, even wheelbarrows and on their backs; and all tired out with traveling perhaps a couple of days.

"It was enough to make a man want to fight."

Cliff Cates, former college-man-about-town, law grad, and the would-be heir to Cates Landing, Tennessee, took in the scene from the back of his bumping, grinding truck and also was moved.

"It was the most pitiful sight I have ever seen, and there is not a man in our bunch that didn't grit his teeth and say, 'Vive la France,'" he would write. "'Do or die' is our motto—and the mother that can furnish a boy should say—'America—here's my boy, God grant that he may come back, if not, I am glad he died for a noble cause, and I am willing to give him to you.'"

Almost four years before, a similar caravan of troops—these French, and some traveling in a vast line of Paris taxis—had rolled along the same route to hold the advance of the Germans in a desperate, last-ditch battle at the Marne River, now sparkling as it coursed through the florid fields that rolled just ahead beyond this maze of misery.

Now the Germans, the Boches, were back, and they were marching with grim determination toward the Marne and also trending southwest toward Paris in a great, gray tide of destruction.

The French armies before them pushed back as long as they could and then collapsed, men in raggedy groups of twos and threes, exhausted, heading west by any means they could find and now encountering fresh-faced Americans on the road, marines who rejected the entreaties of the defeated *poilus* to turn tail and flee, lest they, too, should become engulfed in the seething, murderous German advance.

This clash of Old World and New, of heroic Americans riding to the rescue of the French, on the Paris–Metz highway on May 31, 1918, was exactly what the Germans had hoped to preempt.

By that spring, Americans were safely arriving in French ports by the boatload, and their presence had not gone unnoticed by the German high command, which had been certain its submarine campaign would prevent a large American entry into the war.

That had not happened, as some three hundred thousand Americans were already in-country and either training or holding a line somewhere, and now the focus of Erich Ludendorff, the Germans' military architect of the war, was focused on ending things before the Americans could tilt the balance.

Where the Germans had devoted much of 1917 to pulling back from their farthest advances, straightening lines across the center of the western front to reduce the amount of square footage that had to be defended, and fortifying an ultimate line of defense known as the Hindenburg Line, the new year brought with it urgent designs for a new plan of attack on the Allies.

Though there were only five American divisions deemed ready to fight—among them the 2nd—in France as spring approached, Ludendorff hoped to end things by the summer, and at the least force the war-weary British and French to the negotiating table, or, at best, seize Paris.

Ludendorff had new weapons at his disposal: some forty-two German divisions—five hundred thousand men—that had been tied up in the war with Russia. Following the Bolshevik Revolution of the previous November, an end to hostilities on the eastern front was declared on December 15, 1917—and on March 3, 1918, Russia sealed the deal, signing a treaty with the Central Powers at Brest-Litovsk.

On March 21, 1918, while the marines were just entering the front-line trenches in the quiet Vosges, Ludendorff's carefully laid plans exploded on the Somme north and east of Paris, the scene of horrifying British losses in their own desperate offensive during the latter half of 1916.

In an offensive dubbed Michael, the Germans aimed for the junction of the French armies to the south of the Somme River and the British armies to the north. With the two forces split, the Germans then planned to wheel right, envelop the Brits, and pin them to the French coast.

To that end, at four forty a.m. on March 21, 6,700 artillery pieces opened up with a deluge of gas and high explosive along a forty-mile front from the Sensee River to the north to the Oise River below. At nine thirty-five a.m. heavy mortars began pounding the British lines, while mines that had been set under the protective wires were blown.

Just five minutes later, the German first waves left their trenches and flitted with deadly intent across No Man's Land toward the French and British outposts. Three separate armies, a total of sixty-nine German divisions, would advance this day, Ludendorff's great gamble to end the war in Germany's favor riding on the soldiers' feet and nerves.

As the barrages lifted, fourteen-member teams of German storm troopers carrying light machine guns, flame throwers, and automatic weapons appeared out of thick fog and crossed the trenches, ignoring the deadly strongpoints and, instead, leaving them for strong mop-up teams, who reduced them with mortars and automatic weapons.

On the first day, results were better than hoped for, with great advances made all along the line, but especially in the south, where the German tide rolled four and a half miles through the British 5th Army and beyond. Twenty-one thousand British soldiers were made prisoner that day, and untold hundreds or even thousands more were wounded and killed, many of whom would be buried where they huddled in their trenches.

Over the next two weeks, a hole forty miles deep would be punched through the formerly nonbudging western front, 164,000 British soldiers would become casualties and another 90,000 be taken prisoner, and hundreds of newfangled tanks and thousands of artillery pieces, machine guns, and rifles would also be lost.

It was a brilliant stroke, and a real-life mirror of the theoretical open warfare John Pershing espoused and even planned upon.

Ironically, though, even as Ludendorff's *Sturmtruppen* were racing through and across the British lines and toward the French coast, the average American doughboy in France was far from the action, learning the soon-to-be anachronistic and static "art" of trench warfare in their holes in the quiet front lines at Seicheprey, the Vosges, and around Verdun.

By April 5, when the great German onslaught had run out of steam and rolled up at the edges of a small village called Cantigny—short of the forest of Compiègne and the strategic Allied centers of Amiens and Arras—the American mission in the war had changed.

Though the Allies had clamored for Pershing to pass his soldiers on to them almost piecemeal for insertion into their lines, he had steadfastly refused, and dug in his heels on the point of keeping under his command an all-American army.

Even during the bleak early days of the German offensive, he had held fast against renewed pleas for troops, gambling a possible German victory on the principle of keeping his army American.

But by March 28, just as the German push began breaking against stiffer Allied resistance and falling prey to exhaustion and supply issues, Pershing saw the light. On that day he went to French Marshal Ferdinand Foch, just recently made commander of all the Allied armies, and in halting French told him, "All that we have are yours."

Within days, the U.S. 1st Division was ordered to entrain from a passive area of Lorraine and sent first toward Paris and then to Picardy, where French colonials were holding the line where the German assault had petered out around Montdidier, fifty miles north of Paris.

There, in a ghastly landscape pocked with shell holes, and smothered in bodies of Moroccan soldiers blackening and swarming with bluebottle flies under the increasingly hot spring sun, the Americans on April 24 began digging in under the eye of the Germans who held the tiny village of Cantigny, which teetered on the edge of the Cantigny plateau and overlooked the verdant farmland to the west. The 1st would hold that position for a little more than a month; the 2nd Division, meanwhile, continued to hold the lines in its sector outside of Verdun.

While the Germans paused to reorganize before launching another series of audacious drives to the northwest, and the outcome of the war teetered on their success or failure, Cliff Cates and his marines continued to wade in and out of various sections of mucky trench line.

"We do not mind fighting the damn Boche, but this rainy weather and mud gets our goat," Cates would write. "We get very little sleep while up front, as the time that we are not on post, we are working on our trenches trying to get them in a better condition. We have to pump water out of all of the dugouts and we do not have fires during the day, so you see that it is real muddy and damp."

The trenches were also fronted by barbed wire—"worlds" of barbed wire, Cates would write—and on one night he would again prove his luck while out in front of his line inspecting the condition of the wire. There he fell and became entangled in a grabbing, stinging circle of wire, "and I thought I would never get out."

The wire, thick and heavy with large barbs, impaled his clothing and ripped his skin. Cates went to work trying to get free of the wire, all the while worrying the racket he was making in the still night would catch the attention of the Germans across the way.

"It was as dark as pitch and they couldn't see me, but a skyrocket flare would have made things as bright as day," he wrote. "When they shoot up a flare, the only thing to do is to drop into the nearest shell hole, or lie flat on the ground, and pray that they do not see you." Cates somehow extricated himself and made it back to his line without incident.

Once again, Lucky Cates's luck had held.

On May 1, the 96th Company pulled out of the lines and headed to a reserve position. "The men have well earned a rest," Cates would write his sister. "We stayed in the line a good while for our first time in. Our men all did good work and are 'sure-enough' soldiers."

The men rested and drilled until May 10, when the 6th Regiment began a long journey by foot, truck, and rail that by the last week of May would find it in a training area north of Paris.

The weather had turned warm, hot even, and the marching over miles and miles of French countryside was grueling—but after the relative physical inactivity of the trenches, and the long hours of sitting, watching, and waiting in the dark, the physical work returned muscle tone to the marines' frames.

And oh, the things they carried. . . .

"A person who has never carried a full pack cannot imagine how heavy it is," Cates would write after a long, hard day of picking them up and putting them down.

"Here is an average of what one man carries—his rifle, 100 rounds of 30-30 ammunition, pistol, 21 rounds of 40 [caliber] ammunition, wire pliers, shovel . . . canteen, canteen cup, meat can, condiment can, bacon can, knife, fork, spoon, 4 boxes of hard bread, 32 ounces of bacon, coffee, sugar, salt and pepper (emergency rations), first aid package, 3 pistol clips, poncho (raincoat) overcoat, pr of shoes, 2 pr socks, pr of leggings, suit of underwear, O.D. shirt, toilet articles, towels, cigarettes, etc., English gas respirator, French gas mask, steel helmet, overseas cap, bayonet, scabbard and blanket. . . . Besides all that, each platoon has 14 pouches of Chauchat ammunition and clips, that weigh 30 pounds each, that the men divide equally."

By May 21, the 6th Regiment was concentrated around the village of Serans. There was much talk of the 2nd Division heading north to Picardy to relieve the 1st Division around Montdidier and Cantigny, and to that end the marines were instructed in "French combat drills"— specifically, open-terrain attacks on fixed emplacements, aka Pershing's open warfare.

But the methods and tactics as taught were reminiscent more of Pickett's doomed charge over open ground at Gettysburg in July 1863 than any novel approach to attacking an entrenched enemy that had any number of death-dealing machine guns at hand.

Instead, the men were drilled in columns of platoons and companies, and small-unit tactics were foresworn until the time came that the mechanical, larger-formation drills were perfect.

"Unfortunately few of these dated maneuvers would fit the war we were entering," Corporal Don Paradis of the 80th Company would remember.

As the marines—"youthful, idealistic, slightly dated," to use Paradis's words—continued to hone their French-style drills and prepare for their turn in the trenches in Picardy, the sky seemingly fell in on May 27.

Four thousand German guns, massed for twenty-four miles on an east-west line on the Chemin des Dames above the Aisne River, opened up with a thunderous roar, and soon thirty-six German divisions, many released from duty in the East, advanced against just six French and four British divisions that had been depleted from the fighting of March and April and sent to the supposed quiet area below the Chemin des Dames to rest and refit.

The Allied opposition quickly melted away.

Ludendorff originally had sought to lure south the French divisions that had been sent to bolster the British lines to the north, then pause that offensive and attack the weakened fifty-mile British front in the Ypres salient and drive the Brits to the Channel ports in the north.

But by the second day of this supposedly limited offensive spilling south from the rugged heights of the Chemin des Dames, the Germans had drilled a bulge fifteen miles deep and forty miles wide into the Allied lines. Ludendorff, now seeing a greater opportunity to end the war, ordered the advance continued south to the Marne River at Château-Thierry and southwest toward Paris.

Soissons soon fell as the French 6th Army sacrificed division after division in fighting below the city, while Reims, to the east, barely hung on. By May 30, the vanguard of the German onslaught was at the Marne, thirty-five air miles from Paris; on the same day, the marines were just north of the capital and fifty-six miles northwest from where epic disaster loomed.

The marines cheered jealously on May 29 when told of the 1st Division's successful assault on Cantigny the day before, then resumed their training and drilling in the area around the 2nd Division's headquarters at Chaumont-en-Vexin.

Then on May 30, as the Germans tried to force a crossing of the Marne at Château-Thierry, the marines celebrated Memorial Day, holding parades and commemorative services to honor the dead of previous wars.

When those were done, the men found themselves free to pass the day as they liked, some heading off on sightseeing hikes, some writing letters, some engaging in games. All were ready for a fifty-mile march north to begin the next day to Beauvais and then the Cantigny sector to relieve the 1st Division.

Their reveries were broken at five p.m., when a French staff car, caked with dust from speeding over unimproved roads, raced up to the headquarters of 2nd Division commander General Omar Bundy. A French staff officer hurriedly disclosed the dire situation at the Marne, where a motorized machine-gun battalion from the 3rd Division was even then barely holding off the German advance at the river at Château-Thierry while French engineers blew the Marne bridges.

"We had been reading the Paris papers and we knew the situation," the 6th Regiment's commander, Albertus W. Catlin, would write. Bundy and his staff quickly forgot about the pending move toward

Picardy, and orders were sent across the area recalling marines to their billets.

The marines packed, locked, and loaded, and then waited for a convoy of trucks that would spirit many—hundreds—to their final resting places in the coming long days, and etch a small piece of woods into the national consciousness, and into Marine Corps lore.

"DO YOU WANT TO LIVE FOREVER?"

THE 2ND DIVISION rode all day and all night—"an awful cold and dirty trip," Cliff Cates would write when some of it, but not the worst of by any measure, was over.

"We (the whole division, 27,500 men) were jammed into French trucks and started out. . . . If you can, imagine about one thousand trucks lined up one behind the other and running as fast as possible. We passed through the outskirts of gay Paree and on thru numerous towns. The French people would cheer us as we passed through the towns, and the children would throw us worlds of flowers—it is a sign of good luck."

The trucks, or *camions*, driven by the exotic Anamites and other colonials had not arrived at the 2nd Division staging area until four a.m. on May 31. With their canvas tops, the trucks looked like "prairie schooners," Albertus Catlin would write. It took about fifty *camions* to move one battalion, thirty men to a truck.

At five thirty a.m., the engines were revved, gears engaged, and the long convoy of trucks headed out at the astonishing speed of between ten and fifteen miles an hour, "according to the roads and the temperaments of the drivers," a marine with the 5th Regiment, John W. Thomason, would recall.

Pershing had ordered the division to engage, acting finally at the request of the ever-desperate French, and when the marine 4th Brigade went in, it would be under a new commander, not one of their own marines. Instead, Pershing had selected his own good friend and Chief of Staff, General James Harbord, to take over the job when the original brigade commander, Charles A. Doyen, was deemed physically unfit for active service.

There was some grumbling among the marines at the affront of some *army* character taking over—but Harbord quickly won their respect.

"He seems to be an extra good man," Cates would write. "General Pershing said to him when he put him in command of us, 'My boy, I am giving you the finest command in France. You will have the best troops in the world.'"

Harbord was quickly won over by the marines, and their way of doing things, as well. He appreciated especially the marines' camaraderie and democratic spirit, which ran from top to bottom.

"No Marine officer ever pulled any of that 'My man' stuff, which, when I was an enlisted man, made me feel like doing murder," he would write. "The habitual marine address was 'Lad' or 'My Lad.' No Marine was ever too old to be a 'Lad.' . . .

"At our Brigade mess there was hot coffee on the fire day and night. No runner or other marine brought there by duty ever failed to receive the invitation, 'Go back to the galley, lad, and get a cup of coffee.' It was the same at every officers' mess that came under my observation."

(What Cliff Cates and his fellow marines may not have known was there was more to Pershing's pep talk to Harbord: When he turned over the 4th Brigade, he warned Harbord: *If it fails, I'll know where to place the blame.*)

Harbord was determined to succeed, but as his staff car preceded the convoy of marines and regulars down the Paris–Metz highway that last day of May 1918, he wasn't even sure exactly where he was headed.

With decent maps scarce and the situation beyond fluid, all the Americans could do was head in the direction from which a flood of dejected, spent humanity was coming toward them.

"We passed through Meaux, and the main body of the French army in full retreat," the 96th Company's Harrison Cale would write. "All semblance of formation had disappeared.

"Soldiers mingled with civilians in a mad rush to safety. Beyond Meaux the road was filled with refugees. A motley-looking mass of men and women and children and cattle and carts.

"Toothless old women and aged men struggled under heavy burdens. Young girls dragging little children scurried along the edge of the fields. They watched us pass, without emotion, pausing only to cry, 'Tue le Boche,' and draw their hands across their throats, suggesting this method as the most effective means."

Twenty-six-year-old Private Orley M. Dunton of the 96th Company would remember one woman who resembled his own aged grandmother back in Michigan. The woman was "hardly able to move across the room, and here were a score, equally feeble, being pushed ahead by the onrushing tide of Huns.

"A fellow directly behind me said, 'Damn 'em, damn 'em!' and there was a murmured re-echo down the line. 'Quiet back there!' the platoon leader shouted, but there was a bit of sympathy in the command."

"No traffic in N.Y. city [sic] can compare with the few miles that we covered that afternoon—truck after truck, automobiles, motorcycles—thousands of troops and lots of airplanes overhead: also lots of artillery and machine guns moving into new positions," Cliff Cates remembered.

At four a.m. on June 1, the 2nd Battalion disembarked in the village of Montreuil-aux-Lions on the Paris–Metz highway, about four miles from the leading edge of the German advance. The men fell out, and, the occupants of the houses having joined the exodus west, went to work slaughtering chickens and rabbits and cooking a feast. It was the first food many had had in the past twenty-four hours.

"[A] lot of wine cellars were located also," Cates would recall.

Then the men of the 96th Company hit the villagers' feather beds and haystacks, some to sleep off the exhaustion brought not just from the road but from the bottles of wine they had liberated from cellars as well.

All that previous day, confusion had reigned. The officers of the French 6th Army, harried and harassed and distracted, had been little help in telling the vanguard of the 2nd Division where it was needed most.

Initially, the German tide was expected to come streaming south on the Soissons–Meaux road, and so elements of the 2nd Division were assembled at the village of May-en-Multien. But the Germans were rolling down more from the east than the north; amid the flood of conflicting reports and the fog of fast-changing events, the French issued four separate orders of assembly.

"Having been brought up on Santa Claus, I was not so hardened as to believe what the cynical marines told me, that one should not begin to obey orders from the French until the third edition had arrived, as there were always at least two changes," would write Harbord, who spent much of the day madly dashing about on the conflicting instructions of the French.

Finally, it was realized that the main German thrust and pressure were coming from the east, and mainly north of the Paris–Metz highway west of Château-Thierry.

While Cates and his men feasted on rabbit and wine and hit the hay, elements of the 2nd Division that had preceded it to the area began moving east to intercept the German drive around a tiny village called Lucy-le-Bocage, just north of the highway and a little southwest of an ancient hunting preserve called the Bois de Belleau.

There, the French commanders on the scene urged the Americans to throw their men into the action piecemeal, but they were rebuffed by 2nd Division commander General Omar Bundy and his Chief of Staff, Colonel Preston Brown, who insisted on forming a cohesive American line behind the French withdrawal.

To that end, the 9th Regiment, first to arrive on the field, took up positions south of the Paris–Metz highway and below a German-occupied rise called Hill 204, as the 5th and 23rd Regiments streamed cross-country east from May-en-Multien toward Lucy-le-Bocage. Meanwhile, Cates and the 2nd Battalion under Thomas Holcomb took to the Paris–Metz highway by foot at about two p.m., moving to the sound of the guns.

Hoping to speed the advance, James Harbord personally commandeered a convoy of trucks that was dumping a load of rations and ammunition farther east along the highway, and, seated in the cab of the first truck, led the convoy west to scoop up Holcomb and his men, who gladly hopped aboard. The trucks then turned east and retraced their steps to the developing battle zone.

The 2nd Battalion's marines were the first of the regiment to arrive at the hot zone. They deployed above and to the left of the 9th Regiment, the 96th Company placed the farthest to the right and connected with the regulars on the highway at the village of Le Thiolet. A thousand yards behind a thin line of French infantry that continued to battle the advancing Germans, the battalion began to stretch itself to the northwest and take up a line that ran twenty-two hundred yards from the highway through Triangle Farm to the village of Lucy-le-Bocage and almost to the southern tip of the Bois de Belleau.

As they settled in, they could see the Bois de Bouresches to their front and right, as well as the village of Bouresches itself. The Bois de Belleau, a roughly mile-square kidney-shaped blob of thick, dark woods and rocky, uneven ground that had been maintained for centuries as a hunting preserve for the local royals, was now owned by a wealthy Paris businessman. Just yards from the front left of the battalion's line, at that moment the woods were sparsely held by the French.

As the battle, unseen but heard, raged through the rest of the afternoon above the villages of Bouresches and Belleau and along the Clignon brook to the north, the rest of the 6th Regiment slowly trooped in, caked with dust from marching with sixty-pound packs behind trucks and looking "more like miners emerging from an all-night shift than like fresh troops ready to plunge into battle," Albertus Catlin would write.

As they arrived, Catlin ordered the 1st Battalion, temporarily under Major Maurice Shearer while Johnny Hughes was away at school, to deploy to the left of the 2nd Battalion. Its marines raced to man positions that began sixteen hundred yards west of the ravine in which Lucy-le-Bocage sat, and meandered to the left to a prominence called Hill 142 a mile to the northwest. The 3rd Battalion under Major Berton Sibley was put in support.

The 23rd Regiment, meanwhile, was put in place on the far right next to its brigade-mate, the 9th Regiment, to block any German movement up the Paris–Metz highway from Château-Thierry. Colonel Frederic "Fritz" Wise's 2nd Battalion of the 5th Regiment would eventually be posted on the far left of the American line, from Hill 142 west to Les Mares Farm, beyond which French troops were in line.

A French general suggested to Harbord that he should have a second line dug several hundred yards behind where the brigade had established its positions. But Harbord quickly rebuffed him, telling the general his men were prepared to die if necessary to hold the line, but if they started digging trenches, "they would know that it could have but one purpose."

The marines, Harbord added, "will hold where they stand."

Even while these dispositions were being made, the hard-pressed and dispirited troops of the French 43rd Division continued to filter through the American lines, some weaponless after having thrown away their rifles while on the run, and some armed only with bottles of cheap red wine they had scavenged from the cellars of the dispossessed.

They'd been fighting almost constantly since May 27, and were, indeed, *finis*.

"As we passed a clump of trees near the Triangle Farm, a French officer at the head of a company of horsemen dashed up to my section and shouted, 'Go back while you have the opportunity. There are many Boches!'" Harrison Cale would write.

"'Many Boche[s],' I answered, 'why that's just what we came here to see.'"

Cale may have been embellishing his own role in the affair; all along the line and in the days to follow, stirring words would be spoken that would ring into the annals of marine legend and history.

Retreat, hell—we just got here! was one such utterance, spoken, most agree, by the 5th Regiment's Captain Lloyd Williams (though many others, including Wise, claimed speakership) to a French counterpart who urged him to turn back with his men. *Come on, you sons of bitches! Do you want to live forever?* is its equal, shouted by the two-time Medal of Honor recipient Dan Daly as he urged his machine-gun company forward during another attack.

But for the marines there was little such drama for the remainder of June 1, which was spent trying to dig holes into the hard, flinty French soil with whatever implement or utensil one could find. The line traversed open ground and patches of woods, neither safe from the rounds of artillery and machine-gun fire that would find targets over the next days as the Germans pressed the attack to the southwest.

"There were no trenches and the only protection we had were the holes which we dug to lie in," the 96th Company's Private John T. Miller would remember. "Things were flying and I did not take time to get my shovel, which I had in my pack, but used my mess gear instead."

By the time each hole was finished, it measured roughly six feet long, two and a half feet wide, and three feet deep. Whole days would be spent lying low in these refuges, which, under the circumstances, the marines only half jokingly referred to as "their graves," Catlin would write.

That night would be the last relatively quiet one for the next three weeks. With their rolling kitchens still stuck on the roads, the men reluctantly resorted to chowing down on their emergency rations—hard bread and tinned, red Argentinian beef, which the marines spitefully called "monkey meat."

That night, Thomas Holcomb walked the line and checked the double rows of holes—they would come to be called "foxholes" before the war was done—and approved each man's billet. Shortly, the exhausted marines drifted off, each one no doubt wondering what tomorrow held.

BOCHES

FIRST IN THE red glow of dawn on June 2, it was the French soldiers, *poilus*, loping across the fields below Bouresches and the Bois de Belleau and coming straight for their lines, once again some of them shouting warnings that the Germans were coming, the war, *la guerre*, was *finie*, over, and the crazy *Américains* should make a run for it while they still could.

Behind them came waves of said Germans, pushing now toward Bouresches and its screening wood, and rolling south through the browning wheat from the northwest of the Bois de Belleau, long lines filled with inviting targets unaware they were about to encounter not just Americans, but marines, and each one a well-schooled rifleman, if nothing else.

"Blame me if they didn't come off that hill, and the Huns after 'em," the 96th Company's Private Joseph Greenburg would write of the French retirement. "But we could do nothing, for if we fired we'd hit the French, too. So we waited.

"As luck would have it, the French outran the Huns and got to us first. The Huns, fagged, stopped opposite us in a wood, expecting to finish the job tomorrow. They didn't dream the Americans were there. And especially the marines."

"Hardly a lad of us didn't boast a 'Marksman's' badge, many qualified as 'Sharpshooter' and 'Expert Rifleman,'" the 96th Company's Private Orley Dunton would write. "The boys did not just simply raise their rifles and shoot in the general direction of Germany.

"They adjusted their sights, coolly took aim and shot to kill. I cannot believe that one shot in ten missed a mark. The Prussians dropped as if Death were wielding his scythe in their midst, rank after rank."

"I could not but admire the precision and steadiness of those waves of men in grey with the sun glinting on their helmets," Albertus Catlin would recall. "On they came, never faltering, apparently irresistible. But they were not irresistible. Back of the French was a force they had not reckoned on, a force as steady and confident as themselves."

All along the line, but particularly in front of the 2nd Battalion of the 5th Marines posted below Hill 142 and in front of Les Mares Farm on the left, the carnage was extreme.

"I guess the Germans didn't realize they were coming against Americans," the 51st Company's Second Lieutenant Lemuel Shepherd—destined to succeed Cliff Cates as Marine Corps commandant one day—would say. "We could actually hear them yelling about it."

"We just mowed them down," the 96th Company's Private Clarence Weismantel would add.

After standing as much of the American fire as they could, the Germans backed off. "The flower of the Germans broke ranks and took refuge in the woods," Dunton would write. "But our impudence could not be allowed to go unpunished. They whipped and slashed that field of waist-high wheat with such a concentrated machine-gun fire as I never expected to encounter again."

For the rest of that day and the next three, the marines held the German advance as they waited for . . . well, nobody was really sure. Supplies were brought up, and the divisional artillery, and subsequent artillery duels, ruled the skies, the machine guns on both sides were active, and Germans in airplanes and balloons provided coordinates for pinpoint artillery fire.

"We laid [sic] in those holes for three days and dared not stick our heads up," Private John Miller would write. "If we did, it meant 'taps,' and that we would have to answer 'reveille' in the morning."

"Things were comparatively quiet for four days—of course, both sides of artillery were active most of the time and we had a few casualties," Cliff Cates would write. "We could not get food for the first sixty hours, so we ate the emergency rations that each man carries."

Cates's 96th Company lost nine men over those four days. It could easily have been more.

Corporal Julius Steinberg, the "Count" from Omaha, was wounded by shrapnel in the leg during the fighting on June 3, while the next day, Sergeant Ollie Henry Johanningsmeier of St. Louis, Missouri, was killed. On the same day, four more from the 96th were wounded.

The 96th's John T. Miller would recall one private deciding to change his "boudoir" one evening and almost paying the ultimate price.

"About that time 'Heinie' saved him the trouble by sending an eight-inch [high explosive] which made a hole big enough to put a regiment in," he wrote. "So 'Tex' decided to take up quarters in it. He had just arrived at his new home (or hole) when 'Heinie' duplicated the order, which hit on the edge of the first hole. 'Tex' came sailing over my head.

"I first thought he had joined the aviation, and was going to Heaven, but when I looked around there was 'Tex' sitting on the ground trying to find out if he was all together, and cursing Heinie for being so attentive. Looking at me[,] he said:

"'Can you imagine those Dutchmen sniping at me with an eight-inch gun[?]'"

While the marines and regulars of the 3rd Brigade lay in their holes, the Germans on the night of June 2 took the village of Bouresches, to the right of Belleau Wood. With their right-rear flank now threatened with envelopment, the French began quietly filing out of the wood and toward the American lines.

The Germans saw an opportunity and quickly took over the crags and gnarled crevices of the wood and, unseen through the thick green screen of trees, spent June 3 and June 4 building deep lines of enfilading machine-gun emplacements, sited well to cover the wood from east to west.

Except for a tentative foray in the direction of the 5th Regiment on the left, which provoked a rude refusal provided by machine guns and well-aimed rifles, they settled in and waited for the marines to make a move.

But there was no movement, even though 4th Brigade commander James Harbord remained certain that the woods were clear—despite plenty of evidence that they were occupied by a less-than-desirable element.

A French aviator had told of being shot at by a machine gun as he flew over the wood on June 3, and the next night a four-man patrol led by the 6th Regiment's intelligence officer, Second Lieutenant William Eddy, reported "considerable activity" in the woods, as well as a German presence on the west edge of the wood.

Harbord remained convinced, however, that only a small portion of the northeast corner of the wood was occupied; retreating French soldiers had said so. On June 5, the 2nd Division was ordered to prepare for an assault north from Hill 142, west of the Bois de Belleau.

The 2nd Division's Chief of Staff, Colonel Preston Brown, met with the regimental and battalion commanders picked to lead the attacks, and advised them to employ the tactic of infiltration by small groups, instead of advancing in waves.

His advice, when it came time to attack, was largely and tragically ignored.

Despite scanty intelligence on the nature of the ground and the disposition of the German force before them, Harbord made his plans for the assault, to begin early on the morning of June 6.

A French division, the 167th, was brought up and placed on the left of the marines, allowing them to shorten their lines to a seven-kilometer (four-mile) front in preparation of the assault, which would begin with an advance on Hill 142 by the 1st Battalion of the 5th Regiment under Major Julius Turrill.

Major Benjamin Berry's 3rd Battalion of the 5th would advance on Turrill's right and "conform" to Turrill's progress, while the French on the left were also to advance.

At three forty-five a.m., Turrill's depleted battalion—he had only the 49th and 67th Companies, as two more remained behind at Les Mares Farm waiting for relief by French troops, which was supposed to have occurred at nine p.m. on June 5—stepped from the relative shelter of the woods in its line and into the wheat, advancing dumbly in waves up the slope of Hill 142, supported by covering fire from the 18th Machine Gun Company before Champillon.

"The platoons came out of the woods as dawn was getting gray," the marine John W. Thomason would write. "The light was strong when they advanced into the open wheat, now all starred with dewy poppies, red as blood.

"To the east the sun appeared, immensely red and round, a handbreadth above the horizon; a German shell burst black across the face of it, just to the left of the line. Men turned their heads to see, and many there looked no more upon the sun forever."

After just fifty yards, all hell broke loose. The 1st Battalion's marines went flat as withering German fire coming from a small wood to their front—"more machine guns than I had ever heard before," the 49th Company's Captain George Hamilton would write—sliced through the grass at a rate of one thousand bullets per minute.

Hamilton bravely went along the line, urging his men to rise and race for the guns—becoming, as historians Susie and Meirion Harries would write, "the first to demonstrate the chilling marine theory that the only sure way to overcome machine-gun positions of this kind was to rush them."

It would surely not be the last time the "chilling" theory would be demonstrated; many a marine would die while both proving and disproving it.

"I don't remember clearly what happened," a still-dazed Hamilton would write after the assault.

"I have vague recollections of urging the whole line on, faster, perhaps, than they should have gone—of grouping prisoners and sending them to the rear under *one* man instead of several—of snatching an iron cross ribbon off the first officer I got—and of shooting wildly at several retreating Boches."

Marines took the machine guns in mad dashes, using their bayonets, fists, grenades, pistols, and whatever else was at hand. But after passing through the first danger in the wood, the marines entered another field flooded with red poppies, and again were pasted with machine-gun fire, this time from their front and right.

"Again it was a case of rushing across the open and getting into the woods," Hamilton wrote. He would find later that three German machine-gun companies were present and accounted for—and mowing down his men.

Hamilton continued to advance, but soon found he had outrun his flanks and was isolated and alone and under heavy fire. Hamilton and most of his remaining men—"it was every man for himself"—now turned tail and sought the safety of the reverse slope of the previous hill they had crossed.

Three more marines continued north toward the village of Torcy, where they encountered fire coming from the first home they came upon.

One of them was sent back to tell Hamilton they had taken Torcy while the other two marines jumped into a hole in the farmyard from which rocks had been excavated, and returned fire; their remains, and those of two German soldiers, were found in the hole in 1927 when the landowner cleared brush from the edge.

Hamilton, meanwhile, found the tables turned and an angry swarm of Germans coming right for him. Five "nasty" times, they counterattacked. They were preceded by grenades, one of which threw off a piece of rock as it exploded and caught Hamilton behind an ear "and made me dizzy for a few minutes."

The fog enveloping his head evaporated when one of Hamilton's gunnery sergeants let out a yell as he jumped into a patch of thick bushes and began "shooting to beat the devil. Not twenty feet from us, was a line of about fifteen German helmets and five light machine guns just coming into action. It was hand-to-hand work for several strenuous minutes, and then all was over."

Hamilton, who had gone six hundred yards farther than his objective, and what remained of the 49th and 67th Company began digging in. Soon reinforced by the two missing companies—the 66th and the 17th—and by elements of the 5th Regiment's 2nd Battalion, and supported by the French who had finally come up on the left, the 1st Battalion hung on through several more counterattacks.

Dead and wounded from both sides littered the field, but neither side would allow their retrieval, firing at anything and anyone that moved. Meanwhile, Benjamin Berry's 3rd Battalion of the 5th Regiment, on Hamilton's right, had advanced just two platoons of the 45th Company fast enough to keep pace with Hamilton.

These were now pinned down two hundred yards short of their objective, however, and the 3rd Battalion remained in place on the right of the 1st Battalion through the morning.

The tally of dead, wounded, and missing that day came to 8 officers and 325 men for the 5th Regiment's 1st Battalion, a portent of what would become the marines' deadliest day until the assault on Tarawa in 1943.

"Gee, but it was a long day!" Hamilton would write.

INTO THE WOOD

"LET'S GO!"

The wheat below Cliff Cates's feet seemed to be moving, shaking and shimmering from a thousand small breezes created by passing machine-gun bullets.

It was almost stupid the way they zinged and whiffed as they cut the tops of the grass, sending tufts gamely aloft to swirl and spire, but it was terrifying when they slammed with a muffled thud into the body of a marine and hit bone or a lung, sending sprays of pink blood to mingle with the hard brown earth.

"Let's go!"

Cliff Cates had perhaps stupidly followed Robertson's command forward—crazy, hardened, and worldly First Lieutenant James Robertson, who had his right arm extended in a sweeping motion and pointing toward a collection of stone buildings gleaming dully in the bright sun like the ruins of Mycenae.

It was maybe stupid, but Cates didn't hesitate, nor did the men of his 4th Platoon. They followed Cates, and Cates followed Robertson, while around them men were lamed or died in the grimacing paroxysms of last agonies.

Don't think, Cates told himself. *Just move.*

June 6, 1918, had begun in the deep dark of the predawn, when Cates was roused by advance scouts from the 23rd Regiment. A battalion of regulars would relieve the 96th and 79th Companies, and they, in turn, would march to and assemble in a corner of the Bois de Clerembauts near La Cense Farm, where the 2nd Battalion of the 6th Regiment was headquartered.

It was cold, and in the pitch-black, Cates headed for the back lines, happy to be out of line after five days of being bombarded by the German guns and having few targets to shoot back at.

As he and his men marched, they could hear the sudden racket of machine guns to the northwest that marked the 5th Regiment's deadly foray into the dawn. That fire would rise, and ebb, and rise and ebb through the morning.

They spent the morning making rude crosses and fences for the graves of the several 2nd Battalion men who had died. It was good to be back of the lines, good to do some bathing, maybe, or just lounging under the trees while a world war raged in front of them.

But at four forty-five p.m. the idyll was ended; Cates and the 96th Company were ordered to assemble and advance at five p.m. on Bouresches. At the same time, the 5th Regiment's 3rd Battalion, which had already made a move west of the woods that morning, was ordered to pivot right and hit the western side.

Meanwhile, Berton Sibley's 3rd Battalion, 6th Regiment, would assault the woods from the south-southwest. The ambitions of Harbord and the French were high—it was hoped and expected that the marines could in one sweep pierce into and through the Bois de Belleau, exit on the eastern side, and continue on to Bouresches and, it was hoped, all the way beyond to the railway station one hundred yards east of the village.

The 6th's 2nd Battalion would guard the right flank of this audacious move. The 96th Company was to lead the advance toward Bouresches, with Cates's 4th Platoon touching on the left of Sibley's easternmost company just on the right of the wood. Randolph Zane's 79th Company would support Cates, while Captain Bailey Coffenburg's 80th Company supported Berry's attack and Robert Messersmith's 78th Company remained in place and in contact with the 3rd Brigade on the right.

Despite evidence to the contrary, Harbord was still certain that the Germans held only a toehold in the far northeast section of the woods. Catlin, though, would write after the war that "the wood was strongly held," and that the marines could only wonder "what terrible destruction the Hun might be preparing for us within its baleful borders."

In fact, the Bois de Belleau was a veritable fortress. "The Bois," Harbord conceded after the war, "proved to be fully occupied, with many machine-gun nests, in positions well chosen among the giant boulders."

The Germans manned three east–west lines in the wood—one on the southern edge that faced Lucy, one in the center, and a third 150 yards south of the high, wooded bluff that marked its northern reaches, and where an old hunting lodge still stood. Barbed wire had been strung in front of the lines, and sharpshooter pits dug.

Even if Harbord had known the position's strength, it no doubt would not have mattered. Those in charge, Catlin among them, were certain the wood needed to be taken. For one thing, Catlin would write, the wood was a "dangerous salient within our curving line." For another, "it formed a base of attack that threatened our whole line to the south.

"So long as they held it, a sudden thrust was possible at any time, and such a thrust might mean untold disaster, probably the quick advance on Paris. . . . The Allies could not advance with that thorn in their side. . . . An assumption of the offensive was the only solution."

Few at the time seemed to have promoted the ridiculously simple idea of simply holding the lines while the artillery pounded the wood into sawdust, saving many marine lives in the process. Some would also question why the marines hadn't simply taken the wood first, instead of standing by idly as the Germans took over and fortified their defenses in the first days of June.

The most probable answer is that the priority of the French and the 2nd Division was to stop the German advance. The French were on their heels, and the marines' first job was to provide some backbone and order, establish a strong line, and worry about going on the offensive later.

Even as late as the morning of June 6, things were still in something of a jumble along parts of the 2nd Division's line, as the understrength assault of the 5th Regiment's 1st Battalion indicated. But there were other considerations in play—among them a desire on the part of the AEF and marine hierarchies to show the Allies that the Americans meant business and could fight, as the 1st Division had shown at Cantigny just a week earlier.

Simply put, the marines were there to fight and kill Germans.

And that was what they would do over the next three weeks, though at great cost.

Two battalions—two thousand men—of the German 461st Regiment held the woods in strength along its western face, some forty machine guns at their disposal, but they had left the farthest south and southeastern portions out of the defensive alignment because the ground was too broken by rocks, gullies, and ravines to allow for adequate fields of fire.

Because of this, Berry's battalion on the left would face the most difficult job, advancing over open fields of wheat, with nowhere to run and nowhere to hide if Harbord was wrong. Ominously, they would advance not only over open ground but under the clear observation of German sausage balloons, from which artillery spotters directed fire on the marines.

"I was fully aware of the difficulties of the situation, especially for Berry," Catlin would write. "He had 400 yards of open wheat field to cross in the face of a galling fire, and I did not believe he could ever reach the woods."

Going along for the ride with Berry in the assault was *Chicago*

Tribune correspondent Floyd Gibbons, who had learned of the marines' plans and raced from Paris that morning to watch the spectacle. Before the day was out, his presence would, ironically, do more to raise the profile of the Marine Corps than any single assault the marines would make.

Catlin's "considerable anxiety" over the assault was quickly borne out. At exactly five p.m., both battalions of marines advanced on Belleau Wood in waves, marching into the wheat as the sun began to sink behind them, putting each marine in silhouette as they traversed the open ground toward the foreboding and sinister-looking woods. They moved stoically and in perfect—if fatal—formation through the tall grass over open ground, each step bringing them closer to they knew not what.

Berry's battalion was almost immediately consumed by a storm of machine-gun fire from the woods to its front. As the first lines wavered under the galling fire, a shout rang out to the right. "Come on, you sons of bitches!" the venerable Gunnery Sergeant Dan Daly, possessor of two Medals of Honor, yelled. "Do you want to live forever?"

Among Berry's battalion, living forever was not much of an option. One hundred yards from the woods, the German fusillade intensified, driving many men to the ground. Berry himself ordered his men to hit the dirt, but as he did, he gripped his left wrist and shouted, "My hand's gone!" Gibbons, raising his head from the earth to see what had happened, yelled for Berry to get down.

A few men managed to roll and stumble to the edge of the wood, in which some safety could be found behind the rocks and trees lining the western edge. "They had us enfiladed," Sergeant Merwin Silverthorn of the 45th Company recalled. "It was absolutely like a shooting gallery and not a single marine of ours firing a shot. We weren't trained that way. We went on."

Silverthorn and his platoon commander managed to make it into a small ravine, still one hundred yards short of the Bois de Belleau. Six men remained from his fifty-man platoon; the others had been killed or wounded, or they remained behind, desperately hugging the ground.

The lieutenant told Silverthorn he was going to retrace his steps through the annihilating fire and get the hell out of there. He suggested Silverthorn follow him.

Silverthorn demurred.

"I thought, 'Here's where you and I part company, because we just got across this place, and that's the last thing I'm going to do—go back,'" Silverthorn would write, adding, "Nobody ever got in trouble for going toward the enemy."

Silverthorn made the wood, taking a machine-gun bullet to a knee in the process. Correspondent Gibbons was not so lucky; as he crawled through the grass to reach Major Berry, he suddenly felt a stinging burn in his upper left arm, where a bullet had gone clean through. Another nicked the top of his left shoulder . . . and then his world suddenly went white.

A bullet had pierced his left eye and smashed through his forehead. Blood coursed over his face, and sharp pain flooded his senses. Still, he looked for Berry, though there was no way he could reach or help him now.

Before long, with his one good eye he saw the wounded Berry rise into a hail of German lead and race for the woods. Gibbons, meanwhile, lay in the field until nightfall, when he found his way to the rear with the aid of Lieutenant Oscar Hartzell, a former *New York Times* correspondent who had accompanied him to the battlefield.

Sibley's battalion on the right, meanwhile, was having more luck. Advancing from north of Lucy-le-Bocage to below Bouresches, the men went in, "and it was one of the most beautiful sights I have ever witnessed," Catlin, watching from his headquarters at Lucy, would write.

"I say they went in as if on parade, and that is literally true. There was no yell and wild rush, but a deliberate forward march, with the lines at right dress. . . . Before them were the dense woods effectively sheltering armed and highly trained opponents of unknown strength. Within its depths, the machine guns snarled and rattled and spat forth a leaden death. It was like some mythical monster belching smoke and fire from its lair."

As pretty and dramatic as the advance might have looked, at the same time the enemy within could not have desired better targets, one German officer recorded.

And Catlin, although far behind, watching his men parade toward the Bois de Belleau from a forward observation post, made a fine target himself. As Berry's marines approached the wood, a sniper's bullet smashed into his chest and wheeled him around. Grievously wounded and his right side temporarily paralyzed, he found that his part in the war was quickly over.

With no idea their regimental commander was down, Sibley's marines continued on. They at least had some advantage over Berry. Orchards and scattered trees north of Lucy screened some of the battalion's one-thousand-yard approach to the woods, and though some casualties were endured as it crossed open ground above and below a ravine running from Lucy to Bouresches, the steady advance kept on and made good time to the wood.

The 82nd and 83rd Companies on the left plunged into the wood, while the 84th and 97th Companies skirted the wood to the east over exposed ground. The left companies cleared away scattered opposition in the southwest extension of the woods before running into the main German line of defense just beyond a deeply wooded prominence known as Hill 181.

Armed only with rifles, the marines stopped and dug in beneath the wood's many rocky ledges, while the Germans sent machine-gun fire and potato mashers their way.

The two right companies, meanwhile, had been scheduled to continue the assault all the way to Bouresches once the wood was cleared—

which it was not. Enfiladed now from the German strongpoint north of Hill 181 inside the wood, the 84th and 97th Companies went to ground in a sheltering ravine, where they spent much of the night under intense shelling.

For the marines still inside the wood, it was "a hell of a night," battalion adjutant Captain David Bellamy would write. "It had been impossible for men to overwhelm machines and our position was uncertain."

BOURESCHES

DUNCAN WAS ONE of the first to fall. Captain Donald Francis Duncan of St. Joe, Missouri, had walked carelessly into hell, swinging a cane and puffing on his pipe.

He had made a fine target, had Don Duncan.

So had the rest of them.

While Benjamin Berry's men were advancing, then dying, then trying to burrow through the grass and earth to China on the west face of the Bois de Belleau, and Berton Sibley's marines were attempting to probe its nefarious and unknown depths, Duncan was leading his 96th Company out onto open fields to the east and beginning an advance of eight hundred yards toward Bouresches, five hundred yards east of the wood.

He had almost been late in getting there; 2nd Battalion commander Thomas Holcomb had only at four thirty p.m. met with Albertus Catlin in an orchard, where he was told to put one of his companies on Sibley's right during the coming advance. Holcomb wasn't able to get his hastily scribbled order to Duncan until four forty-five p.m. That gave the 96th Company just fifteen minutes to race the kilometer (half a mile) from its resting place in Clerembauts Wood north to where Sibley was assembling his battalion for its assault from the Lucy-le-Bocage ravine.

"So we double-timed part of the way and got into position," Cliff Cates would recall.

Cates was ordered to lead his platoon on the left and maintain contact with Sibley's farthest-right company, while the rest of the 96th spread itself to the east. As he was trying to find Sibley's left, however, Cates's men became entangled with men from the 79th Company holding the left of the 2nd Battalion's line. Captain Randolph Zane, the son-in-law of the governor of California, told the upstart Cates to get the hell away from his company.

This Cates did, leading his men to the right and putting himself on the left end of the company's 500-yard-wide advance line. At five p.m., with Berry on the left and Sibley in the center, the marines advanced; years later, Cates would say they "didn't actually know our objective or where we were going or what."

The 96th's objective was in fact Bouresches, which consisted of some sixty stone buildings that offered plenty of shelter for two companies of the German 398th Regiment, which manned it with six to eight well-sited machine guns and plenty of available rifle power.

A look at the open, tawny fields of wheat that guarded the approach to the village put a lump into the throat of each and every man in the 96th—Cates included.

Luckily, there was little time to think too much about it.

Just before jump-off, a barrage of American shells hit Bouresches, and the men cheered. Before long, Captain Duncan blew his whistle, and it was on. Three platoons of the 96th followed the La Cense ravine north toward the Bois de Triangle just south of Bouresches, where they began taking fire. Cates and the 4th Platoon, farther west and in the open, also came under fire as they approached within six hundred yards of the village.

"At a certain time and signal we got up and swept over a ground literally covered with machine gun bullets," Cates would write. "It was my first charge, and . . . it is a wonderful thrill to be out there in front of a bunch of men that will follow you to death. A lot of men went down; most of them only wounded, but a few dead."

Among the latter was Captain Duncan. Leading his men toward Bouresches, he had paused at the eastern tip of the Bois de Triangle to confer with the 1st Platoon's leader, Second Lieutenant George B. Lockhart, while bullets sang around them.

Sergeant Aloysius Sheridan, an old pal of Duncan's from St. Joe, Missouri, jokingly asked Duncan if he thought the company would see much action that day.

"Oh! yes, we will give and take," Duncan told him. "But be sure you take more than you give."

"I guess he meant lives," Sheridan would add.

Duncan, wearing his best suit, holding a swagger stick, and pulling on a straight-stem pipe, continued on into the rain of shot and shell coming from Bouresches. Within a minute of talking to Sheridan, he crumpled over, a bullet in his abdomen.

Lieutenant Weedon Osborne, a naval dental surgeon who had been with the marines for just a few days and was serving as a medic, went immediately to Duncan's aid, and with the help of Sheridan, Sergeant Joseph Steele (aka Sissler), and Corporal Peter Ward, dragged him to a small clump of trees clearly in view of the German artillery near Bouresches.

"We no more than laid him on the ground when a big eight-inch shell came in and killed all but myself," Sheridan wrote. "I was knocked down, but my helmet saved me."

Holcomb, taking shelter in a ravine on the east side of the field, wept when he received the news of Duncan's death.

"My battalion did wonderfully, especially dear old Duncan's company," Holcomb would write to his wife, Beatrice. "There was never anything finer than their advance across a place literally swept with machine gun fire.

"Poor old Duncan, my favorite company commander, was killed."

Sheridan would write that the 96th Company "had the reputation of being a wild bunch of Indians that didn't give a damn for anything. And it was true. But a more loyal bunch of men can never be gotten together again. . . . He was the idol of the regiment, and every private and every officer knew him, for his company surely advertised him."

"He was surely a soldier and a regular fellow," the 96th Company's Private Thomas L. Stewart would write. Duncan was also "too careless of his own safety," Stewart would add.

Duncan's death left First Lieutenant James Robertson in command of the company, which had gone to ground in the face of the heavy fire coming from Bouresches. While Cates and his men lay hugging the earth, his friend, Second Lieutenant Thomas Reed Brailsford—designated as the liaison between the 2nd and 3rd Battalions—crawled over.

"Cliff!" Brailsford yelled. "Where in God's name is the third battalion?"

"I don't really know," Cates replied, "but I think they're over on the left."

"I've got to find them," Brailsford said, and was up and running through machine-gun fire and toward Belleau Wood. Cates tried to stop him, yelling, "For Christ's sake don't be ridiculous! Get down and stay down!"

"But he ran on," Cates would remember, "and that was the last anyone ever saw of him."

The situation remained perilous—ridiculous really; the 96th Company couldn't go forward, and it couldn't retreat. But as another marine would later write, there was always one good solution to any pickle in which one found oneself on a battlefield:

Charge.

After clinging to the wheat for what seemed like hours, Cates finally arrived at the same solution. He stood up, looked to his right, and yelled, "Come on Robertson, let's go!"

The 96th Company rose as one and swarmed toward the village, each man bent forward as if leaning into a hailstorm—which it was, but a storm of lead.

"There was very little teamwork," Cates would say years later of Great War tactics. "You usually just got up, rushed in, fired, and there wasn't any covering fire, any maneuvering. You just got up and went forward."

Cates and the rest of the 96th went forward—but not for long. Within minutes, artillery fire and machine-gun bullets scythed the lines, leaving the crumpled, bleeding bodies of dead and wounded Americans in their wake.

"As my section advanced, eight of the twelve men were killed before we had gone a hundred feet," Corporal Harrison Cale would remember. "In the screen of trees directly before Bouresches, the foliage and branches rattled and vibrated with the *pup-pup-pup* of concealed machine guns.

"We pushed on. The bullets whipped and cut our clothing and clipped the ammunition from our belts. Men fell fast upon that field."

"Pretty soon machine gun bullets began to spatter around us," twenty-three-year-old Private Gerald Waples of Omaha, Nebraska, would recall. "One struck a sergeant just in front of me in the mouth, cutting open his cheek and the side of his neck."

I expect it's my turn next, Waples thought.

Sure enough, it wasn't too much farther on that Waples, one of eight automatic riflemen in the 96th Company, got his. "We had gone 200 or 300 yards when I felt something like a drop of hot water on my arm," he would say. "I looked down. Blood was spurting from my arm."

Waples didn't yet know it, but the bullet had pierced his right lung, bounced off his right shoulder blade, and then ricocheted downward, breaking six ribs before lodging under the skin on his back. Still, he knew he was hit badly enough and, trained to hand off his weapon to another marine in the event of being wounded, Waples told a private next to him to take his rifle.

"He didn't hear me and I started after him," Waples recalled. "'Take this gun, I am shot,' I shouted.

"'So am I,'" the marine told Waples, and then fell forward with bullet holes in each shoulder. Private Sidney McIntosh, who had been working as a clerk for the Union Pacific Railroad in Council Bluffs, Nebraska, when he enlisted on the previous June 22, came to Waples's aid.

"I handed the gun to Sid and dropped on my face," Waples said. "Sid went only a few yards and fell." McIntosh, twenty-two, died of his wounds that same day. Waples lay on the field, painfully oozing blood, until eight the next morning.

Despite the company's rush to the jump-off line, Private John T. Miller would remember anxiously awaiting the signal to attack. "I cannot describe the feeling one has while waiting for the word," he would recall. "It seemed to me that the time would never come."

Suddenly, "the silence was broken by the blast of a whistle and we were on our way. The sun was shining and the country looked wonderful."

The deaths of Duncan and his tenders sobered Miller. "I began to realize then what we were up against, for 'Heinie' must have had a million machine guns and they were all working.

"The boys started to fall and all that was heard was, 'I'm hit,' or 'Heinie got me.' A lad beside me 'got it' in the ankle, and said to me, 'Kid, what do you think of that dirty bunch of Dutchmen. They won't even let me get started. When you get into town, kill ten for me.'"

Cliff Cates, meanwhile, continued leading his 4th Platoon toward Bouresches. But two hundred yards short of the village, a machine-gun bullet clanged off his tin hat, and he fell forward into the wheat, unconscious. Robertson picked up the charge and continued on to Bouresches with about twenty of Cates's men.

Cates came to after about five or ten minutes; just how long he couldn't tell. All he knew was that the war had not yet ended; German machine guns were still pumping lead at the company's thinning ranks, the bullets spraying the ground all around him.

His first thought was to run to the rear. "I hate to admit it, but that was it," he would sheepishly admit years later.

He tried to put his helmet on, but the dent made by the bullet was so large, "the doggone thing wouldn't go on," he would later laugh. Looking east, he saw that four of the company's men from the 1st Platoon, among them Sheridan, had taken cover in a ravine on the far right, south of the village.

"So I went staggering over there," Cates would recall. "I fell two or three times, so they told me."

Sergeant Tom Orgo, seeing that Cates was still reeling from the blow to his head, took out his canteen and began pouring cheap red wine over Cates's head. Cates told him, "Don't pour it on me—let me drink it!"

Cates grabbed the canteen and took a big gulp. Suddenly revived, he began to consider his situation.

There was only one thing to do.

Charge.

He picked up a discarded French rifle, told the others to follow, and then the five marines began crawling toward Bouresches, the ravine covering their movement. "About that time we saw a bunch of Germans on the edge of town," Cates would recall. "We let go at them and they ran."

Just then, Cates also saw Robertson leaving the west end of Bouresches with about twenty marines. Cates blew his whistle and yelled at Robertson, who double-timed toward his subordinate with his small group.

Robertson handed over the reins and told him, "All right, you take your platoon in and clean out the town and I'll get reinforcements."

"Which I thought was a hell of a thing," Cates would shake his head and say years later, still wondering why the company's senior officer would essentially hand over the unit to his subordinate in the face of the enemy.*

Battalion commander Holcomb also wondered what the hell Robertson was thinking. When Robertson reported to him, Holcomb "had to direct him to return to help his own men and hold the town," Sergeant Don Paradis, a battalion runner, would write. "He thanked him for coming back to tell him but told him his place was back with his men."

Cates, meanwhile, didn't hesitate to act on Robertson's orders. Leading twenty-four men, he raced into and through Bouresches, cleaning out machine-gun nests, throwing grenades into buildings, and putting most of the Germans—about one hundred men—to flight.

The village, five hundred yards across, had three main avenues. Cates told his gunnery sergeant, Willard Morrey, to take eight men and clear the northwest corner. He sent Sergeant Earl Belfry on a

---

*Further fueling Cates's ire was the fact that just a few weeks later, he had to attend a ceremony at which Robertson—"a very difficult man, the men hated him," Cates would say—was awarded the Distinguished Service Cross for showing "marked courage and resourcefulness" in capturing Bouresches and then "heroically" withstanding "vigorous attempts of superior forces to dislodge him."

Another marine would also earn several dubious awards for his actions that day. Sergeant John Quick, who'd earned a Medal of Honor in Cuba in 1898 and was attached to the 6th Regiment's Headquarters Company on June 6, would receive a Distinguished Service Cross, Navy Cross, and Silver Star for bringing a truckload of ammunition and "material" into Bouresches "over a road swept by artillery and machine-gun fire."

In fact, Quick dumped his load on the southern approach to the village; Cates didn't even know about it and didn't need it, having captured a large number of guns and significant amount of ammunition from the Germans. Cates would only run across this supposedly vital store of ammunition four days later, after being relieved.

similar mission to the eastern part of town. Cates took his own small bunch north on the road leading toward the railway station.

"We took heavy fire going down the streets," Cates recalled. Somehow having managed to screw his lid back onto his head, he took another direct hit to it. Another bullet, this time from a machine-gun sniping from the town's church tower, clipped one of his shoulders, severing the strap and the attached gold bar from his shirt.

Lucky Cliff Cates . . .

He now split his group, and four men, including his orderly Herbert Dunlavy, took the tower sniper out with grenades and rifles.

"I ran down one street with a lieutenant who had the bars shot off his shoulders," Harrison Cale would recall proudly. "Every street had its fight; sticking—slashing—banging. Machine guns in the doors of the buildings, in the church steeple, behind piles of rubbish, and sharpshooters in every . . . vantage.

"In a cellar a number of the enemy hid with a machine gun. I tossed a hand grenade into their midst and it was 'Fini La Guerre' for them."

"[I]t was no easy job, for every 'Heinie' had a machine gun," Private John T. Miller would write. "But it was the same old story, they would fire their guns until we were on top of them, then throw up their hands, shout 'Kamerad' and beg for mercy. But after you go through as far as that, you cease to be human and don't know what mercy is."

Cates had once again proved himself to be perhaps the luckiest of marines. As he would write on June 10, he was unwounded, except for "two bum fingers and a face which is skinned up," the result of his rifle exploding when he tried to load a rifle grenade onto it to take out a machine-gun emplacement.

The fight was furious, but short. The Germans fled "like rabbits; dropping their equipment as they ran," Cates wrote. Among Cates's booty were a "big German pistol, gas mask, and raincoat," which the Germans left behind them.

With the town consolidated, Cates's problems were just beginning. Bouresches was a key prize—it guarded the eastern flank of the Bois de Belleau, where Sibley's men had only just gained a toehold. From Bouresches, Belleau Wood could be enfiladed. Surely the Germans would counterattack the village, and quickly, to seize it back.

In fact, they didn't. Not in force, anyway. Now leading fewer than twenty men, Cates, who would crow that he was "colonel of this town for one night," established "Cossack posts"—one in an apple orchard just east of the village, one to the north behind a stone wall, and the others to the east.

He also had his small force constantly change its positions and fire from them so the Germans "couldn't tell how many men were in the town," the 96th Company's Sergeant Joseph Stites would remember.

Within a few hours, reinforcements arrived for Cliff Cates and his hardy, if small, band of marines. The remainder of the 1st Platoon filtered in from the ravine on the east side of the field, the same that Cates had used to reach Bouresches.

The survivors in the 2nd and 3rd Platoons, which had been badly shot up while crossing the wheat field, came in as well. Cates—whom Private Miller would praise as "a pal to all the boys"—counted heads, finding that he'd lost thirty-two men out the fifty-six who'd started out with him that day.

According to a company history compiled by Cates and Morrey after the war, eight of the company's men were killed and forty-two wounded on June 6. More, however, would die of their wounds at base and field hospitals and in the days to come.

Besides losing its captain, Donald Duncan, the 96th Company had lost Second Lieutenant John D. Bowling, who'd been wounded, and Second Lieutenant Thomas Brailsford, who was missing.

"He was one of the finest fellows we ever had with us," Sergeant Ernest Wolf would say of Brailsford. "To meet him was to like him.

He talked to you like a buck private. When we were going to have inspection: 'Fall in, gang,' he'd say. 'We're on parade today.' You'd never meet a finer fellow."

"So long, fellows," was all Brailsford had casually said to his men as he started out across the open field before the village, a cigarette dangling from his mouth.

"We never saw him again," Wolf would say.

BESIEGED

CLIFF CATES WOULD be surprised that there were, actually, no meaningful attempts to retake Bouresches. It was still light, and he expected a counterattack at any moment. Instead, the Germans decided to pound the village with artillery, knocking apart each house stone by stone over the next three days.

Meanwhile, Cates's command slowly grew, until by eleven p.m. he had at least six hundred marines, whom he split up and posted throughout Bouresches. When thirty-year-old Captain Randolph Zane of the 79th Company turned up with the remainder of his unit, Cates relinquished command. He was no longer "colonel" of the town.

The 79th had tried to support the 96th Company in the assault on Bouresches, but had had to halt halfway toward its objective in the face of the withering fire that also stymied the 96th's 2nd and 3rd Platoons. Lloyd Pike, a sergeant with the 79th, remembered fierce machine-gun fire coming from the Bois de Belleau putting many of his men to ground.

Even so, "Men who had dropped to the ground unhurt were wounded or killed where they lay," he wrote. "Those already wounded were hit again, as were those already dead."

Ordered to take the gun, Pike and a two-man Chauchat crew bolted toward the wood. Taking heavy fire from the German gunner within, they dropped into a life-saving shell hole seventy-five yards from the woods and began digging furiously to build a dirt parapet.

Each time one of them stuck his head up for a look-see, a spray of bullets hit the ground around the hole. The ammunition carrier for the Chauchat was quickly wounded; the gunner eventually was shot through the head and died at his gun.

At one point, Pike ventured out to get a good look at their tormenter. After painstakingly locating the German, who wore a small gray cap with a red band that only made it easier to locate him among the greenery, Pike aimed his rifle and fired.

"I only remember seeing his head drop forward to the left side of his gun," Pike recalled sixty-one years later. Looking at his watch, Pike was stunned to find that his cat-and-mouse ordeal had lasted for more than four hours.

"We got a hell of a lot of machine gun fire after we started out, and it just cut us to pieces," Pike's then platoon commander, twenty-year-old Second Lieutenant Graves Erskine, would recall.

As the company lay helpless in the green wheat, one of Erskine's privates came crawling back, shot through the nose. "He was such a bloody mess," Erskine would say. Erskine bound him up as best he could, and sent him to find Zane and tell him his platoon was pinned down and could not advance.

The private came swishing back through the grass twenty minutes later. "I told the captain what you said and he said, 'Get going, goddamnit!'" the marine told Erskine.

At about eight thirty p.m., the company was notified that the 96th Company's "Lieutenant Robertson"—there he is again—had taken the town, and Zane finally led his men in. At the western edge of the village, Erskine—who had just arrived on the field after taking "French leave" from an army school at Gondrecourt—captured a German soldier, and his machine gun.

He told one of his men to take the captured soldier back to headquarters, and the marine took off. He returned "in much less time than he should have been back," Erskine recalled.

"I said, 'Slattery, you shot that prisoner.'"

"He said, 'How did you know?'"

"I said, 'You didn't have time to take him back to battalion headquarters. Don't you know you're not supposed to kill prisoners?'"

"He said, 'Yes, but I haven't had a chance to kill one of the bastards all day, all they are doing is killing us, and I can't go back to Minnesota and tell them I didn't kill a German.'"

"That's how cold-blooded he was," Erskine would write in wonder.

Erskine entered the town and was met at the central fountain by Zane, who ordered him to "go out and locate the Germans."

Erskine told him he already knew where the Germans were: "They seem to be all over the goddamn world."

Zane told him he was serious. "Take what you have left of your platoon and go out and locate the Germans."

By God, this is my last trip, Erskine thought.

Meanwhile, the Germans shelled Bouresches as reinforcements continued to file in, including men from Benjamin Berry's 84th and 97th Companies that had been in support in the fields just east of the wood.

"From then on, there wasn't any question about holding the town," Cates would say. "I mean, in two or three hours we had enough men in there to hold half a dozen towns."

Among the reinforcements were replacements fresh to the battle, and to the war. The 96th's Corporal Harrison Cale would write that five of these unlucky greenhorns assigned to his outpost were killed that night during the German bombardment. "Few houses in the town escaped the destructive fire of the artillery that hammered us incessantly," Cale wrote.

"The Germans laid it on us," Cates would remember. One gun, in particular, remained a mystery. Every twenty minutes or so, a twelve- or fourteen-inch shell would land inside the town, "and the people in the rear swore and be-damned it was a German gun but there wasn't any question about it.

"I went way back down the ravine and I could hear the damned shells coming from the south and I'd watch it go right over and hit in the town. We understood it was one of the big railway guns—naval guns.

"Luckily the thing was hitting right in the center of the town and practically ninety percent of our men were out on the perimeter, so it didn't do too much damage except to morale."

Cates over time would hear all kinds of stories about the mystery gun—one being that the officer in charge of it had to be killed because he refused to stop firing or change the range. No one knew if it was French or Americans blasting at them, but it didn't matter. "We would have been only too glad to have killed the whole gun crew if given the opportunity," Cates wrote.

While the town's defenders huddled in their posts around town after nightfall, waiting for a German advance, Graves Erskine led his small group of three volunteers out beyond the village to locate the German positions.

One of them, Private Oscar Rankin, had been a minister and was called "the Preacher" by the other marines. After Rankin's best buddy, Corporal Thomas Gragard, was killed during the advance on Bouresches, Rankin "sprang to his feet and swore as no parson had ever sworn. He took command of what was left of his squad and headed for Berlin," Erskine wrote.

As they set out into the dark from the northwest corner of Bouresches, it wasn't long before Erskine and his patrol drew German rifle fire and turned southwest. After crawling one hundred yards, they were fired on again, and turned back toward the village.

He had sure enough located the Germans.

As they neared Bouresches, they heard movement in a ravine and immediately decided it was a great opportunity to take a prisoner or two. Erskine and company approached in the dark, when suddenly "we were stricken dumb by a barrage of real seagoing profanity," Erskine would write.

He recognized the voice as that of an "ex-sergeant" named Richard Mazereeuw, who had enlisted in the Marines from Grand Rapids, Michigan, in February 1908, but had more recently been demoted to the rank of private on account of "an overdose of cognac."

The ex-sergeant "was quite a character in our company," Erskine would say. "He was tall and thin, Irish, smoked a pipe with a long stem; he could be very military, but he had the vilest mouth, I think, of any man that I have run into in a long time."

Mazereeuw, one of Preacher Rankin's men, was wounded in the knee while advancing toward Bouresches, and now he rudely abused his own company mates, who were there to save him.

"You goddamn bastards," he told them, "if you'd stayed with me, you would have been in Berlin."

The former sergeant also expressed his opinion, in no uncertain terms, "about an army that couldn't afford an ambulance to pick up a wounded man," Erskine wrote.

"He was an old marine, and he had his fighting blood up that night for we had a most difficult time carrying him back to the ravine, and later to the town."

Erskine wound up smacking Mazereeuw several times in an effort to quiet him: "I couldn't sacrifice a whole patrol to listen to his profanity."

Erskine and his squad returned to the village at one thirty a.m., having traversed the northern end to the railway station, which was being "grazed" by heavy fire from a German .88. During the night, "every street in the town seemed to be enfiladed by machine guns firing from the east, north and west."

Erskine, defending a post on the northern edge of Bouresches, was surprised to hear German soldiers calling out to the defenders in English, trying to confuse them and lure them into the open.

"Ninety-sixth Company, forward, march," they called repeatedly. "Ninety-sixth Company, assemble over there!" "Right this way, boys."

Their identification of the unit defending Bouresches may have resulted from the capture of the unit's Private Leslie Cunningham, who after being wounded was placed in an ambulance that got lost, and wound up in German hands. He would be the only member of the 96th Company to be made prisoner during the war.

Leslie's brother, Robert, was one of those wounded on June 6. He would die on June 10, becoming just another name on the list of those marines killed or wounded on June 6, 1918, which to that date was the single worst day in Marine Corps history: Thirty-one officers and 1,056 men became casualties on that day, 6 officers and 222 men making the supreme sacrifice.

After a perilous night spent holding Bouresches through heavy shelling, Cates had "the scare of my life." While making his rounds of the village checking on the disposition of his men the next morning, he searched several homes to see if there were any "stray heinies."

Alone, he pushed open the door to a stable, and "a rough, dirty looking character stood right in front of me, and as I had my pistol in my hand, I almost shot him, as I was sure he was a German," Cates would write.

The villager was saved when Cates noticed a woman standing behind him. "To make a long story short, they turned out to be an old French couple which had not been evacuated, and had been hiding in the hay. We had a really hard time to get them to leave," he would add. "In fact, we had to do it by force."

Throughout June 7, the Germans continued to pound Bouresches, as Cates and his men hung on. The constant pounding was trying— physically and emotionally.

"A fellow can't fight back at a high explosive shell and it's the hardest thing to endure continually," the 96th Company's Thomas L. Stewart would write to his uncle, the Reverend D. H. Stewart, in Wellington, Kansas.

"A fellow has got to have something to hang on to or he goes to pieces as some of them do. I am thankful that my parents have taught me what that something is to be. . . . You wonder what is saving you from a direct hit and you've simply a Divine Providence to thank for it."

The Germans also tried infiltrating attacks, but were beaten back by marine rifle and machine-gun fire. "They put on a lot of smaller attacks and they'd fire and we'd fire," Cates would remember.

On the afternoon of June 8, one of Cates's mess cooks prepared him a meal that under the circumstances would have been fit for a king—chicken, rabbit, green vegetables, and honey. Cates sent for a friend, former University of Michigan all-American fullback John West, now a second lieutenant with the 79th Company. "We enjoyed our first meal in three days," Cates wrote proudly.

That same night, Cates, who hadn't slept since the morning of June 6, was just stretching out on a feather bed in one of the village's homes right after dark when tragedy struck. The Germans sent over a ferocious barrage, and the marines at their posts began firing wildly into the night.

Cates jumped up and ran to the nearest frontline post with his orderly, Herbert Dunlavy, certain that an all-out German counterattack was finally under way. "Shells were falling all around us, and soon one exploded right on top of us—either just over us or in a sand pile which was about twenty feet behind us—and the concussion was terrific," he wrote.

The shell flattened Cates, as well as all of those near him. When they stood and dusted themselves off, Dunlavy didn't stir. The concussion had killed him. "There wasn't a mark on his body," Cates wrote.

Once again, the increasingly famous Cates luck had held. Cates would see to it that Dunlavy would be awarded a posthumous Distinguished Service Cross for his heroic actions on June 6.

Earlier on June 8, the 6th Regiment's 3rd Battalion had made another try to clear the Bois de Belleau, attacking from the eastern edge with some semblance of security now that the Germans in Bouresches were no longer squarely on its right flank. Stokes mortars tried to prepare the way, plopping their loads on suspected strongpoints within the tangled woods, but it was really guesswork.

At four a.m., the 82nd and 83rd Companies made their dash, jumping and tumbling over rocks and ledges while a mostly unseen enemy poured fire and hurled potato mashers at them. It was no use. The Germans of the 461st Regiment had the advantage in the dark woods, and they fended off the marines in desperate, sometimes hand-to-hand fighting.

At ten twenty-seven a.m., battalion commander Berton Sibley reported to Colonel Harry Lee, who had taken over for the fallen 6th Regiment commander, Albertus Catlin: "They are too strong for us. Soon as we take one machine gun, another opens."

At twelve thirty p.m., Sibley was ordered to withdraw to the southern end of the wood, which was then pounded by artillery through the rest of that day and the next, turning it slowly into a twisted miasma of toothpicks.

Sheer human willpower and marine bravery and sacrifice had proved no match for entrenched machine guns. It was time to get serious.

There was to be little rest and no relief for the defenders of Bouresches, which continued to be slammed by German artillery and subjected to attempted night infiltrations by small groups of German soldiers. Machine guns from both sides fired until they were empty through each long night, and men remained at their posts until they were past exhaustion, a little sleep being available only in the day.

Lloyd Pike was assigned to a gun pit that held a French Hotchkiss machine gun. To his right was another, and between the two of them a cross fire was established. One night, though, two Germans somehow slipped between the bursts and approached Pike's station unnoticed. He didn't see them race out of the inky night until they were almost upon him.

"Large shadowy forms began to materialize right in front of my gun pit," he wrote. "By the time I got my Colt .45 out of the holster, two big men carrying rifles [with] bayonets were in the right side of my gun pit coming toward where I stood. I fired at one, and he appeared jolted. Then I shot the other and he dropped. The first one kept coming, and I dropped him with another shot."

Not used to killing men, and overcome with delayed stress, Pike became sick. "I shortly went off to the right, leaned up against the building, and heaved up everything I had eaten recently and tried for more," he wrote.

"They are dropping a shell about every minute into the town just now—they are tearing it down," Cates would write to his family from Bouresches on June 10. "It's a shame. I am sitting here writing on a dining room table and trusting a shell doesn't hit near. I am pretty well worn out, as I have had only four hours sleep the last four days. A man can live on excitement for a long time."

There was at least one bright spot: Even as they continued to hold out in Bouresches, they learned that they had become heroes. Fresh replacements had brought with them the latest editions of the overseas *New York Herald* that told of the marines' furious, if less-than-successful, assaults.

Correspondent Floyd Gibbons, wounded in the eye on June 6, had written a sensationalized advance story before going in with Berry's battalion, filed it with the censors, and asked that he be allowed to identify the marines.

The AEF's strict censorship did not allow the identification of

American units, but as a tribute to Gibbons, who was thought to have been killed, a censor in Pershing's headquarters allowed through Gibbons's copy and his mention of marines doing the fighting.

"This is the last thing I can ever do for poor old Floyd," the censor sadly murmured.

Gibbons's dramatic dispatch, and subsequent accounts of the unfolding battle, brought everlasting glory to the Marine Corps. But the implication that marines, and only marines, were in the fray rankled the regulars—not so much the soldiers of the army's 9th and 23rd Regiments in the marines' own 2nd Division, but the division of regulars, the 1st, that had taken Cantigny somewhat anonymously the week before, as well as elements of the 3rd Division that had held the Marne at Château-Thierry.

The marines, of course, were quite happy to see their efforts publicly applauded, and Cates would report that their morale soared sky-high.

"It was truly wonderful," Cates wrote. "We lost heavily, but so did the Boche and we gained ground."

As always, Cates did not neglect to mention the bravery and endurance of his men. Showing the selflessness that caused his men to revere him, Cates wrote:

"All the men should get decorations and the men of my platoon will get more than one. . . . I am very proud of my men and they deserve a lot of credit."

Later that same day, Cates and the remnants of the 96th Company were relieved by elements of the 5th Regiment's 3rd Battalion, and were sent back to a support position in some woods south of Bouresches. They received more badly needed replacements right out of Quantico, washed up, dug new holes—and rested.

"I wish you could look out at my bunch now—some are in their holes, some writing, some working on their little shrapnel[-]proof dugouts, some reading of our new success, two shooting a friendly crap game, some cleaning their person and equipment, while others are just sitting looking into space—thinking, no doubt, of home and some girl," Cates would write.

"I heard, just now, that we would get mail tonight. I hope so, as nothing cheers us up more than to get mail from the ones we love."

They would thus pass the next few days, some wondering, no doubt, whether the worst was over for them.

HELLWOOD

ONE SNIFF, THEY'D said, and you'll die. One sniff, one whiff, one momentary inhalation; it was like cyanide, like a bite of Black Plague, a drop of instant death.

One sniff of mustard gas, they'd said, *and you'll die.*

Mustard gas. It wasn't really a gas; it more of an oil. The Germans had invented it, using a mixture of seventy percent dichloroethyl sulfide and thirty percent sulfur and related compounds.

It was brown, viscous, evaporated slowly, and its vapors were five times heavier than air. Some said it smelled like garlic; others mustard, ergo, its name. First used by the Germans in April 1915, it would become "the king of battle gases" and cause four hundred thousand casualties in sixteen months of use.

The Germans had sent over 250,000 shells laden with mustard gas on British positions on the Somme outside of the attack zone prior to launching their March 21, 1918, offensive, cascading canisters of the stuff for a whole five days, but they withheld it from the narrow path areas over which infiltrating *Sturmtruppen* would cross, not wanting to disable their own men.

Mustard gas burned the eyes and any open skin it touched. It got into clothes, loved to work its way into crotches and any places khaki touched the body; men would go out into an affected area to do their morning's morning, not knowing it had been gassed.

The resulting wipes and swipes of private parts made for agonizing, weeks-long suffering, boils and burns erupting almost immediately. The only remedy was a good lathering with soap of the areas affected, and even then it would take weeks for the burns to heal.

Mustard gas was so insidious that anyone who even just passed through an area that had been gassed was instructed to beat and shake his clothing before going into a dugout. A man whose eyes came in contact with the gas could lose his vision for three days or three weeks, depending.

Or a man could get one sniff, they'd said, and he'd die, die a slow, suffocating, strangling, lung-burning death.

The only prevention, gas masks, were almost as bad as the afflicting gas. Hard to breathe through, almost impossible to see through, British versions, developed after the Germans first introduced gas warfare— chlorine—on the Ypres front in April 1915, were doled out to each arriving American soldier.

"You might as well piss on a handkerchief and put it over your face," Cates would say derisively of the masks.

Not really sure why, marines and regulars trained in them, drilled in them, marched in them, were told to keep them on for a full four hours after a mustard gassing—and hated them.

And now mustard gas was tumbling from the black starless sky near Lucy-le-Bocage, tumbling and rolling and thudding amid the pluming as well of high-explosive German shells. Clouds of the oily droplets were searing and blistering and burning and suffocating his men—and for once, Cliff Cates didn't know what to do.

The 96th Company had spent three days and nights out of the line in reserve in woods south of the battle zone after being relieved at Bouresches. Lazing, writing letters, playing craps, feeding themselves with food finally brought up in the rolling kitchens, they were happy to be out of the fray, happy to have made it through those nights in the village.

Meanwhile, many of their marine brethren had continued to hammer away at the Bois de Belleau, in which the Germans continued to hold much of the rocky, frightful ground. Artillery had blasted away at the woods through June 10, after which Johnny Hughes's 1st Battalion of the 6th Regiment plowed its way in and managed to make it to just south of the German strongpoint on Hill 181.

Hughes reported that the American artillery fire had blasted the woods into "mince meat" [sic].

On June 11, Colonel Fritz Wise's 2nd Battalion of the 5th Regiment, sent to the western face of the wood, attacked the Germans along the deep indentation that gave the wood its kidney shape. The intent was to hit the wood at its narrowest part, then continue the attack against the Germans holding the eastern face of the wood.

Wise watched as the men of the 43rd and 51st Companies formed in two leading waves, the supporting 18th and 55th Companies behind them. A barrage of shells flew overhead and deposited themselves in dirty bursts in the cultivated ground.

As German machine guns in the wood began their blind but deadly probes, the barrage began walking east, fifty paces every two minutes. Finally, the company commanders blew their whistles, and the marines marched toward the wood.

"The Germans couldn't have had better targets if they had ordered the attack themselves," Wise would write.

Walking 250 yards behind the barrage, "the battalion went on, men dropping, men dropping, men dropping. Yard by yard they advanced. Minutes after, I saw them disappear into the woods."

Soon, the barrage lifted and disappeared, and the German machine-gun fire ebbed. "Across those fields from the woods I could distinguish machine-gun fire, rifle fire. A sudden ripping burst of machine-gun fire would break out. That meant the marines were advancing on a nest. It would die down. That meant the nest was taken."

The operation was effective, if, as usual, very costly. "The woods were so thick that all action was local and individual," marine John W. Thomason would write.

The Germans, having snipers and machine gunners in trees, guarded every path and small clearing with machine guns, and the natural depressions and dense foliage that still remained offered almost endless opportunities for ambush. Captain Lloyd Williams of the 51st Company was mortally wounded, and a long string of marines lay dead in front of countless machine-gun emplacements.

There were fewer Germans dead; they notoriously whipped their machine in frenzy at the advancing marines before throwing up their hands and yelling, "Kamerad" as the marines' steel bayonets aimed for their chest.

During the action, two companies of the German 40th Regiment were destroyed in separate attacks by Wise's and Hughes's men, Hughes's men advancing on their own to the north after Wise's men had pierced east.

The 2nd Battalion managed, within a few hours, to cross the wood to its eastern face, and much of the enemy took flight through the trees north. Attempts to reinforce were broken by intense American machine-gun fire coming from the force at Bouresches to the east. For once, the marines could claim victory, though it was limited; more than half of the Bois de Belleau remained in German hands.

That evening, 150 replacements were sent to the 5th's 2nd Battalion (and what an awful place to get one's feet wet in battle that must have been). Germans filtered back into the wood through the night, using the blinding darkness for cover. Their lines just fifty yards apart, marine and German jibed at each other in the darkness until exhaustion overtook all.

The next day, June 12, Wise was ordered to continue the advance north through the wood at four thirty p.m. after artillery had had a chance to hammer at the suspected German positions. Not satisfied that the artillery preparation was sufficient, Wise asked for, and received, another hour's barrage on the woods; unfortunately, most of it fell far to the German rear, those plotting coordinates for the American artillery thinking the marines had advanced farther than they actually had.

At five thirty p.m., the 2nd Battalion led the attack north, once again fighting in local, Indian-style actions in the wood's dense thickets and ravines.

"The Boche heard us coming and gave us all they had," First Lieutenant Elliott Cooke of the 55th Company would write. "Light machine guns camouflaged in trees, heavy guns on the ground, grenades, rifles, pistols; everything was turned loose at once. . . . A burst of bullets smashed into a man's face beside me, carrying away the lower part of his face. A grenade fell on the other side, tearing a youngster's legs to shreds. Someone shot a Boche officer out of a tree. He came down all spraddled out, bouncing off a low sapling."

The battalion had taken hundreds of mostly grateful prisoners the previous day; on this day, however, there would be few.

"When he rushed through the underbrush," Cooke would write, "there wasn't time to argue about surrendering. We either killed the Boche or they killed us."

The attack was hugely successful, though marines continued to drop, dead or wounded, into the underbrush as they pushed through the Bois de Belleau. The attack carried almost to the northern edge of the woods, where, from a clearing, marines could see Germans racing about in the streets of the village of Belleau below.

The two-day push bagged more than four hundred prisoners, fifty-nine machine guns, and ten Minenwerfers, but the toll was ghastly:

Not counting the replacements that had come up the previous evening, the 5th's 2nd Battalion had just three hundred "old men" left from the thousand or so that had begun the fight on June 11.

The 6th Regiment's 1st Battalion, meanwhile, had followed in support during both days of fighting, and at the end of June 12 had seven hundred men still deemed fit for duty. Fritz Wise reported to James Harbord that he didn't think he could hold his positions against any aggressive counterattack by the Germans, and reported that a captured German officer, wounded, had told him that the German 237th and 28th Divisions were readying just such an assault for the next morning.

While plans were being made and orders written for the relief of the 5th's 2nd Battalion, the survivors of the June 12 assault came under the most severe bombardment they had ever known, and men huddled in their clawed-out holes and cowered behind rocks and trees as the artillery rounds smothered their position at the north end of the wood, and German infiltrators worked around to their rear left, where the flank was open.

"There followed a night and day of pure, unadulterated hell," Elliott Cooke would write. "Six officers and three hundred men left in a battalion that had thirty officers and a thousand men the previous three days. Corpses lolling grotesquely in the dirt, no water, no food, ammunition almost gone, and Germans creeping closer and closer.

"We lost the sense of emotion. Dull-eyed, resigned, lacking the courage to go forward or back, yet we clung desperately to that rocky edge of woods. It seemed to be all we had left in the world and we would not give it up. Not for Heinie, Kaiser Bill, nor the devil himself."

Help was on the way. Sibley's 3rd Battalion of the 6th Regiment was sent to relieve the 5th's 1st Battalion on Hill 142, with the ultimate intention of pushing the marine line forward and to the east to eliminate the yawning gap on the marines' left in the wood.

Cliff Cates and the 96th Company, meanwhile, were rousted at twelve fifteen a.m. on June 13 from their comparatively cushy position around Maison Blanche, directly south of Lucy-le-Bocage and the Paris–Metz highway, and ordered forward to the woods northwest of Lucy in preparation for the expected German counterattack.

However, at three fifty a.m., the Germans launched an urgent attack on Bouresches, which was preceded by heavy artillery fire. By four ten a.m., reports came in from both the marines in the town and the adjacent 23rd Regiment that the village had been taken.

The reports turned out to be false; two companies of the German 109th Regiment had pierced the defenses, but the marines managed to kill many and sent the survivors packing. Fifteen German dead lay in the streets of the town, and another forty lay sprawled outside of it.

Harbord, disturbed by the reports that Bouresches had been taken, ordered Thomas Holcomb to move two companies of his 2nd Battalion to the woods southeast of Lucy in preparation for a counterattack on the village.

Holcomb paid a visit to Cliff Cates.

"Cates, can you take Bouresches again?" Holcomb asked him.

Cates gulped hard. "Yes," he said finally.

"All right, take your company and the 79th, Zane's company, and recapture it."

Once again, First Lieutenant James Robertson, the supposed hero of Bouresches, was off the screen. "I don't know where Robertson was," Cates would later say. He was making a name for himself, whether he liked it or not.

Cates and the two companies headed off cross-country toward Bouresches, under the ominous watch of four German observation balloons floating north of the American lines. By the time they reached their jump-off, though, word was finally received that the marines of the 3rd Battalion, 5th Regiment, still held the town. The 96th Company turned back west toward Lucy, and bivouacked on the side of a thickly wooded hill just southeast of the village. There, they endured some intermittent German shelling during the day.

Restless, Cates spent much of the day walking the fields between the wood and Bouresches in a vain attempt to locate the body of his friend Thomas Brailsford, gone missing during the assault on June 6.

He went alone. "I found that it's much safer than to have other men with you," he would write. Even as he walked the fields alone that afternoon, "I had some very close calls as I was shot at repeatedly."*

That day at about five thirty p.m., Holcomb was ordered to have two companies of his battalion enter the Bois de Belleau and relieve Wise's men, who had spent the day enduring more heavy shelling—this time laced with mustard gas. The 96th and 78th Companies would do the job.

James Robertson, meanwhile, had returned to the company, but, upon receiving orders, he once again left Cates in command and went into the wood to reconnoiter the way to Wise's battalion.

Just prior to midnight, the companies' rolling kitchens arrived, and Cates told his men to "saddle up, put on their equipment," get something to eat, and then get ready to enter the woods at one a.m.

As they lined up for chow, though, a salvo of shells tore out of the black-as-pitch night, headed right toward them. "I realized that they were no ordinary shells—the gas shells make a different whine to it," Cates would recall.

"So they hit and there was no detonation so I knew it was gas, but I waited to smell. By that time, there were more salvos coming in. So I got the first whiff of gas and I yelled 'Gas' and everybody passed it along."

Worse, the Germans were sending over more than just gas shells— "gas air bursts, shrapnel, and high explosives," Cates wrote.

---

*Various reports had Brailsford either being captured or killed by a shell. Second Lieutenant John Bowling, wounded during the advance, would report that a friend of his saw Brailsford fall from a shell near Bouresches. His body was ultimately located, and he was buried in the Aisne-Marne American Cemetery at the northern tip of Belleau Wood.

In the next hours, between six thousand and seven thousand such shells rained down on Cates and the two companies. "There was no standing such fire," the 78th Company's Private T. S. Allen would recall. "It meant annihilation for the whole unit and perhaps a hole in our line."

One whiff . . . and you'll die. The marines scrambled to put on their gas masks in the deep night as tiny droplets of mustard gas enveloped them in a deadly fog.

Cates reached for his mask, too, and . . .

"MY COMPANY IS DEFUNCT"

WHEN HE LOOKED at them now he broke down and cried. He cried like a baby. These men, these few now gathered on the Paris–Metz highway, shuffling quietly and speaking in low tones and all wondering how they'd survived, were all that remained. The others . . .

The others of the 96th and 78th Companies were mostly in the hospital, though a good number were being buried. They'd not been so lucky on that early morning of June 14, 1918. Some had panicked and torn off their gas masks as the shells rained down into the darkness. Others were ripped apart by shrapnel, some almost obliterated. The suffering had been horrible, unearthly.

"The strain has been terrible," Cliff Cates would write, "but the few that have come thru will soon recuperate back here. . . . At times I wished that one would knock me off, but still life is very sweet at its worst."

Life is sweet. . . .

Cates had almost been one of them, had almost lost it as the shells came down and he reached for his gas mask and found only his tunic. He suddenly remembered he had left his mask in "this hole" fifteen feet away, but with the darkness and the gas-laden mist and the shrapnel tearing the very air apart, there was no hope of finding it.

Panic rising in his throat, he crawled desperately amid the poisonous fumes, searching for the only thing that would save his life. Then he remembered Virgil A. Hall, the redheaded private who had come across a German gas mask back in Bouresches and taken it as a souvenir.

Hall! Cates yelled. *Private Hall!*

Came a muffled reply: *Here I am, sir! Here I am!*

Cates groped in the darkness toward Hall's voice and asked him where the German mask was. Hall handed it over, and Cates wound up wearing it for the next five hours—all but suffocated and blind, but alive.

He jumped in on top of Hall in his pitiful hole and waited it out— and made, he would admit later, "the mistake of staying there and taking that gas."

Cates should have gotten his men out of the wooded ravine and away from the gas and explosives. Instead, many of them lay in their holes, enduring salvo after salvo. "We took terrific casualties," Cates would say later, in one of military history's great understatements.

Some obeyed the natural instinct to go to ground, burrow into the sweet-smelling earth while havoc rained around them. Some understood what Cates could not: It was better to risk the shrapnel than remain there as the poison slowly wrapped around them from ankles to their tin hats, soaking their clothing and burning into their skin.

Corporal Harrison Cale would write that some did better understand their predicament and risked the high explosives to find relief from the mustard gas.

"When the shells began to fall, a lieutenant ran over to me and gave orders to move the men in our platoon out of the woods and onto a road a hundred feet distant, where they might find some protection from the shells," Cale would write.*

---

*The 78th's commander, Captain Robert Messersmith, would later claim that "permission to move the companies into another area or to proceed with the relief" of the 5th's 2nd Battalion in the wood was "requested, but refused." By whom, he didn't say.

"He had scarcely shouted the order when a shell burst near him and I never saw him again." Cale removed his mask briefly so he could tell the men in his squad to move out. One by one, timing the intervals between falling shells, about forty men made it through the barrage to safety.

"The others had shifted for themselves," Cale added—among them the veteran gunnery sergeant Fred W. Stockham, who "walked back and forth through the woods that night, driving men out of their fox holes and making them get up and go to me, as all were loath to leave the shallow holes which provided at least a little protection.

"The woods was a mass of crashing shells and falling trees as the gas, mingled with high explocives [sic], swept through the branches," Cale wrote. "But the brave sergeant never stopped until he had made every man he could find move out to the road."

Another of the 96th Company's sergeants, twenty-five-year-old James M. Finn, also tried to get his platoon away from the deadly gas. "He could have saved himself, but took off his mask to help direct the platoon out of the woods," his friend Corporal Harold D. Powell would write to Finn's family and friends back in Granby, Missouri.

Finn made it to Base Hospital #30; he fought for life for six days before he died at eleven thirty p.m. on June 19. "It is usually such as he who pay the full price, and it is an honor to know the one who paid the price in the fullest, as Jim did. . . . There is none, officers or men, who do not feel the loss of Jim," Powell wrote.

Even moving out to the road did not guarantee safety. The 96th Company's Gus Turngren, a stocky private whom the men called "Bullet Head," made it to the road, but then made a fatal mistake.

"He came out of the gas area and tore off his gas mask and threw it down and stepped on it saying he would never wear it again," Private Joseph Greenburg would later report.

The insidious gas emanated from his clothing, and soon Gus Turngren found himself in an ambulance racing toward a backline field station; he died en route.

Twenty-year-old Private Theodore LeGrande Guerry, whose grand-father and namesake was president of the Georgia State Senate when the state seceded in 1861, and whose great-uncle John B. Guerry was killed while fighting for the Rebs at the Second Battle of Manassas in 1862, was also stricken by the gas, but managed to stumble to the road and supposed safety.

"He came out of the gas area and walked a little way but sat down," Private Greenburg would say. "We tried to get him to walk farther back but he sat down and could not get up and died in a few minutes."

Others fell while trying to get their stricken comrades from the scene. "The sacrifice was enormous," the 78th Company's Private Walter Shanley would write.

Answering Captain Messersmith's call for volunteer stretcher bearers, Shanley and another private "ran into trees, due to our clouded gas masks, so we did what everybody there did, threw away our gas masks and carried them back until we fell and in turn were carried off the field."

As the four-hour barrage began to slacken, Gunnery Sergeant Stockham went to the aid of a badly wounded private. Stockham had only recently refused an offer to attend officers' school at Gondrecourt, and would have been there, instead of in this hell, had he gone.

But Stockham had refused to leave his men.

"I've lived with them and goddamnit, I'll die with them," he had said.

The marine was not so grievously injured that he couldn't move, so Stockham gingerly lifted him onto his back. "He couldn't have been more than eighteen or nineteen," Cates would recall.

Stumbling into the dawn and out of the gas-soaked ravine, both went flat when a high-explosive shell exploded above them. Stockham, dazed, quickly sprang to his feet and located the private. He hadn't been wounded further—but his gas mask was shattered.

"Well, there it was," Cliff Cates would write. "The area was thick with mustard gas, and even a linthead could figure that chances for survival without a mask were precisely zero. Fred Stockham knew that. No man in flaming hell knew it better."

Stockham without hesitation ripped off his own mask and placed it on the face of the wounded marine. He picked him up and began carrying him toward safety, "with his own face bare and grim," Cates wrote.

Fred Stockham delivered his load at a backline aid station . . . and then returned to the gas-laden ravine that had become a perfect hell on earth, where men moaned and writhed in agony as the oily gas did its work, and where others were up and moving around now, carrying the dead and badly wounded from that hideous den of torture.

Before long, Stockham collapsed from the effects of the gas, which took "four mortal days to kill him," wrote Cates, who would be instrumental in getting his gunny a posthumous Medal of Honor.

The gas had a delayed effect on others as well. "The gas, while I was inhaling it, did not feel so disagreeable," Harrison Cale would write. "It made me feel quite sleepy, but aside from the burning sensation in my eyes, I experienced little pain."

But as Cates called for the 96th and 78th Companies' survivors to follow him into Belleau Wood, still intending to carry out his relief mission for Wise's battalion, Cale suddenly felt weak.

"An officer"—Cates, perhaps—"noticing me stagger, ordered me to the rear. I took about twenty men with me, all suffering from the effects of the gas."

They removed most of their clothing, "in order to escape the severe body burns that follow mustard gassing," Cale wrote.

Nevertheless, nine men died on the way to aid.

Both companies had lost well over half of their men or more; more would fall as the gas went to work through the morning.

Once in the wood, the remnants of the 96th Company were detailed to carry off the wounded of the 5th Regiment, which had also suffered a bombardment of mustard gas the previous day.

"It wasn't over an hour until all of my men became casualties," Cates wrote. "The mustard gas had saturated their clothing, and when they started sweating it made bad body burns. Also, the fumes caused temporary blindness. The gas was in the clothing—the ones that didn't get it in the lungs . . . got it from the clothing."

"This gas goes right through your clothes and burns worst where you are perspiring or the least bit warm," twenty-four-year-old Corporal Joseph Stites of the 96th Company wrote.

Stites managed not to breathe in the gas, but was badly burned over much of his body—and in his eyes. By the time he and his fellow marines made their way to a field hospital, "we had begun to blister and my eyes were closed.

"We were given a hot bath and our burns dressed and we were then sent to another hospital and it sure was not a pleasant ride for there was not a spot on my body that was not blistered. Every time the car would hit a rough place in the road I could feel the blisters break and water run down my back."

He found little comfort even once in the base hospital, where his burns tormented him. He had castor oil dripped into his eyes every thirty minutes for six weeks.

"It was quite painful as there is not an unburned place on my body on which to lie, so I sat in bed for sixteen days," he wrote on July 6. "My eyes were closed for eight days but the doctor said they would be good as new in a short time."

While many of the company's men lay dying or in transit to aid stations, Cates, once more lucky to not be severely harmed, stripped his clothes, beat them and aired them, and soaped himself.

Still, he was "pretty badly burned" on his legs and arms and forehead—"any place where it was wet from perspiration. I do have bad blisters between my legs, around my neck, and on my forehead where the helmet rubbed," he would add. "The doctor has tried his best to evacuate me, but I am not going unless I get worse."

Except for a few of his company's men who had somehow dodged the gas or been detailed to supply work, the 96th Company was "defunct," Cates now sadly acknowledged. Except for a pitiful handful, "I was the only man left out of the company."

Fifteen men of the 96th Company were killed in action or died of wounds as a result of that awful night; another 161 were wounded, or gassed—or both. In the 78th Company, 16 would die and another 190 were wounded or gassed.

Among the casualties was First Lieutenant James Robertson, who most likely was gassed while he was reconnoitering the relief route in the Bois de Belleau, and Robert Messersmith, who was blinded by gas—a common occurrence.

Temporary blindness was one delayed effect of mustard gas. As Harrison Cale would write, by the time he and scores of his company mates had arrived at hospitals in Paris, "we had all become blind, and it was ten days before we again saw daylight." Cale spent the next eight months in the hospital.

By June 16, Evacuation Hospital #8 at Juilly, France, had received almost seven hundred men suffering from mustard gas, most of them marines and "some of them badly gassed in the lungs and fighting horribly for breath, which could be prolonged a little by giving them oxygen," wrote ambulance driver Frederick A. Pottle.

Nearly all were blinded, "many delirious, all crying, moaning, tossing about. For most of the patients, there was nothing to do but frequently renew the wet dressings which relieved somewhat the smart of the burns, and to try to restore their lost morale. For those who had been gassed worst, nothing effectual could be done."

The June 1918 muster roll for the 96th Company reveals the catastrophe that visited its men in the early hours of June 14. Over and over, the date and affliction—"14 gassed in action" or "14 wounded in action"—tell the tale in black and white.

Among the names are those of Lieutenant Robertson: "Acute, bronchitis, bilateral, catarrhal, due to exposure to mustard gas." And this for Second Lieutenant George B. Lockhart, commander of the 96th's 1st Platoon: "Gas absorption of deleterious enemy mustard, inhalation and surface contact . . . skin burns, scrotum and thighs."

The heroic Gunnery Sergeant Fred Stockham expired at Base Hospital #30 at nine forty-five p.m. on June 22. Two more of the 96th's sergeants also died at the hospital from the mustard gas—Alcide St. John at twelve forty-five a.m. on June 24, and James M. Finn at eleven thirty p.m. on June 19.

Despite the disaster, Holcomb still intended to carry out the relief of Wise's battalion in the Bois de Belleau, and to that end, on the morning of June 14, he sent for the 79th and 80th Companies, then resting in the southeastern edge of Belleau Wood northwest of Lucy.

Don Paradis, a gunnery sergeant with the 80th Company, would remember arriving at the southern edge of the woods and being greeted by "the sight of dozens of men trying to alleviate the burns caused by the mustard gas.

"Some were stripped trying to wash the mustard gas burns from under their arms and down their backs and around their eyes and in the grime many were coughing terribly. We had only had a couple of medics and one of them was badly gassed."

Filing through the gas-infested woods, parts of it burning, Holcomb reported to Wise with less than two full companies, more casualties having been taken from German shelling during the 2nd Battalion's trip to the front line. Wise remained in line with his battalion and placed what was left of the 79th Company on the eastern edge of the wood.

Wise then placed Bailey Coffenburg's 80th Company on the left of his battalion's line, bending it to the south in the form of a hook.

Holcomb attached Cates and the few of his remaining men to the 80th Company; they would fight with that unit for three days and nights.

"The company I am serving with is in the tip of Belleau Woods, and the Germans are only about forty yards from my hole to my left rear," Cates wrote from the lines on June 16.

"They have a very strong machine gun nest which we have practically surrounded, but other units have been unable to take it. They refuse to surrender and every so often we have a grenade battle. Sometimes they cut loose with about a dozen machine guns.

"Then the Germans to our front also open up, and it is bedlam, as we are getting fire from our front and rear. The bullets sound like a swarm of bees as they ricochet off the big boulders and the trees around our position."

There was plenty of shelling to go around as well.

"In the town a one pounder tore a hole in arm's reach of my post and I thought that a narrow escape[,] but over in the wood one night a Boche .77 exploded not 15 feet from the hole where I was sleeping . . . not much sleep, I'm not fooling," Private Thomas Stewart, one of the few men able to survive the gassing and make it into the wood with Cates, would remember.

"Some of the shell holes are terrific—20 or 30 feet across, and half as deep. The big shells are the easier to dodge for you can hear them coming longer, the 3 inch or Boche 77 mm is mean as it comes pretty fast and there are lots of them.

"The one pounders are impossible, the whizz-bangs as we call them. They shoot at such short range that they're on you by the time you hear the report."

The marines fought off two German attacks on the night of June 15.

"Each time we met them with the hottest fire imaginable—you cannot possibly imagine the roar that our rifles, machine guns and artillery made," Cates would write on June 18. "They never reached our lines at all—they fell back with considerable losses while we didn't lose a man.

"They kept a constant stream of bullets cutting over our heads—you should hear them whiz over and cut thru the woods. That is, what used to be—a few trees are still standing, but our artillery cut it to pieces before we drove the Boche out. Today the bodies of Boche are laying all over the woods—it's suicide to get out to try to bury them, so we let them stay."

Cates and the 80th Company held the line at the northern edge of the woods until the night of June 16–June 17, when they and Wise's battalion were relieved by the 1st Battalion of the 3rd Division's 7th Regiment.

The relief did not go off without incident. The 7th's men had not seen action and could have no idea what kind of hell they were about to endure, or die within, and as they approached the lines, "all hell broke loose," Cates wrote.

"The Boche in our rear started firing, then our men returned it, the Germans to our front started firing, we answered, then both their artillery and ours opened up. We thought they were attacking, and they probably thought we were. It kept up for over thirty minutes, and it was a madhouse. Imagine the poor army boys that have not been under fire before."

During the excitement, Cates sent up flares from the company command post within the lines. Running out, he raced to his "hole" down the line and heard a fresh salvo of shells coming in.

He jumped into his hole, and "a bayonet went right up through my legs almost ripping my trousers off. I thought he was a Dutchman, but it turned out to be an army boy, and he had been shot through the hand. He had set his rifle down in the hole with the bayonet pushing upward."

Once again, it was a close call for Lucky Cates: "I could have received a nasty wound."

Cates once again had also proved to be a popular presence among his men, these temporarily of the 80th Company.

"The most optimistic person I ever saw was Lieutenant Cates of the 96th Company in our battalion," Private Carl Brannen of the 80th Company would write. "In one of the gas attacks his entire command was wiped out, and he was attached to my group until more men could be brought for him to command.

"With his winning personality, he was able to cheer us when everything looked as dark as it possibly could. His lion courage in the face of any danger was enough to bolster one's morale. I hated to see him leave us."

On June 17, Cates walked fairly unscathed from the Bois de Belleau and went into reserve with what remained of the 2nd Battalion in the Bois Gros Jean on the Paris–Metz highway.

Decompressing after the events of the past four days, he thought of the men from his mostly now-defunct company, tears welling in his eyes.

"Honest," he would write, "when I look out at the few men left I really cry—I am the only officer out of two companies and I am in charge of the remains of both companies—one good platoon. I didn't realize how much I loved the old bunch until it had been broken up. . . . I am hoping that we can get a lot of them back in a few weeks."

By then he had learned to hate—hate what the Boches had done to his company, his men; hate an enemy who refused to surrender until at the point of a bayonet; hate the men who killed and maimed his men.

And by then he had learned to kill, and to not be bothered by it. He had killed one German during the taking of Bouresches in what seemed like a year before, and with the 80th Company in the Bois de Belleau, he killed another, sniping from his position at a soldier running across the fields south of the village of Belleau.

"My first shot hit right under him," Cates would write, "[and] the next one dropped him. . . . I now have two notches cut on my pistol grip, and I hope to make it fifty.

"A man gets to be a hard hearted [sic] brute over here," he would add, "but has to be, so don't think I am so very inhuman when I tell you all this. A person can get used to most anything."

But he would allow that the stresses of the past week had gotten to him.

"If a man had to stay at the front very long at a time, he would go crazy," he wrote on June 23. "It is an awful strain and men break real often. I was scared at times that I was going nuts. At times I wished a shell would get me, but a man soon changes his mind and looks forward to one time—the time he will be home with the ones he loves."

For the time being, Cates would have to get used not to home but to handling new men, as the third wave of Quantico recruits since he and the 2nd Battalion had marched out of its gates in January arrived in the back lines.

So much had changed since then, so much life lived, so many men gone to dust in the Bois de Belleau and its surroundings.

He had changed, too. It was impossible to be otherwise. Cliff Cates had become a bona fide leader of men in combat, a marine's marine, and had found that he loved his job; and so on June 26, Cates led his new 4th Platoon back into those woods with a spring in his step, but a hole in his heart for those many marines who had followed him before, and who had been lost.

"VIVE LES MARINES!"

THREE CHEERS NOW for the red, white, and blue; three cheers for the valiant United States marines who had saved Paris; *trois* cheers for Cliff Cates and the twenty of his men from the 96th Company who paraded, smiling, laughing, and still alive though looking "like a bunch of bums" in their greasy dirt-and-blood-smeared uniforms through the City of Light to calls of *"Vive les Américains!"* and *"Vive les marines!"*

"Gee!" Cates would write excitedly. "I am glad that I joined the Marines."

Thirty-five miles up the Paris–Metz highway, men were still sleeping on the gas-infused bare ground, surrounded on all sides by the detritus of battle and the decomposing bodies of marines and Germans; thirty miles up the Paris–Metz highway, some 650 Americans were sleeping in their graves, those whose bodies had been located in the woods, anyway.

Thirty-five miles up the road, at a place that would soon be renamed the Bois de la Brigade de Marine, thirty-seven hundred marines had entered that flesh-sucking black-hole patch of woods and been gassed or decapitated or had their eyes gouged out, or had had their legs and arms blown away, or had been shot in the stomach and the head and the groin, and died agonizing, lonely deaths.

Thirty-five miles up the road, Cliff Cates had virtually lost his entire company, and now here he was in Paris, parading on the Fourth of July over cobblestone streets and playing to an adoring crowd of Frenchmen, some of whom just one month before had been packing up for places south as the German drive appeared unstoppable.

Thirty-five miles up that road, the almost brand-new 96th Company was still holding the line in the north end of that stinking wood. But for Cliff Cates, life was sweet, at least for the moment.

"Vive les marines!" said the most optimistic man many marines would ever meet.

Thirty-five miles up the road, the Bois de Belleau was in American hands. Or what was left of it, anyway. In the end, they'd had to destroy the wood in order to save it; they'd had to blast it to beyond smithereens, had to lay a fourteen-hour barrage on its northern reaches before the 3rd Battalion, 5th Regiment—used and abused more than any single battalion, including Cliff Cates's—could report, momentously if anticlimactically, "Belleau Woods now U.S. Marine Corps entirely." These were the words Major Maurice Shearer, who'd taken over for the wounded Benjamin Berry, messaged to James Harbord on June 26.

They'd damned near had to destroy the Marine Brigade to take the wood; as hard-nosed as Harbord and the marines had been about grabbing the Bois de Belleau as a symbol of American resolve and commitment, the Germans had almost equaled them. As one of their battlefield commanders, General Max von Boehm, told his troops in a special order:

"An American success along our front, even if only temporary, may have the most unfavorable influence on the attitude of the Entente and the duration of the war. In the coming battles, therefore, it is not a question of the possession of this or that village or woods, insignificant in itself; it is a question of whether the Anglo-American claim that the American army is the equal or even the superior of the German army is to be made good."

Cliff Cates had certainly earned the right to feel superior, and the right to parade. He'd taken Bouresches; he had experienced more of the wood and its incessant, localized battles than anyone in the 96th Company; he'd heard and seen the blasts from the Minenwerfers and the *pup-pup-pup* from one hundred unseen machine-gun nests, seen bodies strewn here, there, and everywhere like beached whales, covered with bluebottle flies and whitening and rotting and moldering under the quickly decreasing canopy.

Cliff Cates had alone felt the emotional brunt of the company's losses—the 96th's June 30 rolls would count thirty dead, just about everyone but Cates wounded or gassed—and had alone seen and understood just how many were lost, and had now more than half a dozen times himself almost been killed, at Bouresches and on that goddamned hillside near Lucy and within the wood itself.

He'd lost a captain, a good friend in Thomas Brailsford, all those 4th Platoon men he'd learned to love, and who would have followed him anywhere. He'd survived that awful night of June 14 and then gone into the wood as almost the lone survivor of the 96th Company.

He'd earned something; a trip to Paris would certainly do.

Two weeks earlier, Cates had been resting in the Bois de Gros Jean with his few remaining men when 135 men from Company B of the 4th Replacement Battalion turned up. These were swallowed into what amounted to a new 96th Company, the unit being reborn in that wood on that day and under the command of a new captain, Wethered Woodworth, who brought with him a new lieutenant, Robert Duane.

If Cates felt he'd earned the right to a promotion and command of the new 96th Company, he never said; "I like the new officers fine," is all he would write.

As for the new men? They were "a good looking [sic] bunch and I am sure that they will uphold the honor of the 'fighting 96th.'"

Cates took his new men into the wood on June 25 and huddled on the eastern edge while artillery barraged the north end for fourteen hours, stunning and demoralizing the Germans who had tenaciously denied attempts by marines and regulars of the 7th Regiment alike to root them out.

The same day, Maurice Shearer and his 3rd Battalion of the 5th Regiment advanced at five p.m. The half-day barrage preceding them had demoralized those Germans it had not annihilated. Shearer's men took prisoners in bunches; one, Private Henry Lenert, took seventy-eight Boches all by himself.

Shearer the next morning declared the woods American; what one author called the "heroic tragedy" of the battle for the seemingly insignificant French forest was over.

Cates and the 96th Company relieved Shearer's men that evening, and they spent the next few days mostly stringing barbed wire to their front just in case the Germans wanted to try to assert their supposed superiority one more time. Twice the Germans shelled him and his men as they tried to lay new wire; Cates finally gave up and brought everyone into the lines.

There, they found to their delight that coffee, ham, steak, bread, and potatoes had been delivered from the rear. "We get one hot meal a day here," Cates would write on June 26 from the front line.

"They bring it in in big thermos cans on a Ford truck. They also bring canned meat, bread, bacon, sugar, candles, and solidified alcohol. During the day we take either the alcohol or candles and cook the bacon in our mess gears; then we fry the bread in the bacon fat, and put sugar on it—it's a swell dish."

It was hardly the Ritz, but all things being equal, Cates and his men had an easy time of it when compared to the lives that had been wasted and destroyed in that wood over the past three weeks.

The condition of the Bois de Belleau itself told the grim story of the fight, as it now hardly resembled the leafy, peaceful enclave it had once been.

It resembled more the aftermath of a natural disaster, having been "gassed and shelled and shot into the semblance of nothing earthly," marine John W. Thomason would write. "The great trees were all down; the leaves were blasted off, or hung sere and blackened. It was pockmarked with craters and shallow dugouts and hasty trenches.

"It was strewn with all the debris of war, Mauser rifles and Springfields, helmets, German and American, unexploded grenades, letters, knapsacks, packs, blankets, boots; a year later, it is said, they were still finding unburied dead in the depths of it."

The living now endured the usual salvos of Minenwerfer and machine-gun fire sent their way. They also exhibited the attire and equipment needed to survive in the troglodyte world of Belleau Wood.

"I wish you could see your son with his equipment on," Cates would write his mother from the front line, "dirty, torn, ragged suit; wrapped puttees, shoes, that used to be boots, but are now cut off; steel helmet, with a hole thru it and a big dent; pistol belt and suspenders; first aid package and cover; pistol and holster; canteen, cup and cover, knapsack, which holds toilet articles, maps, message books, extra cartridges, etc.; field glasses and case, two extra pistol clips and cases; German gas mask (which saved my life); French gas mask; big German luger pistol and holster; big musette bag with cigarettes, chocolate bars, magazine, writing paper, condiment can, malted milk tablets, comb, little clothes brush, alkaline tablets (for gas) and other junk; a blanket roll which contains a poncho, blanket, air pillow, handkerchiefs, socks, underwear, etc.; and a German raincoat slung over my arm. A nice load, but I need every bit of it. Gee! how I would love to walk home with it all on."

Even as he wrote, there was now a flicker of light at the end of the tunnel, at least for him and a few other soon-to-be-lucky men: On the evening of July 1, battalion commander Thomas Holcomb told Cates that the entire battalion would be relieved as soon as the front was wired.

Cates and thirty-two of his men spent the long dark night working at it, and strung 450 yards before dawn.

"They are a fine bunch," he would write of his new command, "but still a little green and excitable. Gee! I wish I had the old men back."

At first light, while Cates and his men were still out front, the Germans began shelling the American line, and Cates and his men rushed back toward their line. Cates was knocked down by an exploding shell, but again his amazing luck held.

As he entered Captain Woodworth's dugout, another shell burst directly overhead, knocking him flat once more. "God only knows how they missed me," he would write, "but I did not get a scratch." However, the left side of his face was sore from the concussion—"it even gave me a toothache."

No Germans tried the wire, and soon the ruckus died down. The 2nd Battalion's men passed the day in their holes, waiting to be relieved. At five p.m., word came from the 6th Regiment that twenty men from each company were to proceed to Paris to parade on the Fourth of July as part of a composite company of marines.

One lieutenant from each battalion would accompany the men. Lots were drawn, and Second Lieutenant Johnny Overton, the former captain of the Yale track team, won. Overton, though, had only joined the battalion in mid-June, so Holcomb overrode the pick and selected Cates to go.

Cates selected those who would accompany him, and took "as many old men as possible, as they deserved it," he would write. "I was some happy mortal."

Getting to Paris wouldn't be a problem; getting out of the Bois de Belleau during the bright light of day would prove troublesome. The Germans weren't in an attacking mood, but they were always watching, artillery spotters at Torcy and Belleau still looking to plug anything that moved.

Including Cates and his merry group of dirty, exhausted marines bound for "gay Paree."

Sticking to the woods and ravines as much as possible, the bunch was spotted emerging from the tree line at dusk, almost out of range but not quite. Quickly, three shells screamed toward them.

Well, Cates thought, *I'm damned. I've come all this way but now I've had it.*

Lucky Cates: Two of the shells missed by 150 yards, but the other almost nailed Cates and one of his sergeants. During the following lull, the whole bunch got up and starting running like hell.

Finally, Cates's groups, and the others from the brigade, reached the safety of the Paris–Metz highway, three miles from the German guns. On foot, by train, and by truck almost five hundred very happy mortals trekked to Paris, reaching a camp on the outskirts the next afternoon. There they ate and bathed, and many slept in bunks for the first time in weeks.

"I didn't feel natural as I had been sleeping on the bare ground so long," Cates wrote. "I will never be able to sleep in a decent bed again— I will have to dig me a little hole out in the yard, before I will feel natural."

The morning of July 4, they arose and tried to clean themselves off, "but we still looked like a bunch of bums," Cates wrote. They marched to their jump-off—a familiar word—only this time it was not to advance on the German guns, but into a swelling, screaming, cheering crowd of Parisians.

"Vive les marines!"

"They literally covered us with roses," Cates wrote. "I would carry each bouquet a piece and then drop it—then another girl would load me down with flowers. It was truly wonderful and it made us marines feel very good as they gave us all of the credit. . . . We have certainly made a name in France."

As they passed the Red Cross hospitals, familiar faces from the 96th Company, those wounded at Bouresches or gassed in the wood, stood outside or hung from windows and cheered their comrades. "As we paraded by[,] all would yell and I would turn and answer, parade or no parade," he wrote.

The parade coursed the Champs-Élysées and the Grands Boulevards.

"It was pretty good to hear 'La Marseillaise' and old 'Semper Fidelis,' and to see those fine old gray-haired Frenchmen take off their hats to Old Glory as we passed," the 79th Company's Private Douglas Mabbott would write.

"I was glad to find how well the French people knew and appreciated the great part the marines had taken in stopping the German drive." (For that, Mabbott could thank one-eyed Floyd Gibbons, and a sentimental censor at Pershing's headquarters.)

At noon, the joyous procession fell out and traveled to a large ammunition plant. The place employed ten thousand "girls"—"a very good class of girls, and not the kind a person usually finds in factories," the scion of Cates Landing would fairly sniff.

The factory floor was set up for lunch. One American flag adorned a chair at each table, and one man would be feted at each table, the women taking the other seats. The officers ate and watched from a balcony above.

A band played, the lunch was "swell"; "we ate with a lot of generals, colonels, etc.," Cates wrote, adding, "Also a lot of pretty girls."

He didn't mention in letters home the bacchanalia that followed, as two thousand sex-deprived men drank two thousand bottles of champagne that had also been provided and went wild, "screwing whenever and whatever they could," in Cates's words as paraphrased by author Robert B. Asprey.

The scene below, Cates would add, was "simply fantastic, because the officers could watch them."

Afterward, the marines were given liberty until six a.m. And here Cates proved himself to be not only lucky, but, once again, a natural leader.

The eighty men representing the 2nd Battalion were busted, flat broke. They hadn't received their pay for two months while on the march and then while doing that bit of fighting in the Bois de Belleau.

Cates, though, had saved his previous pay and had ninety-six hundred francs. He told his gunnery sergeant to take four thousand of these and dole them out, fifty francs to a man—the equivalent of about nine dollars at the time. "That gave them enough money to go out and have a good dinner, and go to a show, or pick up a gal—whatever they wanted," Cates recalled.

He didn't ask to be reimbursed, and the men were duly impressed. "My reputation was made from then on, I can tell you that," Cates would say many years later. (More than half of the men did repay him, one just prior to a victory parade in New York City the next year.)

Cates took on the town with three other officers and two pretty girls. They had a nice dinner and went to a show, and he returned to camp at one a.m.

The man who'd almost missed the boat to France wasn't about to take a chance on being left behind again.

Although this time, he just might have wished he had been.

A BON FIGHT

AND HE'S A pretty sight now, isn't he? With his trousers half blown-off, his hand bleeding from yet another near hit, racing to and fro on a godforsaken beet field dodging snipers—yet again.

They keep trying, but they don't seem able to kill Cliff Cates. Lucky Cliff Cates. Cliff Cates, "the luckiest man that ever was in the Marine Corps," his pal First Lieutenant Samuel Meek of the 82nd Company would one day recall.

"I guess he was being saved to become commandant."

Once again, on this day, Cliff Cates will be left as the last man standing—or last officer—and the only officer left in the whole god-damned 2nd Battalion, for that matter.

And they say God works in mysterious ways, but Cates isn't God, and no matter how hard he tries, he can't get the line to move farther against the Germans lining the low hills to his front.

Too much artillery, too many damned Germans in the way, the men just hanging on and trying to stay low.

And no cover.

Just like at Bouresches.

It's a hell of a place to be, and not one that he had anticipated being in while traveling the Paris–Metz highway back to his company exactly two weeks before, his head still a little woozy from all of the champagne, his belly filled with French delicacies, the image of a certain mademoiselle—*what was her name?*—hovering in his memory.

He'd almost, for one night, forgotten there was a war on. And for a while—a week—after rejoining the 96th Company, life had been comparatively good. There were new faces all around, the new captain, Woodworth, to get to know better, and new lieutenants—among them Robert Duane, whom he'd gotten to know a little in the wood, James C. McClelland, and thirty-two-year-old Bernard L. Fritz, a transfer from the 79th Company who had just been promoted to a second lieutenancy from sergeant after thirteen years in the Marines.

A German native, Fritz had been brought to the United States by his parents at the age of two. After first studying to become a priest, he changed his plans and joined the Marine Corps.

"He had a presence that was superb," Second Lieutenant Graves Erskine of the 79th Company would remember. "He was very sharp and very much to the point in everything he said."

Fritz's German heritage kept him from advancing past the rank of first sergeant—"and they suspected him of being an intelligence agent and never found any reason to continue this suspicion."

As well, he didn't get along well with the company's captain, Randolph Zane. Fritz confided to Erskine his frustration about being passed over for promotion for no good reason. Erskine would claim he got Fritz commissioned as a second lieutenant.

The 96th Company also welcomed back—probably not the correct term—First Lieutenant James F. Robertson, the supposed "hero of Bouresches." By the time of his return, Cates had won the admiration of marines new to the company and those old-timers who would return to it over the coming months.

"He was the type of officer that the men admired and loved," James M. Sellers of the 78th Company, Cates's friend and fellow lieutenant, would write, providing an example of just why they loved him so: "When a German plane would come over us, Cliff would pull out his Colt and fire at it."

On July 9, command of the hard-won area around the Bois de Belleau was passed to the 26th Division, and the Yankees took over the defensive position while the 2nd Division went into reserve north of Bézu-le-Guéry, just a few miles southeast of the wood.

On July 13, the 96th Company moved just below the Marne River at Nanteuil-sur-Marne, where for the first time since May the few original men left in the company—excepting Cates—"slept under cover, ate regular meals, and thoroughly enjoyed bathing in the Marne River."

And on at least one occasion, there was a diversion and entertainment that the movies couldn't beat. One afternoon, Cates and his men watched, enraptured, as four American planes protecting an observation balloon took on a single "Hun" aircraft over the Marne.

The German "ducked and evaded" the Americans and then dived in to take down the balloon, blasting away with his cannons. He missed, and returned with a "loop-the-loop" maneuver, Cates would write, and fired again as the two observers jumped out and parachuted to safety.

The Americans now returned, machine guns blazing, and the last Cates saw of the German plane, it was tumbling and trailing smoke as it dived behind some hills.

"He was a nervy rascal anyway," Cates wrote. "I sure am glad they got him."

If nothing else, the scene was a reminder that a war was still on—and in fact, for the marines, the war was stirring, its deadly tentacles about to reach out toward the Marne once again.

German military architect Erich Ludendorff, his move toward Paris stymied by the 2nd Division, sought to enlarge the gains made that spring east and west of Reims and push south of the Marne. Once again, he hoped if nothing else to draw French reserves from the north, and then relaunch a drive on the British.

A new German offensive would begin early in the morning of July

15—just hours after the conclusion of the Bastille Day holiday. Massed artillery, of course, would announce the beginning of the attack.

This time, though, the French and their American allies would be waiting and ready. German prisoners divulged the plans for the attack, and massed artillery opened up on the German guns and attack infantry huddled in their jump-off posts before the German guns could respond in kind.

When the enemy guns did fire, their shells found few victims among the French and men of the American 3rd Division on the southern bank of the Marne and those of the 42nd Division east of Reims.

In many places, a false front had been created, the forward trenches left sparely populated; the few "suicide" troops were overrun, but the attacking Germans were annihilated as they approached the new Allied strongpoints farther on.

The 3rd Division held the Marne, blowing up German pontoon bridges and slaughtering those who tried to cross in boats. On July 17, Ludendorff called a halt; the massive casualties incurred were not worth the paltry gains his men had made.

By then, a new offensive was already well into play—this time an Allied effort.

In the latter days of May, the Germans had pushed their drive below Champagne well past Soissons and just to the Marne, where its movement east and south had been halted by men such as Cliff Cates.

Marshal Ferdinand Foch and his Allied command had weeks before seen a great opportunity awaiting if the Germans' southeastward movement and the Marne could be checked; with the latest German attack quickly falling to pieces, it was time to spring the trap and bring the war to the enemy.

The Germans had, in their haste that early summer to get south of the Marne and to Paris, created a large, hanging pocket from Soissons across to Reims and below to the Marne.

It looked like a large balloon, and Foch decided he would try to pierce it, assigning his ruthless general Charles Mangin to do the job. Mangin was known as "the Butcher," the nickname not necessarily referring to the slaughter of Germans but to that of his own men.

The 1st and 2nd Divisions, bloodied but battle-hardened, were attached to Mangin's 10th Army, which in this assault also would include the 1st Moroccan Division, consisting of numerous colonial regiments from Africa plus a regiment of the famed French Foreign Legion, which were already holding the line on the eastern edge of the Retz Forest.

This Allied force would attack due east-southeast below Soissons, at the point where the bulge narrowed, crossing wide, rolling plains cut and crossed by numerous ravines that sheltered numerous villages. The objective was the severing of the Germans' supply line, mainly the railway that carried twenty-two trains per day through Soissons and to points south.

With great luck, the neck of the bag would be closed, the German supply lines cut, and those Germans remaining inside the pocket trapped. At the least, the bold move, it was hoped, would cause a German retreat north.

The 1st Division's ultimate objective in the north was the eastern edge of the Soissons plateau at Berzy-le-Sec and the railway line just south at Buzancy. The Moroccans, meanwhile, would press east toward Lechelle, while the marines would advance to Beaurepaire Farm, wheel to the southeast and take Vierzy, and then push on toward the heights guarding the Soissons–Château-Thierry highway.

It was to be a surprise, the assaulting troops bursting from the Retz Forest and following not an hours- or days-long bombardment but a quick, cursory barrage that would stand for several minutes on the enemy front line for several minutes as the French and Americans closed, then roll forward at a rate of one hundred yards every two to four minutes, depending on the terrain.

As well, in what was a novelty for the men of the 2nd Division, forty-eight rumbling Renault tanks snorting noxious black exhaust would lead and accompany the offensive (the 1st had used the French machines with mixed results in its assault on Cantigny). They would also, it would be found, make excellent targets for the German artillerists.

Barring the way were several exhausted German divisions recuperating after the massive drives south in May and June. Artillery emplacements and carefully sited machine-gun pits and emplacements pocked the five miles of front over which the Allied force would advance, but there had not been time, or inclination, in the heady days of the German offensive to dig anything like a trench system.

Opposite the 2nd Division would be a consolidated force drawn from the German 14th and 47th Reserve Divisions—about six thousand men. They would have 140 light machine guns and 200 heavy ones with which to rake the advancing lines of marines and regulars.

Major General James Harbord, who had replaced Omar Bundy as 2nd Division commander just days before the offensive, wondered privately if the French architects of the operation weren't crazy. He would later complain that the staff officers even on the eve of the attack could not name debarkation points or say whether final attack orders would reach his men.

He also foresaw the huge problems in transporting tens of thousands of troops over a single forest highway in the middle of the night. "They said the division would undoubtedly be in place," he would write. "I doubted it and said so, and was reassured by many shrugs of French shoulders."

General John Pershing, though, was more certain of the coming offensive, and was ecstatic that it would involve two American divisions. The attack embodied Pershing's dream: open warfare, cocky Americans and vicious Senegalese and other French colonials racing forward across open ground, sweeping all that resisted before them.

All of this had been planned while the marines rested and dreamed of a long stay in backline reserve—somewhere beyond the *"Pas Fini"* sector, as Cates would laughingly say.

On the afternoon of July 16, those pipe dreams were thrown to the wind as, almost as one, noncoms and second lieutenants stirred, and gruff orders were given to all to grab their gear and get ready to move.

When a convoy of dreaded French *camions* with their colorful Asian drivers—among them a twenty-eight-year-old named Nguyen That Thanh, whom the world would later come to know as Ho Chi Minh—pulled up, a soup of fear and excitement arose in thousands of throats.

Their war was far from *fini*. . . .

"We knew the minute we saw those that it was bad news," Cates would say later. "You never ride to the rest area."

Before long, caravans of regulars and marines were flooding the roads leading to the Retz Forest below Soissons, the 1st Division's men coming from the northwest, the 2nd Division's men—fewer now and still in need of replacements after the ordeal at Belleau Wood—from the south.

The converging traffic—hundreds of troop *camions*, horse-drawn artillery rigs, exotic legions of French cuirassiers on horseback—caused a massive traffic jam that would threaten the timing of the operation, which was set to begin at four thirty-five a.m. sharp on July 18.

The 2nd Division's men rode from seven p.m. on July 16 until midday on July 17, when they were dropped in the depths of the Retz Forest, its great black and gnarled trees blocking the sunlight and turning the ancient roadways into dark tunnels. Climbing from the back of the tormenting trucks, they stretched legs and, stomachs grumbling, immediately thought of food.

But there was little time for either food or relaxation after the sleepless, bone-jarring ride. After a pause, orders arrived, and battalion commanders gathered their company commanders together to tell them what was up.

In the 55th Company, Captain Elliott Cooke felt his knees go weak as the "brief and businesslike" directive was read by his new 2nd Battalion commander, Major Ralph Keyser, who then spread a map on the ground and pointed out the battalion's assault line.

Cooke was floored by what Keyser said next: "One officer and twenty men from each company will be left behind."

"I only have a hundred and sixty men now, Major," Cooke protested. "Why leave any behind?"

Keyser didn't beat about the bush in answering. "They will be needed as a nucleus to build new companies, after the attack."

"Well," an unnerved Cooke would later write, "I got what I asked for and wished I had kept my mouth shut. So did everybody else."

Twenty minutes later, the 2nd Division was back on the road, this time on foot and headed back into the swelling traffic jam, heading eastward "in the general direction of Germany," as an otherwise officious and somber division history would put it. The 6th Regiment, placed in reserve, followed in the wake of the others, who would carry the attack in the morning.

After a hot day, the skies let loose in the evening, and the great and ancient beeches and oaks shivered and shook high above as lines of exhausted, starving men stumbled and slithered through the pitch-black toward some destination, each man holding on to the back of the man in front in order to stay with the column.

They marched through side ditches, the cavalry and tanks and wagons taking up the road; they marched half-asleep through a pelting, bombastic, thundering rain. Men tripped and fell in the dark, breaking legs and arms. At one point, the column halted when a marine, sound asleep yet moving, stumbled into the back of a cavalryman's horse in the blackness.

At ten p.m. the 6th Regiment was ordered to fall out and bivouac in the woods. The others kept on, picking up French guides who would, they hoped, guide them to their final positions on the eastern edge of the forest.

The 5th Regiment would attack along the division's northern boundary, keeping in contact with the right flank of the Moroccan Division above; the 9th Regiment would advance in the center, and the 23rd Regiment on the southern flank. All were racing through the night, now facing the additional obstacles of retiring French troops that had given up their places for the Americans moving east and past them.

By four a.m., thirty-five minutes to zero hour, only the 9th Regiment was in line. Half an hour later, the 23rd Regiment raced up, having double-timed the last ten minutes.

At exactly four thirty-five a.m. there was a thunderous roar from artillery emplaced in the woods several hundred yards to the west; whistles shrieked, and all along the front, men pitched into the wheat and toward a bulbous orange sun just then awakening.

The roar of the guns "went to the blood of the men like wine, and they stepped swiftly forward, erect and eager," Marine Corps historian Edwin N. McClellan would write.

All, that is, except the men of the 5th Regiment; they arrived on the run as the assault was under way, and managed to go from column formation to attack position—the 1st Battalion on the left, the 2nd to the right, the 3rd in reserve—almost without stopping.

After the initial bombardment of the German front line, parts of which extended into the very eastern edge of the forest, the barrage began walking forward one hundred yards every three minutes, pounding each successive line for fifteen minutes or more.

The German outpost line, holding two battalions from the German 218th and 219th Reserve Infantry, was quickly overrun.

On the northern flank of the assault, the 1st Division jumped off from shallow trenches in front of the village of Cutry. From north to south the 28th, 26th, 16th, and 18th Regiments made quick progress, though there were heavy losses from machine guns hidden in the wheat.

By eleven a.m., however, the mile-wide chasm of Missy Ravine had been crossed, hundreds of prisoners taken, and five miles of ground covered. The advance now lolled short of the Paris–Soissons highway, which cut southwest across the path of the advance. There, bristling resistance stopped the depleted regiments short of the road, where they would remain the rest of the day.

Farther south, similar progress was being made by the Moroccans and 2nd Division. Field Marshal Foch had insisted on surprise, and he attained it, marines and regulars quickly overwhelming the stunned Germans, many of whom were shot or bayoneted—and many of whom quickly threw up their hands while shouting, *"Kamerad!"*

Not to say there wasn't some resistance: held up by a German strongpoint that had killed several of his men, the 66th Company's Sergeant Louis Cukela—a native Serb already famed for his butchering of the English language in telling a subordinate, "Next time I send a damn fool, I go myself"—circled around a nest of machine guns, three of his men in tow.

Alone, he attacked and killed every German with his bayonet, "shocking the Germans by his seemingly maniacal disregard for his own personal safety," one account says.

But Cukela wasn't done: He then grabbed a handful of grenades and went after a neighboring nest of Boches, finally gaining the gun and turning it on the retreating men. Cukela's disregard for his own personal safety would earn him a fistful of medals, among them the Medal of Honor, and he would also gain a lieutenant's commission.

On the left, the assault by the 5th Regiment's 1st Battalion had begun in the edge of the woods, now tangled and torn from shells and dangerously pocked with machine-gun nests. "It was every man for himself," John Thomason would recall, "an irregular, broken line, clawing through the tangles, climbing over broken trees, plunging heavily into Boche rifle-pits.

"Here and there a well-fought Maxim gun held out until somebody—officer, non-com, or private—got a few men together and, crawling to left or right, gained a flank and silenced it."

As Thomason and his 49th Company moved east toward open ground, he ran across a lieutenant chum from the 17th Company. "He waved his pistol and shouted something," Thomason wrote. "He was grinning. . . . All the men were grinning. . . . It was a bon fight, after all. . . ."

Before long, units became tangled as small knots of marines and Senegalese, and even marines, Senegalese, and regulars, moved north, south, east, routing Germans who needed routing and flanking machine-gun emplacements that dotted the ravines and fields.

The black tanks went hither and yon like steely tarantulas, some taking direct hits and exploding in a thick perfume of smoke and gas.

Just for fun, German planes under the command of Hermann Goering, the heir to famed ace Baron von Richthofen, who was shot down and killed the previous April, would harass the advancing men, swooping low to strafe or drop grenades and then peel off under fire toward the sun, which streamed its own hot, devilish rays onto the bizarre, oh-so-human panorama below.

Thomason was right: It was, almost, every man for himself in many places on that field, the blind leading the blinder, second lieutenants sans maps asking the nearest already exhausted and starving and dehydrated lowest private if he thought that farm or that village might be the objective. Meanwhile, German prisoners, many of them boys, headed west, under guard or freely; either way, their war was *fini*.

But there remained plenty of resistance amid the free-for-all. In the center, the 9th Regiment came under strong fire on its left flank at Verte Feuille Farm, and so turned its advance to the north to subdue the German garrison. Marines from the 5th's 2nd Battalion then arrived and helped crush the resistance, after which the 9th continued to drift north into the 5th's zone.

On the left, marines came under fire from their left flank at Maison Neuve Farm and the village of Chaudon just north of it as the bulk of the Moroccan Division shifted north to subdue the Germans in the Bois du Quesnoy.

As the 17th Company, elements of the 55th Company, which was supposed to be on the 1st Battalion's left flank, and twenty Senegalese soldiers moved to eliminate the threat, they came upon an officer and some men of the 1st Division's 18th Regiment who had drifted south and far out of their own zone to the north.

Chaudon was quickly taken, as was Maison Neuve. As the advance continued, a force of several hundred Germans was seen heading toward the 49th Company.

"Pure joy ran among the men," Thomason would remember. "They took out cartridges and arranged them in convenient piles. They tested the wind with wetted fingers, and set their sights, and licked their lips."

"Range three fifty—Oh boy, ain't war wonderful!" one marine shouted. "We been hearin' about this mass-formation stuff, an' now we gets a chance at it!" But the Germans were surrendering, not attacking. "The low-life bums, they all got their hands up!" one marine would say.

The Moroccans—"wild black Mohammedans from West Africa," Thomason would write—were enjoying themselves, too.

"Each platoon swept its front like a hunting-pack, moving swiftly and surely together. . . . They took no prisoners . . . they carried also a broad-bladed knife, razor sharp, which disemboweled a man at a stroke," Thomason would remember.

During a pause, one of these feared, dark Senegalese approached Thomason and offered him "a brace of human ears, nicely fresh, strung upon a thong."

"*B'jour, Américain!*" he told Thomason. "*Voilà! Beaucoup souvenir ici-bon! Désirez-vous? Bon!*"

From Chaudon, some marines turned southeastward according to plan and advanced toward Vierzy, which lay at the bottom of a deep ravine and was well sited by cross-firing German machine guns—and as well by murderous fire from German 150s and 77s.

The 23rd Regiment, having taken Beaurepaire Farm in the center of its line of advance and Vauxcastle Ravine—from which spilled two hundred to three hundred German prisoners—to the south, was stymied at the western entrance to Vierzy.

(Some of these prisoners, being moved west under a light marine guard, encountered an ambling group of Senegalese soldiers, who demanded the Germans be turned over to them. The marines resisted as the prisoners looked around for discarded weapons and lined up with their captors/protectors. The Africans moved on, their hope of securing more grisly trophies quashed.)

Marines arriving at Vierzy saw a French tank, stalled in the bottom of the ravine, swarmed with German soldiers prying at its plates as if trying to open a sardine can. The marines rushed to its aid, and the automatic riflemen "especially enjoyed the brief crowded seconds that followed," Thomason would write.

Soon, the southern slope of the ravine was filled with retreating Germans as marine marksmen carefully took aim. From the tank emerged "a greasy, smiling Frenchman," who casually asked for a cigarette.

At seven p.m., 1st Battalion commander Major Julius Turrill gathered 150 men from the 1st and 3rd Battalions, plus a smattering of clerks, runners, and orderlies from the 5th's Headquarters Company, and attacked Vierzy, in which Germans lurked in numerous posts and strongpoints.

"Somehow we made a running skirmish line and hit across the backyards of the town," Elton Mackin, a twenty-year-old runner with the 67th Company, recalled.

"We were scared enough to make it look like we meant business. Some men picked up rifles as they ran. We reached houses, most of us, and then all hell broke loose.

"From a steeple deeper in town, machine guns opened up. Another started firing from the red-tiled wall of a factory, and shortly German shells were dropping in among the buildings where we hunted. They did damage to their own as well as ours."

The marines went house to house, ultimately subduing the German garrison but not the snipers in various locations, who continued hunting their Allied prey for several more days.

The 23rd Regiment followed on the heels of the marines, and all spilled out of the east edge of the ravine and kept going.

Here a new attack was organized, this time aimed at carrying the vital Château-Thierry–Soissons highway several kilometers (a few miles) to the east. The 5th Marines' 2nd Battalion and the 2nd Battalion of the 9th Regiment moved east toward the German lines hidden across pancake-flat fields of wheat and beets.

The men quickly drew fire from their left, where the Moroccans were supposed to have been but had not yet come up. Tanks arrived on the scene but only made things worse, drawing the attention of the German gunners.

Four were destroyed, and the marines in particular took many casualties—among them Lester Wass, captain of the 18th Company, who was mortally wounded.

A furious German artillery barrage from the front and machine-gun fire from the left in the Bois de Lechelle stopped the drive—that and the condition of the men, marines and regulars. After an advance of about a mile, the attack was called off at dusk, and the survivors took refuge behind the reverse slope of a ridge.

After an all-night ride followed by another all-night march with no rations and little water, and then a long day of hard fighting under a blazing sun, the survivors were not fit to continue—especially against a quickly reinforcing enemy manning scores of machine guns somewhere out there in the ill-lit wheat.

It had been a hell of a day, a bloody day. Many companies were being led by sergeants, battalions were hardly the size of companies, every battalion commander in the 9th Regiment was dead or wounded; "the men were dead for sleep," the division's history says.

Many of them were dead, period.

But the gains had been huge, especially by Great War measures. The 2nd Division had pushed the Allied line from the Retz Forest almost five miles to a north-south line running from Chazelle in the north to Vierzy in the south.

That the day hadn't ended in an Allied disaster was something of a miracle, the 55th Company's Elliott Cooke would write:

"In one of the best-planned and most successful attacks of World War I, no two units jumped off at the same time. And once started, battalions crossed each other's boundaries, seized wrong objectives, and even broke up into small groups fighting individual wars of their own . . . if that was a sample of a coordinated attack, I feel sorry for anyone who has to lead men into an uncoordinated one."

Hundreds of prisoners had been taken, and the Germans had certainly been surprised and were now furiously sending west any reinforcements— among them the German 28th Division, which had opposed the marines at Belleau Wood—that could be scrounged from the back lines.

Tomorrow, the marines of the 5th Regiment knew, would be another hell of a day.

But not for them.

A BAD DREAM

PLANES LIKE BUZZARDS now, sweeping over the tabletop French soil, and he's of course shooting at one of them with his pistol. What was it Lieutenant James Sellers had said? *When a German plane would come over, Cliff would pull out his Colt and fire at it.*

Blam. Machine-gun fire is sweeping the plain and cutting into heaps of dead marines that lie splayed under the brutish sun; it's cutting over the sweaty tin hats of those who've found an old trench, or any old eight-inch-deep furrow in the ground in which to hide; it's raining—streaming—bullets, again, and Cliff Cates is trying to bring down an airplane.

Blam.

The plane swoops so low, Cates can see the pilot's eyes. He fires another shot at the German as he varooms over the line, that thin miserable line of marines there in that beet field, and he's certain he hit him. "I saw the fabric fly," Cates would say.

Blam.

Even if Cliff Cates had brought the plane down, it would have been one of the few things to go right on this day, July 19, 1918, a day that had begun with such promise, embarking on a mission that had seemed so easy but had turned, within the matter of an hour and a half, into a bloody nightmare.

At four thirty-five a.m. the previous day, Cates and the men of the 6th Regiment had awakened in a wood to a resounding booming coming just to their rear. Some five miles ahead, the marines and regulars of the 2nd Division were fighting through the eastern edge of the Retz Forest and out onto the rolling plateau.

They would have little idea of what was happening until they themselves moved east during the day and began encountering the detritus of war—the walking wounded, men and vehicles and horses moving forward and back.

"I never realized what this war was until that day," Cates would write in wonder. "The roads were one solid mass of men, cavalry, trucks, armored cars, tanks, artillery, big naval guns, and many other things."

Most impressive was the French cavalry, whose cuirassiers cut a fine jib but who were, in the new world dominated by the machine gun, rather otherwise outmoded military appendages.

Numerous marines would remember seeing masses of them hovering on the edge of the fields over the next days, saddled clouds of blue forms that stamped and waited impatiently for an opening to charge that never seemed to come. Still, the young Americans found them thrillingly exotic.

"There were at least ten thousand on that road that day and they looked wonderful with their pretty horses, good uniforms, and lances," the 96th Company's twenty-three-year-old Corporal Stanley Williams would write.

Lances.

"On the right side of the road were troops going forward in columns of squads as far as the eye could see. Also heavy trucks, wagons, and even carts loaded with ammunition and shells.

"Artillery and tanks were mixed in, not to mention the Colonels and Majors in their Dodge Bros. cars, Generals in the Nationals, dispatch bearers on motorcycles and French officers in French cars. All this on one side in about as much confusion as I have written it."

Coming the other way as the men moved up were ambulances— "and thousands of Heinies, guarded by grimy, grinning, tattered Americans, some slightly wounded," Williams added. "The American boys were certainly helping the Germans on their 'advance' toward Paris."

One group passed the 6th Regiment following a "Prussian Major, stiffly erect, waxed mustache bristling fiercely and eyes glaring straight ahead," the 97th Company's twenty-year-old Corporal Havelock D. Nelson would write.

Behind the imperious major strode a wounded marine, the officer's helmet placed jauntily on his own head, his shirt in shreds, his left arm hanging loosely in and wrapped in a bloody bandage, and "a wide grin lighting up his unshaven, dirt-smeared features."

Just for fun, the marine "playfully" jabbed the major in his behind, calling to the passing marines, "Watch him jump!" The marines found it hysterical, the major not so much.

He wheeled around and in German protested, only to be jabbed in the stomach. Now others were laughing. "I noticed that the nearest prisoners smiled broadly, seemingly enjoying the discomfiture of their officer as much as we."

After marching for five miles, the 6th's marines approached the previous day's jump-off. Here, the chow wagons had been brought up, and after forty hungry hours, Cates and his men could finally eat.

Then the marines moved on, a handful of grub in one hand and their Springfields in another. They passed dead Germans, dead marines, dead Senegalese, and rifles and helmets and other flotsam from the previous day's fight, before coming to Verte Feuille Farm, the scene of furious fighting early in the advance.

What had been a quaint French homestead was now a scene of horrors.

"Wounded and dead lay all about," wrote thirty-three-year-old Major Robert L. Denig, who on July 8 was assigned as an extra officer to the 2nd Battalion.

"The filth was terrible; wounded were dumped on manure piles, in chicken houses, on rocks, in fact, anywhere and everywhere. Old bloody clothing was strewn in every direction. The roads were so filled with advancing troops that the wounded could not be taken to the rear."

After a pause, the 6th moved on to Beaurepaire Farm, crossing a plain covered with dead marines and Moroccans.

The farm also looked like a scene from Dante's *Inferno*, a way station to the afterlife for soldiers of every tribe—"some hundreds of wounded and dead men, infantry, marines, artillery, Moroccans, Germans and Americans all lying on the ground in the common decency of suffering and death," as James Harbord, who set up his divisional headquarters there, would remember.

The men went into bivouac as the fighting on July 18 spent itself at the eastern edge of Vierzy. At four a.m. the next day, the 6th Regiment's marines were awakened to the wonderful news that they were to be thrown into the attack, which was to continue pushing east and toward the Soissons–Château-Thierry highway.

At six thirty a.m., the regiment took to a sheltering ravine that ran from Beaurepaire Farm to Vierzy. Vierzy was still under German fire as the regiment pushed through the village, the scene of bitter fighting the day before.

"A few German corpses were still lying in the streets," Havelock Nelson wrote. "Houses for the most part were mere shells, roofs gone, some walls bore large jagged holes, windows were shattered, and an occasional shutter hung crazily by one hinge."

Even as they passed through, a German plane strafed and bombed the streets behind the column; they would prove troublesome through-out the day.

"Very noticeably our pace increased," Nelson wrote. "Vierzy was no place to tarry that morning."

What awaited them beyond Vierzy wasn't much better.

In fact, it would soon be an absolute hell.

The 1st and 2nd Battalions passed through Vierzy to the railroad station. There, they were met by Colonel Harry Lee, who was the act-ing commander of the 4th Brigade with Harbord's successor, Brigadier General Wendell Neville, down sick.

Lee issued the orders for the attack: Holcomb would lead the 2nd Battalion on the left, and Johnny Hughes's 1st would advance on the right. They faced a north-south front of twenty-five hundred yards, the same distance that three regiments had roamed across in the previous day's assault.

Berton Sibley's 3rd Battalion would follow in support one thousand yards behind. Twenty-eight French tanks would lead—or be led by—the marines, who would be flanked by the survivors of the 1st Moroc-can Division on the left, and the French 38th Division on the right.

Unfortunately, the 6th was still two kilometers (one and a quarter miles) from the actual front line, where marines and elements of the 3rd Brigade continued to hold. Just as unfortunately, there would be no barrage; it had begun falling at the hour originally scheduled for the push—seven a.m.

While the marines waited for the tanks and the trailing 3rd Bat-talion to move up, the artillery expended its allotted rounds through the next hour and then, inexplicably, stopped, leaving twenty-four hundred marines to advance with no artillery support, and little cover. As was said about the Confederate slaughter of Ulysses S. Grant's troops at Cold Harbor fifty-four years before, this would be not war, but murder.

It would also be a very hot day, and so the men were handed canteens full of water as they passed through Vierzy, and then they began deploying in the fields east of the village. The men were upbeat, nonplussed, and wholly ignorant at that point of what awaited them.

"It is wonderful to see the men marching to the front; they go with a quick step, heads up, and lots of singing," the eternally optimistic war lover Cliff Cates would write when it was all over. "You would never realize that some were marching to their own funeral."

The optimism was infectious that early morning at Vierzy. As Robert Denig passed Captain Allen Sumner of the 81st Machine Gun Company, Sumner told him, "This looks easy; they do not seem to have much artillery."

Looking east as they filtered from the ravine, the marines were faced with a landscape as flat as the Texas Panhandle, as level as Kansas—and took in a panorama that was fascinating in a "very grim sort of way," Havelock Nelson would write.

Fronting them were wheat fields, browning under the summer sun, and beyond those a green sea of beets—all in all "the most open country that I have seen passed over in an attack," Holcomb would write.

A village—Tigny—lay right of center about two and a half kilometers (about one and a half miles) away, and farther south and west of that sat the smaller village of Parcy-Tigny. Another kilometer (half a mile) east, beyond the Soissons–Château-Thierry highway, a range of low hills appeared as a dark green smudge in the shadowy relief of the morning sun.

At least six German sausage balloons hovered ominously over those hills, shortly to be directing the fire of the German artillery.

Just beyond the line where the advance had stalled on July 18, the German forward line was manned by two thousand German soldiers of the 14th Reserve Division.

Behind them was the 49th Reserve Infantry before Tigny; elements from the German 28th Division—which the marines had encountered at Belleau Wood—were in place before Parcy-Tigny in the south and the village of Charantigny just north and east of the marines' jump-off.

More than fifty machine guns were in place in front of the villages of Villemontoire, Parcy-Tigny, Tigny, and the open spaces in between. As well, three artillery battalions were in place northeast of Tigny.

The advance would be made under their direct observation, with no more cover than a few ravines, shallow roads, and a few unfinished German trenches that here and there slit the plain.

And there would be no surprising the Germans on this day.

In the 2nd Battalion, the 79th Company would lead on the left, with the 96th in support. The 78th likewise would lead on the right, the 80th its support. Each company would advance by platoon in four waves, spaced fifty yards apart, each man spaced five yards apart from another so that one burst of a shell or machine-gun spurt might do less damage.

Even as the marines apportioned their ranks into attack formation, German shells and machine-gun bullets dropped and sprayed among them. Orders went out for the marines to lie down and wait for the tanks. Hughes's battalion lay exposed in the wheat; the 2nd Battalion at least had some protection within the walls of the village cemetery east of Vierzy.

Nevertheless, even as they waited to advance, a machine-gun bullet hit Cliff Cates.

Of course.

Lucky Cates: the bullet was nearly spent, and in its dying contrail as it burrowed into the flesh of a shoulder.

"I thought somebody had hit me with a rock," he would later say. "I finally pulled it out and it was a red hot bullet. I went right on over to Major Holcomb and yelled to him, 'Well, I got the first blesse. Here's the first wound.'

"And I handed him this bullet and he dropped it. It was still hot."

As he led his platoon into line, the former Yale track star Johnny

Overton, now a second lieutenant with the 80th Company, called over to a fellow Eli, Second Lieutenant Samuel Meek of the 82nd Company.

"Hey, Sam!" Overton said. "If I get knocked off today, be sure and send my pin home to Mother."

"He meant his Skull and Bones pin, a secret society we had at Yale," Meek recalled. Meek just smiled and waved him off—"we were always saying things like this."

Four tanks appeared from Vierzy, and, not knowing that the men were awaiting the 3rd Battalion, began the attack on their own. They were soon blanketed by German artillery shells, and put out of action.

It seemed a harbinger of the disaster to come. "This was a mighty hard blow to our morale," the 80th Company's Corporal Don Paradis would write.

The men, already dispirited now, "could only lay [sic] on the ground and take it" as the Germans pounded their front. A gunnery sergeant, John Schrank, was killed just ten feet from Paradis as he lay there taking it.

Medics started to bandage him as Cliff Cates crawled over and took Schrank's pulse. "Don't bother," he told the medical men. "He's dead."

Others were hit as well. "One man with an ashen face came charging to the rear with shell shock," Denig wrote. "He shook all over, foamed at the mouth, and could not speak. I put him under a shelter half, and he acted as if he had a fit. He was a pitiful sight."

More tanks came onto the scene, piling up the ravine from Vierzy and taking positions fifty yards apart across the field. "The Germans took this opportunity to get their range with their artillery, then ceased fire," Denig wrote.

At eight thirty-five a.m., whistles shrieked, and the 6th Regiment stepped into the wheat, trying in vain to use the slow, lumbering machines for cover.

"It was a pretty sight to look out at that bunch of men in eight waves moving across the open wheat fields," Cates would write.

Following the tanks, the men instantly found the machines were magnets for the enemy's big 77 mm and 105 mm shells. Their ponderous gaits forced the marines to plod, rather than quick-step, across the fields.

"It was about a thousand yards to the German lines and as we started forward the German shellfire concentrated just a couple hundred yards in (front) of their frontlines," Don Paradis would write.

"The concentration was so great that it seemed like a black curtain, and it seemed to me that Colonel Holcomb was headed for the thickest and blackest part of that German line."

The men walked on, rifles held at high port. "Their advance over the open plain with their bayonets shining in the bright sunlight was a picture I shall never forget," Denig remembered.

As they crossed the American front line that had been established the evening before, the regulars of the 3rd Brigade and marines of the 5th Regiment begged them to take cover. But their pleas were in vain.

As soon as that shallow string of holes was crossed at about nine a.m., the German machine guns ahead and to the flanks—and especially on the left—came into play in earnest.

"The boche had turned their artillery on us and were cutting at us with about fifty machine guns," Cates wrote. "As fast as they would cut our men down, the waves would close up and take up a perfect formation again. Big shells would hit and tear big holes in the lines, but the men never wavered nor lost their formation."

As at Bouresches, the men bent over at the waist, leading with their tin hats, as if being pummeled by a furious and violent rainstorm. In the 96th Company, Second Lieutenant Robert Duanc was hit in the leg with a bullet and went down. Newly minted Second Lieutenant Bernard Fritz took one in the hand.

Denig—"a fat, chubby little fellow and one of the funniest men that you ever saw," according to Cates—yelled over to Pere Wilmer, Holcomb's adjutant, and told him he had a hundred dollars in his pockets and to be sure to get it if he was killed. "Wilmer said that his chances of living that long could be bought for a nickel," Denig wrote.

Not even. They were walking, literally, into a storm of steel.

Soft, pulsing, living flesh had no chance against it.

"The fire got hotter and hotter, men fell, bullets sung, shells whizzed-banged and the dust of battle got thick," Denig wrote. "A man near me was cut in two; others when hit would stand, it seemed an hour, then fall in a heap."

"On we went, losing a man here, another there, then two or three here, and so on," wrote twenty-five-year-old Private Russell Garrison of the 79th Company. "The enemy's artillery . . . was able to get range on us and do full justice without interruption."

Before too long, "I was the only one left of my squad," Garrison would write. "When I learned that, I became nervous and scared."

"It seemed queer to me to see a man drop," one marine with the 6th's Headquarters Company wrote. "It seemed like a dream. A queer or surprised or puzzled look came over a man's face when he got hit.

"No cry as a rule. He simply settled down quietly. I remembered that I was impressed with the idea that all of our men seemed to walk a step forward or at least fall forward and on their faces, hardly ever backwards on their backs."

Losses were so heavy—fifty percent—that in just half an hour reinforcements from the 3rd Battalion were sent forward to fill the gaps in the line. The 84th Company moved in waves to reinforce the left of Hughes's 1st Battalion, while the 83rd Company similarly made contact with Holcomb's right.

Berton Sibley also sent in Sumner's platoon of the 81st Machine Gun Company to support the center. The 82nd and 97th Companies followed in support, encountering dead and dying marines throughout their advance.

"Many times we had to individually make little detours around the dead or wounded lying hidden by the waist-high wheat until we all but stepped on them," Havelock Nelson would write.

"Those killed cleanly by machine-gun or rifle bullets lay stretched out as though in natural sleep, or sometimes sprawled out with arms and legs at awkward, grotesque angles. Others caught by the full fury of a shell-burst were scarcely distinguishable from a heap of blood-soaked rags."

He would remember one grievously wounded marine whom he thought to be a stranger passing to the rear with the left half of his face gone, "so that there was a gaping, bloody hole where his lower jaw had been."

Nelson took a better look at the man and realized he was a man from another platoon whom others had often confused with him. *He'll never be mistaken for me again*, Nelson thought to himself as he moved forward.

The marines had been forbidden from aiding the wounded, but still did what they could. Naval pharmacy mates and medics were following, working furiously and doing whatever possible to aid the wounded all over the field.

The marines, at the least, helped mark the places where the wounded lay as they passed on.

"We could, and did, hesitate long enough to pick up each one's rifle and thrust its fixed bayonet into the ground with the hope that the rifle butt showing above the wheat might mutely beckon some first-aid men before it was too late," Nelson wrote.

As they moved closer to the German front line, "shells simply rained down among us," Nelson wrote. "Every ten square yards of ground within the areas covered by the company appeared to be spouting geysers of dirt and smoke. The din was terrific. . . .

"Squads on both sides of me were melting away, the individuals suddenly slumping forward into the wheat on their faces, spinning about with up-flung arms to collapse on their backs or sides, or simply sinking down in the grain out of sight."

Ahead of Nelson, the marines broke the German front line, shooting and bayoneting without mercy after having come through that diabolical storm of shot and shell. "By that time, though, we were catching billy-hell, and I don't mean maybe," Cates would remember.

"It seemed to rain shells," the 80th Company's Private Carl Brannen would recall. "One hit between me and the man on my left, Red Williams. It knocked a hole in the ground, half covered me with dirt, and left my hands and face powder-burned, but the shrapnel had missed.

"Red was not quite so lucky and received his death wound. I left him writhing and groaning on the ground to continue the attack."

Shortly after crossing the German trench line, Cates noticed Captain Wethered Woodworth and First Lieutenant James Robertson advancing almost in step. He called out to a nearby sergeant, "That's bad business."

Sure enough, almost as soon as the words had left his mouth, a German shell ripped the ground underneath the feet of the two officers, sending them flying.

Robertson was hit by shrapnel in the neck and nearly had his windpipe severed; for him, the war was over. The less severely wounded Woodworth reported to Holcomb on his way to the back line for aid.

"His head was all tied up, coat torn in rags, left arm helpless, thigh cut up and in general he was a mass of blood," Denig wrote. "But his eyes were sparkling, and he was full of pep and ginger."

So was Cates, as usual; also as usual, he was once again the last officer standing from the 96th Company, and the day was far from over. He was also something of a sight himself; as he advanced, a shell hit near him, and shrapnel ripped into his knee. "In fact, it tore my trousers out," he would recall, laughing, years later.

What remained of his pants were wrapped around his waist like a skirt and flapped in the hot breeze. "That's when, after that, they started to call me 'Kiltie,'" Cates would say.

From north to south on a one-and-a-half-mile front, marines continued their hellish march east, taking machine-gun fire and bursts of shrapnel.

Yale's Johnny Overton was quickly hit.

"The last glance I had of Lieutenant Overton, he was walking backward and trying to shout something back to us," Carl Brannen would recall.

Overton held a cane in his left hand, a .45-caliber pistol in the right. Brannen couldn't make out a word Overton was saying amid the din, "but interpreted it from his expression to be some words of encouragement.

"He was soon down, killed."

"I heard his heart was torn out, so his death was without pain," Denig wrote of Overton. The Yalie Sam Meek, hearing of his death, located Overton's body. "There this wonderful guy was, lying on his back with a shell fragment in his heart," Meek would say.*

The 96th Company's Stanley Williams was hit by a machine-gun bullet in his right chest as he advanced. "My first sensation on being shot thru the lung was a feeling that an express train had burst a hole in my side and gone on thru," he would write home to his family in Osawatomie, Kansas.

"I was carrying my rifle by the balance in my right hand, and when the bullet passed thru the muscles it made them contract, twisting my arm into an 'S' shape. I had to pry my rifle out of my hand after going down, I had such an involuntary grip on it. . . .

---

*Meek retrieved Overton's Skull and Bones pin, and that night dug a battlefield grave for him with a bayonet, marking the site with a rifle stuck in the earth. Overton's father found his son's resting spot after the war and had his body shipped home to Nashville, Tennessee.

"My first breath brought a hemorage [sic], of course, which felt like the dam of a river had opened up. I don't know how long I lay there where I fell, but was brought to my right mind by a bullet that hit near me and glanced up, hitting my helmet."

His men falling everywhere, Cates struggled to assert some control over the few not yet hit. But by now, seeing so many of their comrades fall had made their blood boil. When a group of about sixty Germans jumped from a trench and began running east toward Villemontoire, "our men went after them like a bunch of coyotes," Cates remembered.

"Up to that time the men kept perfect formation, but when the boche commenced running[,] the men swarmed after them[,] shooting as they ran. The men yelled like a bunch of cowboys as they chased them."

Cates, as ever nonplussed by the sheer violence of combat, would add, "It was too funny for words. . . . We chased the boche back about two kilometers and then I organized what men were left and had them occupy some old abandoned boche trenches."

Denig would write that the Germans actually had tried to surrender—"but their machine guns opened on them; we fired back, they ran, with our left company after them."

Farther to the front and right, Havelock Nelson and his platoon from the 97th Company made it to the edge of the wheat, where they encountered a beet field that rolled almost all the way east to Tigny, three hundred yards to their front. They hit the dirt.

A gunnery sergeant suddenly stood up with a wild look in his eyes and yelled out above the din, "Come on, boys, we're going to take that town!" Nelson looked toward Tigny and saw nothing but a sea of leafy green, and beyond that the flashes of muzzles and arcs of fire as the German 77s and machine guns fired.

He tried to stand, but his knees went weak. "My legs had turned to gelatin," he wrote. Finally overcoming his fears, he managed to take a few steps into the open beet field. A lieutenant called out, "Hold it, Sergeant!" and ordered the men to retreat fifty yards back into the wheat.

The survivors of the 4th Platoon, 97th Company, never so happily carried out an order.

Many of the ponderous tanks, meanwhile, had been quickly put out of action. All across the field, their hulking black forms stood idle, their tops belching thick, gray smoke, their trapped French crews now just crisped pieces of flesh caught in death's agony while trying to escape from the hatches.

"I do not like to advance with them," Cates would write, "as they go too slow. They are very good when it comes to breaking down barbed wire or destroying a machine gun nest, but otherwise I had rather advance with the infantry alone."

As well, the Moroccans had not been able to keep pace on the regiment's left, leaving the marines' left flank open to terrific machine-gun fire from the vicinity of Villemontoire.

The attack was faltering. Marines everywhere were dead, or dying.

It had been an out-and-out slaughter of fresh-faced American young men.

"In thirty or forty minutes, our regiment had been almost annihilated," the 80th Company's Private Carl Brannen would write. "The field which had been recently crossed was strewn with dead and dying. Their cries for water and help got weaker as the hot July day wore on."

Some kept on; others in the quickly dwindling ranks lost the will under that black cloud of steel and sought refuge in any place the German fire would not reach them.

As he lay pressing his face into the wheat, one marine heard others call out the fates of individuals in his company: "I heard somebody say that Rockwell had been killed. That Copeland was killed. That Madden was wounded. That Denny Thrasher was killed. That Guy Norris was killed. That Fona was killed. That Larsen was killed. It seemed hazy to me."

Don Paradis and some others from the 2nd Battalion found some shelter in the now-abandoned German front line. "We even piled on top of each other to seek cover from that murderous shellfire," Paradis wrote.

The advance was over by ten thirty a.m., melted into the wheat.

The real ordeal was about to begin.

DEAD MEN

PRIVATE LLOYD SHORT was only barely a marine on that day. Twenty-eight years old, he'd left employment in Welch's Café, which his father owned in Watertown, South Dakota, a year before and traveled to Montana, where he tried to enlist in the navy, but had been rejected; he then tried the army, but was again rejected.

Moving on to work in the Washington shipyards, he ultimately was allowed to enlist in the picky Marines in March 1918.

They must have seen something in Lloyd Short that the navy and army missed.

After enduring Parris Island and Quantico, Short was in France with his replacement battalion in mid-June; by July 15, he was serving with Cliff Cates in the 96th Company, just one of the scores of replacements who wondered now at the "constant roar of the big guns," not foreseeing what that roar would mean for them.

By the morning of July 19, all knew, including Short. By the morning of July 19 when the eager recruit stepped out into the wheat, which was convulsing and frothing blackly now under a thunderstorm of shot and shell, Lloyd Short and the other replacements to the 96th Company understood all too fully, if too briefly, what war was, what *this* war was, an awakening that for many would come too late.

Cliff Cates by then understood, but what he knew didn't faze him. He was as alive as ever; invigorated by his surroundings, he remained in an abandoned trench with about twenty men from his own and scattered companies, his pants blown almost wholly off, his knee emblazoned red with a shrapnel wound, his shoulder oozing blood from a machine-gun bullet. He had little idea who else was around, and he wanted to find out.

But doing so could—would—be suicidal; machine-gun bullets continued to play just above the ground all over that field, where the few marines that weren't already dead or wounded had finally, sensibly, gone to ground.

Major Robert Denig had, like Cates and the others, finally gotten the memo that the attack was over.

"It happened for me about this way," he would write. "I noticed the Battalion H.Q. start running towards the enemy; men would jump and disappear."

Denig, wanting to learn just to where they were disappearing from that hellish field, "gathered speed, made a record jump and landed in a shallow 'fox hole.'"

Thomas Holcomb soon joined him, but refused in the best tradition of the Marines to turn his back to the German lines. "I had my back to the enemy while he sat facing them," Denig remembered.

Farther south, the 97th Company's Corporal Havelock Nelson was trying desperately to scratch some sort of cover from the hard-as-concrete French soil in a field facing Tigny. His shovel had proved useless, so he resorted to his bayonet, which gouged two inches at a time. These, he laid in front of him; "I had scarcely laid one of the larger pieces to the right of me before it jumped a few inches toward me as something thudded into it.

"I dug faster."

The 80th Company's Carl Brannen hit the dirt in a sunken road that was less than a foot deep. "A volley from a machine gun missed me by inches, and, falling where I stood in the road, I drew fire which barely cleared my body for the rest of the day."

German snipers posted in trees before Tigny and Parcy-Tigny added to the men's misery—but afforded badly needed cover. "Quite a few were picked off," Denig would write, "but a dead marine helps make a breast work."

Denig himself was nicked several times while digging his hole deeper. Holcomb moved to another hole "that he liked better, next to me." Holcomb's adjutant, Pere Wilmer, "was some way off."

Cliff Cates, "with his trousers blown off and slightly wounded," called out to Denig to say he had sixteen men from several companies. "Another officer on the right reported he had or could see some forty men all told. That with the depleted Battalion H.Q. was all we could find out of a battalion of nearly eight hundred."

There was little to do but lie low—and wait for dark, and relief.

It was going to be a long, hot day.

"From the time we dug in, up to about 8:00 p.m. life was a chance and mighty uncomfortable," Denig would write.

"We just lay there all through the hot afternoon. I wound up my watch. Smoked. Drew pictures and wrote the names of my sons on the clay walls of the 'fox hole' and wondered a great deal on all manner of things.

"It was great; a shell would land near you, and you could feel yourself bounce in the air."

Right. It was great . . . except.

Except for the planes.

They came like vultures, armed raptors, in groups of twenty, dark gray flying machines carrying black crosses on their underwings, with no Allied or American opposition in sight—the late Baron von Richthofen's Flying Circus, now under the command of Hermann Goering.

Swooping and droning and casting their ominous shadows over the field, the pilots strafed at will, and dropped grenades as well, with no opposition but for one brave French airman, who made a cameo over the field, only to be shot down.

"It fell about a thousand feet, like an arrow, and hit in the field back of us," Denig wrote. Soon after the planes left, "we would get a pounding" from the German artillery around Tigny.

The marines were expecting a counterattack by German infantry, but they got only an air war. One plane flew over Carl Brannen, and he flattened himself facedown, pretending to be dead, as the pilot leaned his head out of the plane, searching the ground through binoculars.

"Throughout the day those red-nosed flying devils continued streaking about the sky[,] seemingly eager to make the most of their opportunity to spread death and destruction entirely unhampered by Allied planes," Corporal Havelock Nelson would write. "For the most part we escaped notice by lying motionless with our faces covered."

The airborne devils were starting to irritate Cliff Cates. "They were flying the doggone planes and strafing us and the planes were not over a hundred feet in the air, if not fifty," Cates would recall.

One German pilot zoomed right toward Cates and his pitiful cadre, so close that Cates could see the pilot's eyes as clear as day. But the aviator couldn't get his gun to depress enough for a good strafing of the marines.

Cates, bored and frustrated with the marines' predicament, took the initiative. He fired three shots at the oncoming plane, and saw fabric fly from it as the bullets hit their mark.

"I would have given a million dollars if I could have downed that guy with my pistol," Cates would say years later.

Cates later would have the great satisfaction of watching as a machine gun brought down one of the planes. "That was the finish of him, as he burned up the minute he hit the ground," Cates wrote.

Other marines had more formidable weapons. One marine fell

"heir" to a German machine gun and "apparently an unlimited supply of ammunition," Denig wrote.

"He amused himself all afternoon in shooting at planes, the range made no difference. He had a lot of satisfaction in his efforts, though they resulted in nothing."

Cates's orderly, Private Robert M. Rhodes, had even more fun. He found not one but *six* German machine guns; their previous operators had either been killed or had fled.

Rhodes had earlier tinkered in the back lines with a captured gun; now he spent the day firing in the general direction of Germany, switching from one gun to another in an effort to make it appear he was part of a marine strongpoint.

The Germans directed a plane to investigate. He fired, and the plane veered quickly and took off east; Rhodes would man this arsenal all day, firing bursts center, left, and right toward anything that looked threatening.

On the farthest left of the line, fronting Villemontoire, the 96th Company's Corporal Raymond Hanson had been part of the group that chased after the retreating group of sixty Germans.

A June replacement fighting his first battle, Hanson found himself far forward from the rest, alone except for another marine, near the Bois de Lechelle.

"Our Company was cut to pieces; our Captain hit by [a] shell, only a handful left," that other marine, the 96th Company's William Weaver, would recall. Soon enough, Weaver was hit by a machine-gun bullet in the thigh, breaking the bone.

Hanson and a navy hospital apprentice, Earl Grauer, came across the helpless Weaver while trying to find their own men, and bound his wound with a splint.

"I was nearly gone . . . from loss of blood, but they stayed by me bravely," Weaver wrote. "They also risked their lives to get to a stream and get a canteen of water for me. The Germans were stationed all through the woods. . . . They were in danger of death or capture at any minute, and our own guns had begun dropping shells near us."

Hanson and Grauer moved Weaver to a safer position, but ultimately felt it was best to leave him and get to safety themselves, "for it was impossible to take me back across that open space in broad daylight," Weaver wrote. Hanson and Grauer would each earn a Navy Cross for their actions.

Others also aided the wounded as best as they could. When the 96th Company's Sergeant Harry Manning, himself wounded, saw a stunned and almost delirious Stanley Williams, shot in the right lung and "wandering around bleeding at the nose," he quickly went to him, Williams would remember.

"He said he had to fight me to keep me from getting up out of a ditch which was protecting me from a sweeping machine gun fire," Williams wrote. Manning poured "a half a bottle of iodine" over the hole in Williams's chest; Williams eventually made it to the back lines "on one sylinder [sic]."

Meanwhile, the 96th's wounded Captain Woodworth, still heading back to Vierzy for aid, for some reason thought his company and the 79th Company had broken through and made it all the way to the Soissons–Château-Thierry highway.

"[Ninety-six] and 79 gained objective," he would write in a nine thirty a.m. message to Colonel Harry Lee and Thomas Holcomb.

Perhaps because of such optimistic field messages, Lee had no real idea of the slaughter that was occurring in the fields before Vierzy. He would report that all was well, that the tanks and marines were doing swell work, the Germans were on the run, and Tigny had been taken.

"Casualties normal," he would add; and they were, judging by what had happened in the Bois de Belleau and environs.

Cliff Cates, meanwhile, knew better than anyone that things had

Second Lieutenant Clifton Cates in the trenches, March 1918. In his hands is a German hand grenade known as a "potato masher."

Clifton Cates in his University of Tennessee football uniform, circa 1915. A teammate recalled him as "the most enthusiastic and hardest-fighting lineman on the squad."

A view of the ground over which Clifton Cates and the 96th Company, 6th Marines, attacked toward the village of Bouresches, seen in the distance, on June 6, 1918.   COURTESY OF THE U.S. MARINE CORPS

Splinters were about all that were left at the site of the 6th Marines' signal station during the push to drive the Germans from Belleau Wood.

COURTESY OF THE U.S. MARINE CORPS

Clifton Cates *(fourth from right)* and some of his fellow 6th Regiment officers after the grueling three-week battle to clear Belleau Wood. Also shown are Lt. Graves B. Erskine *(third from left)* and 2nd Battalion commander Major Thomas Holcomb *(center, partially obscuring Cates)*.   COURTESY OF THE U.S. MARINE CORPS

Marines headed to the front aboard the dreaded camions in 1918. "We knew the minute we saw those that it was bad news," Clifton Cates would say later. "You never ride to the rest area."

COURTESY OF THE
U.S. MARINE CORPS

2nd Division commander James Harbord during the Soissons drive of July 18–19, 1918. The first day's assault by the 5th Regiment was a relative breeze, but July 19 would see the marines of the 6th Regiment go to ground quickly in the face of overpowering German resistance.

The 96th Company's first lieutenant James Furgerson Robertson. Robertson was "a fine soldier, fine Marine, but the men hated his guts," Clifton Cates would remember. "He was a hard-boiled rascal."

The entrance to a German dugout on Blanc Mont.

Captain Donald Francis Duncan of the 96th Company, who was killed during the assault on Bouresches on June 6, 1918. "He was the idol of the regiment," the 96th Company's sergeant Aloysius Sheridan would write.

Marines advancing through blasted woods during the Meuse-Argonne campaign.
COURTESY OF THE U.S. MARINE CORPS

The surviving members of the 2nd Battalion, 6th Marines, following their long ordeal at Belleau Wood.
COURTESY OF THE U.S. MARINE CORPS

The site of the 5th Marines' costly crossing of the Meuse River on November 10–11, 1918.   COURTESY OF THE U.S. NATIONAL ARCHIVES

The helmet that Clifton Cates proudly wore in combat throughout the last half of 1918. The deep dent from the direct hit he took while advancing on Bouresches on June 6, 1918 is plainly visible. Painted on its side is the insignia of the 2nd Division, which became known as the Indianhead Division.

COURTESY OF THE NATIONAL MUSEUM OF THE MARINE CORPS

Major General Clifton Cates *(left)* being congratulated by Vice Admiral Richard Kelly Turner, commander of the amphibious force, after the capture of Tinian in 1944. COURTESY OF THE U.S. MARINE CORPS

Clifton Cates being sworn in by Rear Admiral O. S. Colclough as the nineteenth commandant of the United States Marine Corps, December 31, 1947.

not gone well and that he and his small band of marines were in a desperate spot.

"I have only 2 men out of my company and 20 of other companies," he wrote in a 10:23 a.m. message to Lee.

"We need support, but it is almost suicidal to try to get it here as we are swept by machine gun fire and a constant artillery barrage is on us. I have no one on my left and very few on my right."

Before handing the note over to a runner, he added three words that would resound through Marine Corps history: *I will hold.*

The bravado was real, but Cates in fact was worried about a German counterattack and decided to find out the dispositions of the marines hidden in the wheat around him. Stragglers had reported that Captain Egbert Lloyd of the 80th Company was somewhere on his left front, and Cates sent two runners to see if they could find him.

They never returned—"evidently casualties," Cates would recall.

He set out on his own.

He removed his Sam Browne belt "and all kinds of leather," put his pistol in his pocket, and headed north down the trench to a road. "I walked straight into the German lines, walking alongside the road."

Ahead was the Raperie—a sugar-beet mill and storage facility. Closing on the mill, he saw three Germans about 150 yards ahead of him. They soon spotted him, and he was forced to dive into a shallow ditch on the side of the road "just as they cut loose at me."

Bullets clipped overhead; his position was impossible. "There was a mound of earth over to the right and I got all set and made a dive up and over that and jumped on the other side of it," he would recall. "As I did, I went right square on some of my men."

His first thought had actually been that they were Germans; it turned out to be Captain Lloyd with about eight marines. He told Lloyd he had wanted to locate his position so a barrage line could be established that wouldn't hit any marines lurking in the wheat—and then he set out to return to his own hole, some two hundred yards away, while the Germans were "dusting me with everything."

Lucky Cates, of course, made it back.

The 80th Company's Private Carl Brannen saw Cates disappear into a hole after he had skittered across the road on his return to his position, and decided he wanted some company.

He laboriously crawled to Cates's position. Cates asked him where the rest of the 80th Company was. "I don't know," Brannen told him, "but I think most of them were hit."

The rest of the day, Cates and his band waited under a blistering sun, throats parched and dry, for what they were sure would be a German counterattack. Cates made more rounds of the field, but "the damn boche shot at me every time I would get out."

One artillery shell nearly changed his luck, blowing a shovel he was holding out of his hand. "It left me holding part of the handle."

His men, he would write, "did wonderful work in getting the wounded off the field. Every time a man would start in with a wounded man, the damn boche would cut at him with a machine gun or a one pounder."

Such bloodthirstiness enraged Cates: "Someday those damn rascals have got to pay for such things."

The day wore on. At one point, the village of Villemontoire was thought by the Germans to have been taken by marines, and a counterattack was ordered, but it was then canceled when the village was found out to be still in German hands.

Meanwhile, what remained of the 84th Company and the Headquarters Company of the 3rd Battalion managed to get as far as the Bois de Tigny just north of the village, where it captured a trench and dugouts holding twenty-six German soldiers—among them an officer.

They were the very tip of the marine spear point, and had pushed the farthest east; they were also still seven hundred yards short of the objective of the Soissons–Château-Thierry highway and would be "hard-pressed" through the rest of the day, 3rd Battalion commander Berton Sibley wrote.

At three forty-five p.m., Colonel Harry Lee sent a missive to the three battalion commanders, telling them somewhat unnecessarily to "dig in and hold our present lines at all costs. No further advance will be made for the present."

Lee, the message added, "congratulates the command on its gallant conduct in the face of severe casualties."

In fact, of course, the regiment had dug in many hours before; holding on was a case of simple self-survival.

Late in the afternoon, the Moroccans managed to push forward on the regiment's left, and with assistance from the marines, beat back a belated German counterattack spilling from Villemontoire. At five p.m., word came that the marines would be relieved that night by the French 58th Division.

As dusk approached and the shadows lengthened, the marooned marines felt easier about stretching their legs and moving around. Denig then learned something of the state of others in the brigade.

A runner told him that Allen Sumner, the machine-gun captain who had predicted success for the attack, had been killed. Johnny Hughes's battalion, the runner added, "was all shot up."

Denig set out to reconnoiter, and in a shallow trench near his own hole he found "three men blown to bits, another lost his legs, a fifth his head."

At one end of the trench, a marine was still alive. He looked at Denig and with a shrill laugh pointed at his late comrades.

"Dead men," the marine said over and over.

Dead men.

Denig next found Lieutenant Lucian Vandoren, the regiment's scout officer, in a hole not far away. He was alive; he had covered himself "with about a dozen helmets."

They walked to the left of the line and found eight more wounded marines, including one who had lost his eyes. "The others were butchered in various ways," Denig wrote. "There was nothing to do but leave them."

Denig and Vandoren next encountered Cliff Cates and his merry band. Denig thought they had been killed in a shell blast; instead, Cates "stood there and pointed out the sights."

"See that man?" Cates asked Denig. "He's the first sergeant, killed by a shell."

At nine p.m., the marines began to clear their dead and wounded from the field and begin the walk back to Vierzy. "The man who had lost his eyes wanted me to hold his hand," Denig wrote. "Another with his back ripped up wanted his head patted."

One of the wounded managed to get on his hands and knees, and Denig asked him how he could help him. The marine replied only, "Mother—look at the full moon," and fell over, dead.

Other dead, covered with clotted blood and reeking from having lain under the broiling sun all day, were buried where they fell, the burial parties working in the glow of the moon, the fires from burning tanks, and German flares floating high above.

The Algerians of the 58th Division came up at midnight, and Denig and Holcomb showed them the lay of the land and where the Germans were. Then they wished them good luck "and pushed on out."

"It was a tired, happy bunch that was left," the ever-cheerful Cates would write. "Of course, most were dead, wounded, or missing, but the ones that were left thanked God for it and knew that they had done their duty and had gained a noble victory."

Despite the 6th's deadly misadventure that day, Cates's words were, in fact, not hyperbole.

The 1st Division would continue to hammer at the Germans at the Paris–Soissons highway and the heights of Berzy-le-Sec for two more bloody days, the French would continue the push east, and several American divisions coming from the south would face severe fighting while clearing the Marne pocket over the next month, but the lightning offensive below Soissons would come to be regarded as the "turning of the tide" of the war.

Even as Cliff Cates trudged tiredly back toward the Retz Forest, the Germans were pulling out of the Marne pocket and evacuating Soissons. The marines and regulars had advanced to a depth of six miles, garnered hundreds of prisoners, untold artillery and weapons, and cut the German supply line.

With the railway breached and the Soissons–Château-Thierry highway now reachable by artillery, the German retreat had begun.

The Allies' "noble victory" between July 18 and July 21, 1918, marked the death knell of the grand ambitions with which the Germans had set out on the morning of the previous March 21.

But at such a cost; Denig would count heads in the 2nd Battalion on July 20 and find that, of the 726 men who had formed for attack the previous morning before Vierzy, only 146 had come out in one piece: "They just melted away."

The story was the same in every battalion, each now reduced to the size of an understrength company. Some 2,450 marines attacked on July 19. Of those, 1,049 had been wounded, and 142 killed—a casualty rate of almost fifty percent. The 5th Regiment had fared better: On July 18, 472 marines had been wounded, and only 37 killed.

"We got by with charmed lives," Denig would write of those few still standing after the ordeal of July 19.

"When we return to the States people will learn the truth from the few who are left of what really occurred," the 96th Company's twenty-four-year-old Private William L. Sachs of Brooklyn, New York, would write.

"How we advanced in an open wheat field in broad daylight under a barrage of artillery, light and heavy, machine-gun bullets and aerial bombs, the heaviest ever seen. . . . How our comrades fell on all sides of us and still we kept on."

He would add, with some grandiosity: "Were I a Tennyson[,] I would eulogize the marines and their work at that battle alone. You may talk of the Light Brigade at Balaklava, of the Princess Pats at Vimy Ridge, of the Blue Devils at Verdun and of ourselves at Bouresches, but they are all Sunday school picnics as compared to the marines at Soissons."

Havelock Nelson would count the day's toll in the number of un-claimed blanket rolls that the men in his company had left behind early that morning at Beaurepaire Farm. Each one, he would write, "was a mute, but effective, reminder of someone who had not returned.

"Personally I felt that I had received a sudden, but fully unexpected reprieve from inevitable doom. I was most certainly alive and unharmed. But why?

"Over and over my mind reviewed the horrors of the previous day in that wheat field. It seemed impossible, and unreasonable, that any-one could have survived, well and sane."

Not all did. The 80th Company's Carl Brannen remembered awaken-ing on the night of July 20 to the sound of a man next to him "becoming a raving maniac. The strain had been too much and something had slipped in his head. . . . We tried to reassure him that he was among friends away from the front, but he evidently thought he was in the middle of a terrible battle and surrounded by enemies.

"I dropped back down to sleep while he was being carried away."

In the 96th Company, twenty-six men had been killed, and fifty-one—including the captain and five officers—wounded. Almost all were replacements whom, as Cates would write, he and the other offi-cers had not had time to train, "or even know."

Among those was the replacement Private Lloyd Short. He had been one of those buried on the field that night; when his battlefield grave was finally located and his body dug up on December 8, 1921, its condition said more about the violence of July 19, 1918, than Denig or Cates or anyone else could convey.

At least one of those heavy German rounds had caught Lloyd Short as he advanced, shattering his right leg. His left leg was missing altogether, as was his right forearm.

His coccyx was also, like his right leg, shattered.

Lloyd Short of Watertown, South Dakota, the rightful heir to Welch's Café, had not beaten the odds that day.

He was no Lucky Cates, who would write to his family on August 4:

"I was counting up the other day, and I have either been hit ten times or had my clothing or something on my person hit that many times.

"Pretty close, eh?"

WELL AND SANE

SOME CAME OUT of the carnage of Belleau Wood and Soissons bitter, shaken, their worlds gone mad, the well of their core beliefs—in mother, in God, in country—evaporated.

Some turned the bitterness inward, and took to drink, or sought ways out of the war—they went AWOL; they sought a million-dollar wound just bad enough to put them out of the war but not kill them; they dared a lifetime in the brig and shot themselves in the foot.

Others went on enduring the unendurable and wondered at themselves, at their minds. . . .

It seemed impossible, and unreasonable, that anyone could have survived, well and sane.

So Havelock Nelson had written.

No longer did anything matter, neither the bayonets, the bullets, the barbed wire, the dead, nor the living. The soul of Hicks was numb.

So did Thomas Boyd, of the 75th Company, 1st Battalion, 6th Regiment, conclude his 1923 novel, *Through the Wheat*:

Your son, Francis, died needlessly in Belleau Wood. You will be in-terested to hear that at the time of his death he was crawling with vermin and weak from diarrhea. His feet were swollen and rotten and they stank. He lived like a frightened animal, cold and hungry. Then, on June 6th, a piece of shrapnel hit him and he died in agony, slowly. You'd never believe that he could live three hours, but he did. He had nothing to hold on to, you see: He had learned long ago that what he had been taught to believe by you, his mother, who loved him, under the meaningless names of honor, courage, and patriotism, were all lies. . . .

So did the 43rd Company's William March, aka William Edward Campbell, portray a fictional letter of condolence to the grieving mother of a dead marine in his seething 1933 antiwar novel, *Company K*, which also contains episodes of the murder of an officer and the killing of several marines by friendly fire.

The scenes of bloody horror in the Bois de Belleau, in those fields before Vierzy, were enough to break even the strongest of men, turn their minds numb, and leave them brooding and bitter for life.

But not Cliff Cates.

The still quite sane and ever-optimistic Cates was less haunted than beguiled—hell, *energized*—by all that had happened, all that he had seen, on July 19.

"There was something magnetic about him," Corporal Victor D. Spark of the 78th Company would write. "He seemed to take all the danger with indifference."

Cates had dodged death over and over, and come up grinning, writing just days afterward: "I wouldn't sell the memory of that day for any amount of money. It was truly wonderful, even if it was a living hell that day. I wish I could paint a vivid picture of it, but it is beyond me."

Cates was no poet, no Thomas Boyd, no William Campbell. Years later, he would write that he was sorry "that I was not a writer as I felt that my experiences in World War I would have been of much value if I had had the ability to describe them correctly."

Had he had the will or the talent, though, it's unlikely he would have spewed out a vitriolic condemnation of either the war or his part in it.

And there's little chance that Cliff Cates, in command of the 96th Company following Soissons and now writing condolences to the families of the company's dead, would have told Mr. Charles McCreary, father of Private Donald McCreary of East Aurora, New York; or Clara Berg, sister of Private Gustave Berg of Harmony, Minnesota; or Mrs. Mary F. King, mother of Private Eugene J. King of Syracuse, New York; or Mrs. Caroline Short, mother of Private Lloyd Short of Watertown, South Dakota; or relatives of any of the company's twenty-six men who died that day, that their loved ones had been sacrificed in that wheat "needlessly."

Their beloved boys, their brothers, had signed on to be marines, just as he had. They had signed on to fight in a grand cause, and for a noble purpose, and days such as July 19, 1918, had to happen, had to be endured.

Some men died; that was war. Some men lived, and that was also war.

Cliff Cates hadn't hardened his heart to the deaths of his men so much as just learned to expect and accept that some—many, perhaps— would die. Hell, maybe even he would. He'd been born unflappable, unsentimental, and with the flinty soul of a warrior; his was a spirit that sought challenges among the worst, the most dangerous, experiences men could have.

They fed him; they made him feel alive; he was born, he was beginning to see, to lead men in battle—no—to have men *follow* him unflinchingly into battle.

He didn't threaten; he didn't yell; he didn't have to push or pull men.

He simply led the way. Men, seeing his courage and how he fairly laughed in the face of Death, naturally followed; they were ashamed not to.

At Soissons he'd seen and finally realized what war was: grand armies on the march, soldiers clashing in the open, and men of all stripes dying. Where others saw horror, he saw something grand that exceeded all other human endeavors.

It was truly wonderful, he'd written.

Even if it was a living hell.

MOSELLE

WHAM!

September 15, 1918: somewhere, as they used to say, in France.
Wham!

They're gunning for Cliff Cates, again, as he walks down a chalky country lane alongside Second Lieutenant Sam Meek of the 82nd Company. They're out on a stroll in the middle of a war, looking for their front line, when, *wham*, one shell hits to the right of them. *Wham*, and another hits to the left, delivering its white, chalky payload all over the men, who now lie prone.

The men are battlewise and onto the Germans by that point; they know the next incoming shell will split the difference. "Cliff," Meek calls over, "we might just get killed here."

Meek already has a hole in one thigh he could stick a finger through, and he can't move. "Get out of here," he tells Cates. "I'm going to hide in that ditch till it blows over."

Out of nowhere a burly Red Cross man turns up, picks up Meek, and carries him to an aid station. Cates walks on.

"He was the luckiest man that ever was in the Marine Corps," Meek says years later, shaking his head in wonder. "That experience was typical of his World War I days."

Word was getting around. LUCKIEST MAN IN FRANCE, one newspaper story would proclaim of Cliff Cates, noting he'd been hit "ten times" in the last month. He'd shared honors with James Robertson for the capture of Bouresches, "and come through with glory" at Belleau Wood and Soissons, the war correspondent George H. Seldes wrote in the *Atlanta Constitution*.

"He has had shrapnel and machine gun bullets in his clothes, and has been hit by them and cut so he bled, but he has never been a hospital case. Once he got a spent machine gun bullet in his leg and picked it out still hot.

"In the July offensive he saw his captain and first lieutenant hit by a shell. His captain rose and wiped the blood from his face. He was smiling. He motioned to Cates and Cates took command and led the company through two attacks." Seldes first encountered Cates in the back lines around Chavigny in early August. Cates was still battling, though not against "the Boches" this time. All of his grit and determination were coming to play against his own, marines, he having challenged the 3rd Battalion's officers to a baseball game against his 2nd Battalion.

Cates was on the mound; Captain Pere Wilmer played second. Other officers from the 2nd Battalion took up their positions on the field. Other marines watched from willow trees that lined the small field; the odd Frenchman would stop to watch and scratch his head in wonder at these crazy *Américains*, crazee marines.

The 6th Regiment's commander, Colonel Harry Lee, umped, having first objected to possibly placing his face in the way of a baseball, not to mention a possible disputed call by a battle-hardened marine.

"Accustomed as I am to dangers," he said, laughing, "I prefer the others."

Cates wound and threw.

"Stee-rike!" Lee called as a Cates fastball hit its mark.

"Get that umpire," one of the 3rd Battalion's men called out. "He's full of mustard gas."

"He don't know a strike from a minie-werfer."

"Where'd he learn to ump—out near Soissons?"

Cates, nonplussed as ever, scratched the surface of the mound, seemingly taking forever to deliver the next throw.

"Say you Cates, going to dig in for the rest of the war?" some wag of a marine called out.

"Pitcher's up in the air!" called another.

"He's got his parachute out—watch him jump," said another.

Cliff Cates delivered.

Batter out.

Now two men on, two down. Cates at bat.

Slam. *Two men score.*

The 2nd Battalion wins in extra innings, 5–4.

Lucky Cates . . .

Cates and the remnants of the 6th Regiment had filtered back through Vierzy in the early morning of July 20 after enduring the bloodbath of the previous long day.

After bivouacking for several days in the shell-torn woods that marked the 2nd Division's triumphant jump-off from the Retz Forest— in which several marines from other units would be killed in ensuing days from deadfalls caused by the shelling—they entrained for Nancy, and by August 1 found themselves hiking into the village of Chavigny just south.

In reward for having survived July 19, the 96th's men were given a day off on August 3. Cates took his liberty in Nancy, where he spent the day shopping for new clothes and filling his belly in restaurants.

"Gee, but it feels good to get cleaned up and have good clothes on," he wrote the next day. "I have been looking like a beggar the last few months."

During the next days, more of those wounded at Bouresches and in the gas attack of July 14 returned from the hospital.

"I sure am glad to see them come back," Cates wrote of his favored veterans of Quantico, "as it makes me feel a little more at home."

In the streets of the village, marines tried their best to fraternize with the local mademoiselles, promenading in their Sunday finery on a day off from a local armaments factory.

Like a proud father, Cates watched his men's efforts, bemused.

"There are many very pretty girls, and they look very nice today, as they are all dressed up and parading up and down the one main street," he wrote.

Marines who just two weeks before had gone forward with rifles at high port in the hell of July 19 now went on the offensive with English-translation books, this time not trying to take a German line, but a French girl's *coeur*.

"There is one just below my window now," Cates wrote as he watched the international encounter. "Each has a book and they have to look up what they want to say. It is too comical for words. He is trying to learn French and she is trying to learn English."

The war, as always, beckoned. On August 5, the 2nd Battalion was told to pack up and get ready to move yet again; by two p.m., the men were on the road, raising dusty clouds as they followed a dirt road along the banks of the Moselle River, northwest through Dommartin-lès-Toul, and then northeast again to the village of Liverdun.

The boy from the mudflats of northwestern Tennessee was taken with the village and its surroundings, and the beauty of the blue Moselle.

"It was a wonderful place, and the view was one of the prettiest since I have been in France," he wrote. "The town is situated way up on the hill, and you can look down the valley for miles."

The next evening, the marines once more moved on, and arrived later that night in the village of Dieulouard. They were closer now to the front line at Pont-à-Mousson, which anchored the eastern end of the base of the triangular St. Mihiel Salient, above which lay the Woëvre plain guarding the vital German railway hub at Metz.

The 150-square-mile salient had been the site of vicious back-and-forth fighting between the French and Germans in 1915, but was now a backwater of the war, a place for battle-weary divisions to rest and regroup. Still, it remained a thorn in the side of the French, and its shape, with the apex pointing west, seemed almost to represent Germany thumbing its collective nose at France.

On the American side, the southern base of the salient had been used through the spring as a training ground, the 1st and 26th Divisions manning the sloppy trenches that cut through Seicheprey under the watchful eyes of Germans on the eminence of Mont Sec just to the northwest.

Occasional raids were made by both contestants, and forays were sent out at night in an effort to obtain prisoners. As usual, artillery shells and gas rained back and forth, and conditions were mostly miserable, but it had proved a good place to get one's feet wet—literally and figuratively—before the larger contests of Cantigny and Soissons.

Even as American involvement in the war had shifted to other areas, though, the eyes of American military planners often wandered back to the salient, which seemed to invite action; since 1917, and before the spring crises brought by the German offensives, the AEF brass had seen the St. Mihiel Salient as the perfect place to launch an all-American push and show just what the doughboys could do.

John Pershing, ever intent upon keeping his command intact, had by late summer created the American 1st Army, and now he wanted to use it. He pushed the Allies to allow him to have a go at the salient, and they initially acquiesced; plans were laid for a massive blow on both its southern and western sides, with the object of pushing east and taking Metz.

As plans were laid, however, Sir Douglas Haig, the British military commander, consulted his maps and began to see the German line splitting France as a salient unto itself.

He convinced Foch that the Allied initiative needed to be laid on that line from the North Sea to the Moselle, and a great push made to the east by the British in the north and the French in the center, with the Americans exerting their own northward press on the right between the Argonne Forest and the Meuse River, with French help.

An American move on Metz, Foch came to see, would be a move in the opposite direction. Foch wanted the offensive between the Argonne and Meuse to begin on September 15, and told Pershing to limit his attack on the St. Mihiel Salient so American divisions could be released and ready for the offensive.

After some wrangling, a deal was struck: Foch would move the scheduled Meuse-Argonne assault back ten days, allowing Pershing to have his offensive against the salient. With its reduction, the Americans would then turn to the northwest, and be ready to jump off for the second, larger offensive on September 25.

Since some divisions would take part in both attacks, intricate planning for the movement of troops and materiel to the second front would be needed. To that end, Pershing leaned on the 1st Army's chief of operations, George C. Marshall, who almost thirty years later would lend his sweat, expertise, and his very name to a plan that airlifted supplies to a West Berlin stranded and cut off by Russian envelopment and intransigence after World War II.

All of this planning would go on unbeknownst to those who would risk their lives in the attacks, among them the marines of the 4th Brigade, which in the first week of August 1918 made plans to relieve several French divisions on either side of the Moselle River at Pont-à-Mousson, in what was called the Marbache sector.

Cliff Cates and the 96th Company relieved a company of the French

340th Regiment on the night of August 8–August 9, taking up a support position in the village itself.

The next week, the company's history says, would be "thoroughly enjoyed" by all.

"This is what the French call 'a bon sector,'" Cates would write from Pont-à-Mousson on August 12. "It is very quiet and it is a swell place to rest. There is very little firing from either side. Both sides throw over about a dozen shells a day and then rests [sic]. It just suits me, though, as I am willing to take things easy for a while."

They were close enough to the front that the few townspeople—women and children—still left in Pont-à-Mousson carried gas masks with them in the streets. Horses, too, carried them on their harnesses.

Also near the sector was a German "raiding school" that fueled the so-called Hindenburg Flying Circus, a dedicated unit of infiltrators that had caused mischief with the troops that had previously occupied the sector.

"Almost every outfit that went in there lost prisoners," the 79th Company's Graves Erskine recalled. Because of this, a French general bet Colonel Harry Lee that the 6th Marines, too, would lose men in the raids—but Lee enforced strict security, and not a man was captured.

Cates and the 2nd Battalion's other officers took over a large château, with electricity, running water, and nice feather beds. "They can just leave me here until the end of the war if they want to," he would write. "I would be perfectly satisfied.

"This town is full of fruit and vegetables, and we are having fine things to eat. We have an officers mess in our château, and believe me, we sure do eat."

Shortly after moving in, Cates threw a dinner for Thomas Holcomb, who had been promoted to lieutenant colonel and made Colonel Harry Lee's second in command.

There to celebrate was the new commander of the 2nd Battalion, Major Ernest C. Williams, a hard-drinking old-time marine who'd earned a Medal of Honor after storming a Dominican fort with twelve men in November 1916. His marine nickname was "Bolo"; the men soon called him "Bull."

Cates would call Williams "a fine major" in letters home; years later he would say of Williams, "He had all the courage in the world, but I wouldn't say he was the brainiest or friendliest man in the world."

Corporal Don Paradis as a battalion runner had perhaps closer contact with the major. Familiarity had quickly bred contempt.

"He was an alcoholic, drinking from one half to two quarts of whiskey a day," Paradis wrote. "He had some Marine non-coms who served with him before the war whose duties were to keep him supplied with cognac liquor.

"I know he had no love for me and I surely had none for him."

C'est la guerre: Cates provided a wartime feast he defied his family back home to beat. "Champagne, cantaloupe, soup, fish and potatoes, chicken, corn on [the] cob, potatoes, lettuce, cucumber and tomato salad, apple pie, plum cake, honey, biscuits, light wine, beer, real butter . . . Thanks to heinie, the dinner was not interrupted, so we had a swell time.

"If we stay here much longer, we will be fat as pigs."

That went for the enlisted men as well. They, too, shared in the fruits from the gardens the villagers had left behind, to the extent that some of them were able to live off the land, as it were.

Some went fishing in the Moselle, but not with poles. The marines "watched the river for schools of fish and would toss in defensive hand grenades," Paradis wrote. After they exploded, "they would swim around and gather up the stunned fish that floated to the top."

There was also the fun of "reading" one's undershirt under the novel and rare electric lights in the billets. "This occupation started by removing your shirts and turning them inside out and then picking out the cooties," Paradis wrote.

"We'd place pieces of paper in the center of the table and put the lice in a pile in front of us, then bet on who could pick off the most lice."

Cates, meanwhile, was learning the ropes of commanding a company, which he found "not as easy as handling a platoon, but I love it, and I am trying not to pull any boners until I learn the game thoroughly.

"The field part of it is very easy for me, as I know it, but the administrative part and office work is not so easy, as I have never had to fool with it, but I will learn."

Cates had heard from many of the company's officers who had been wounded (he would never be able to properly nail Wethered Woodworth's surname). "I had a letter from Capt. Woodsworth, and he is getting along fine," he wrote. "He had a slight wound in the head.

"Lieut. Robertson was shot thru the neck and will never be able to talk above a whisper again, so he will be sent back to the states [sic]. Lieut. Duane was shot thru the leg; only a flesh wound, so he will soon be back. Lieut. Fritz was shot thru the hand; nothing very serious, but it will take a good while before it will heal."

Lieutenants John D. Bowling and George Lockhart were also on the mend. His pal Thomas Brailsford remained missing. "I do hope he has been captured; if he wasn't, he was blown to atoms."

Helping Cates in the absence of the above would be two new lieutenants: Jesse L. Crandall, who had been a gunnery sergeant with the 79th Company, and Paul J. Ogden, formerly a sergeant with the 80th Company (it was standard for marines being commissioned in the field to be transferred to another unit to avoid any possible issues of fraternization with or resentment among the men of their former companies).

Both, Cates would note, "have been through the whole show that we have gone thru. They were with some other company in the battalion, but they were there just the same. That is a record that no other company can beat."

"I am glad, of course, to become an officer," the twenty-seven-year-old Ogden would write home to his family in Newport, Kentucky, "and doubly glad to have won my commission on the field."

He listed his Marine Corps curriculum vitae thus: "I have been over three times. I came out without a wound. My gas mask stopped a Heinie bullet."

Lucky Ogden . . .

The vacation at Pont-à-Mousson ended on the evening of August 17, when the 2nd Battalion fell in behind Bull Williams, sitting resplendently on horseback, and began an excruciating march south down the Moselle—"one of the longest, hardest hikes that we have ever had," Cates would write. "Luckily it was at night, and it was real cool."

They walked for ten hours, through the deep French night, and then were allowed to stop for two hours. Then it was up and at it again; by ten a.m. it was also hot, and the men began to fall out on the side of the road.

The marines were paying for the fun they'd had in Pont-à-Mousson.

"Up hill and down we went," Cates wrote. "I thought we would never get to our destination." At noon, the vanguard reached their destination, a French training area called the Bois l'Evêque.

Each company's kitchens were waiting, "and believe me[,] that 'chow' sure did taste good. We had marched for sixteen hours without any food and it was very trying."

Seventeen men from the 96th Company had fallen out and were brought in by ambulance, "and there were a lot more that we just had to shove and push in," Cates wrote. "We had many blistered feet to treat that night."

More replacements came in, and Cates would spend the next five days "rounding the company into shape"—working at the rifle range, throwing grenades (he would be hit for the eleventh time in the war when a grenade fragment hit him in the chin, "cutting a small place"), and doing small-scale maneuvers.

More of those wounded at Belleau Wood and Soissons also trickled in, to Cates's delight.

"I am trying my best to have the best company in the battalion," he would write, "and of course I think that I have."

He could hardly wait to show what the old 96th could do, wherever and whenever the next opportunity might come.

NO MAN'S LAND

WHEN THE OLD 96th hiked off to war again, it was without Cliff Cates.

"I am feeling a bit sad tonight," he would write on September 9. "My company has marched off without me. They have gone to attack in the biggest show that we have ever put on.

"God, it is an awful night and I am praying for the boys out there."

In fact, the 96th was no longer Cates's company, though he retained the 4th Platoon. Once again, he'd been passed up in favor of a new captain—John Andrew Minnis, a twenty-seven-year-old Naval Academy graduate who had served with the 3rd Division in its defense of the Marne River just prior to the jump-off at Soissons.

There, Minnis had taken over a unit that had lost its officers and led a counterattack that netted twenty-four prisoners. It was no Bouresches, but it was enough to earn Minnis a Distinguished Service Cross.

Cates had been away on leave when the transfer of power occurred. Granted leave, he and the 2nd Battalion's intelligence officer, Lucian Vandoren, took off for Biarritz—"a person would never know there was a war down there," he would write—and then spent several days in Paris, where he ran into George Lockhart, former 1st Platoon leader; Pere Wilmer, Holcomb's former adjutant; and other old hands. "We ran around together and had a swell time," he wrote.

When he returned to the company, he found Minnis in charge, and he as well found his pal John D. Bowling finally returned from the hospital. "Gee! I was glad to see John B. back again," he would write. "It seems like old times again."

Wethered Woodworth also returned, and the 96th was bursting at the seams with officers. Everyone was on the move, heading toward new fields of battle—the St. Mihiel push (Woodworth would shortly take command of the 78th Company).

Seven American divisions were converging, marching by night in an effort to keep their movements unknown to the Germans, on the southern face of the St. Mihiel Salient, stretching west from Pont-à-Mousson to the village of St. Mihiel more than ten miles away.

The 2nd Division, part of the I Corps, would take its place almost in the center of the American line, flanked by the 5th, 90th, and 82nd Divisions to the right and the IV Corps's 89th, 42nd, and 1st Divisions on the left. Two French divisions held the apex of the salient between Seicheprey and St. Mihiel.

One more American division, the 26th, took its place on the western face of the salient, intending to push east even as six of the other divisions pushed north-northwest, beginning at five a.m. on September 12 after an intense four-hour artillery bombardment of the enemy lines.

A connection between the 1st and 26th Divisions would cut the salient in two and force withdrawal by the Germans; in fact, the Germans had already become nervous about an attack and had put in motion plans for a staged eight-day withdrawal. Coincidentally, the first phase of that withdrawal began on the evening of September 11, even as the massive French-American offensive was about to shove off.

Frontline German units began pulling back in the darkness and taking positions that had been heavily wired, leaving only outposts manned with machine guns in the front lines.

The 6th Regiment reached the vicinity of Manonville, just a few miles south of the designated jump-off, on September 10. The next day, battalion and company commanders received "tank instructions" at 2nd Division headquarters.

"Emphasis was laid on the maintenance of liaison between infantry and tanks," says a 2nd Battalion history written by Lucian Vandoren.

On the afternoon of September 11, battalion and company commanders were shown the plans for the attack, the men were issued extra ammunition and grenades, and then they rolled their coats, toiletries, shelter halves, and other unneeded articles in their blankets, and put them into huge piles.

Afterward, the 2nd Division began moving to its jump-off between Limey on the west and Remenauville on the east, a front of about one and a half miles.

Just before the move, Captain Minnis received a memo telling him to leave twenty percent of his officers and men in the back line, "so as to have a nucleus for another company if the one that went over the top should be wiped out," Cates wrote.

"He decided that I was to be the officer and he left the men that had been thru most of the fighting," he would write to his family. "I was glad in one way and I was sorry in another.

"There is something in a man that makes him want to be with his men. The men that I had left with me were mostly all old 96th Co. men. You might think that it is nice to be left behind, but it is not the case. I would rather take the chance out there with my men."

The 6th Regiment marched off into a driving rain shortly after dark, heading for its jump-off trenches. This time, it would comprise the last wave. The 3rd Brigade would lead the assault, followed in turn by the 5th Regiment, and then the 6th, with Berton Sibley's 3rd Battalion leading and the 2nd in support. The 1st Battalion was out of this fight, being detailed to maintain liaison with the VI Corps on the left.

The leading waves took their places in an old trench line filled with rank, sloshing water. The night trembled with thunder and lightning, and howling winds and slanting rain pierced the ebony blackness.

At one a.m. on September 12 the show began, when nature's thunder was overridden by the stupendous, ear-shattering sound of forty-eight American batteries opening up on the enemy lines. None of those in the American lines had ever heard such a continuous roar, as heavy and light guns sent their steel-cased greetings into the air and toward the Germans for four hours without stop.

"Every time a big gun is fired[,] it lights up the country for miles around and then a few seconds later one can see the shells break over on 'Fritz's' territory," Private John Fischbach of the 79th Company would write. "There is a constant line of fire all along the enemy trenches, showing where the shells are breaking."

At exactly five a.m., fifteen light batteries began a rolling barrage, which would move one hundred meters (328 feet) every four minutes. Whistles now blew shrilly along the American lines, and almost six hundred thousand men stepped out along a ten-mile front.

In the 2nd Division sector, the regulars of the 3rd Brigade stepped from their soaked forward trenches and followed the assigned tanks across the mucky plain into No Man's Land, from which the Germans had already largely retreated, leaving just machine-gun outposts scattered here and there.

These were quickly overrun, and it soon became apparent that this would be no repeat of July 19. Little opposition was encountered, and the few machine-gun nests were rapidly flanked, their occupants killed or captured.

By noon, the 23rd Regiment was already at the designated first-day objective—the village of Thiaucourt—having traveled five miles through pouring rain and after cutting reams of rusting, ancient barbed wire.

Now patrols were sent north and northeast toward the villages of

Xammes and Jaulny—set as the 2nd Division's final objective. The marines followed in support, the 6th Regiment on the left and the 5th to the right. The 6th's 2nd Battalion halted for the night on high ground north of Thiaucourt.

At seven fifteen a.m. on September 13, the scout platoon from the 1st Division's 28th Infantry linked with the 26th Division's 102nd Regiment—led by the legendary "Hiking Hiram" Bearss, now leading regulars—at the village of Hattonchâtel, some five miles northeast of Thiaucourt.

With that stroke, the salient was cut in half.

Everywhere along the American line, the advance had been swift, helped by their having encountered an enemy more concerned with withdrawing than putting up a stiff resistance. The fast-moving Americans had taken sixteen thousand prisoners and 443 guns.

On the evening of September 13, the marines began quietly relieving the 3rd Brigade. The 6th Regiment relieved the 23rd Regiment and placed the 3rd Battalion at the front on a line running east from Xammes, with the 2nd Battalion in support and the first in reserve.

The 96th Company was in that support position near Xammes when a familiar face appeared out of the darkness:

Good old Cliff Cates.

While the marines moved ever forward, he and his lucky fifty-odd men had been detailed to repair the roads leading toward Thiaucourt, taking stones from a nearby bombed-out village to do the job.

"The men worked steadily in a cold rain and without food, but they did not mind it, as they knew that the men out there in front were fighting for them," Cates wrote.

Cates dutifully set to the road-building task, but quietly worried about the men in his platoon. Word had filtered back that the attack was going well; still, he longed to see for himself how his men were being handled.

On September 14, Cates led his band to a small village farther south, where they were able to procure some hot food. Cates then set out north on foot for the front lines.

"I found everything all right, but they suffered at night from the cold," he would write. As for any danger, "The boche had moved most of their artillery back and they had not got it placed, so the fire was very light that day."

Satisfied, he returned to his lucky band of men.

At three a.m. on September 15, the 2nd Battalion was ordered forward to support two companies that had been sent out to reconnoiter the Bois de la Montagne northeast of Xammes and set up forward posts for the marines' eventual relief.

What awaited it was the only scrap Cliff Cates would miss during the entire war.

The new battalion commander, Major Ernest Williams, once again led his men forward while riding horseback. Once again, the men struggled to keep pace, and they were soon dangerously strung out for a mile along the Xammes–Charey road.

Second Lieutenant Graves Erskine, now the battalion scout officer, was familiar with the ground, having done several night patrols. He followed Williams with his scouts, and they were in turn followed by, respectively, the 80th, 96th, 79th, and 78th Companies.

The column passed through the 3rd Battalion's lines and headed northeast through the gray of dawn toward the Bois de la Montagne. Erskine grew alarmed when, at about five a.m., he saw that the major was leading the column toward a bridge that spanned a stream called the Rupt de Mad.

The bridge marked the farthest point of the Americans' advance in that sector; beyond, the Germans were regrouping and fortifying the Hindenburg Line.

What lay between was, simply, the always dangerous No Man's Land.

"I asked the major if he was going to cross the bridge, and he said 'Yes,'" Erskine would recall. "I said, 'By God, that's right in the middle of No Man's Land. I've been out there on patrol.'"

Williams told Erskine he didn't know what he was talking about, and kept riding, Erskine walking along and pulling at Williams's leg in an effort to get him to stop.

Williams continued leading the battalion over the bridge before Erskine irked him enough that he finally halted the column, got down from his horse, and pulled out a map and flashlight.

Shining it on the map, Williams—"not the best map reader in the world"—told Erskine, "Come here and show me where you think we are. I know where I am."

"No, sir," Erskine replied, "the place is full of Germans right up there. I've been there, I know." Smartly, he also told Williams, "I'm not coming near that flashlight."

Williams gave Erskine a "tongue lashing, got on his horse and started the march[,] and we hadn't gone fifty yards before it seemed like every machine gun in the world opened up."

Williams had ordered the 80th Company to send a patrol forward, and the forty-odd men were crossing an acre-sized clearing when the firing began. Half the platoon was shot down, among them Lieutenant David Kilduff, who was shot through the left side and mortally wounded.

The survivors were surrounded on three sides, eating dirt as they tried to remain below the fusillade. The remainder of the column, meanwhile, raced chaotically across the bridge and as if by intuition split in two, half the men turning to the left and half to the right.

Erskine and his scouts kept low as they continued moving forward through the thick, misty dawn. Soon, they saw a contingent of Germans retreating from the marines and heading down a wooded hill.

Erskine relayed this to Williams, who told him, "Well, goddamn it, take a couple of people and go down there and capture them."

Erskine and his German-speaking sergeant, Bill Uhlrich, rushed the woods and encountered between one hundred fifty and two hundred very surprised Germans.

Uhlrich told them in German that they were surrounded, and urged them to surrender. About forty made motions to do so, until "some wise German figured they were being fooled, so they started shooting, and we started firing back," Erskine recalled.

The remaining Germans took off running on the hill's upslope, the marines in hot pursuit. Erskine and his men stopped at a small house, threw in grenades, and bagged about twenty Germans. They then continued on.

Then, "the first thing we knew[,] we were inside the German lines," Erskine would say.

Across open ground lay the main German line, here centered on a strongpoint at a place called Mon Plaisir Farm. Erskine urged his men to fall back as a column of Germans was seen advancing on them from the farm.

"All I had was my pistol, and I got a few of them," he said. Trying to reach cover, he crossed a small patch of open ground and was hit in the leg with a burst of machine-gun fire. He went to ground and tried to become as small as possible as German snipers took potshots at him.

The 96th Company's Corporal Carlos Creed, part of Erskine's scout platoon, tried to advance toward the German strongpoint but was felled by machine-gun fire. A medic, David Hayden, went to his aid, applied dressings while under intense fire, and then carried Creed to the marine lines, where Creed died.

Another from the company, a Missouri private named Lester Nutting, advanced two hundred yards beyond the amorphous front line and scouted German machine-gun positions, signaling their locations to his mates. His work done, the twenty-year-old Nutting was cut down while trying to return to his lines.

He would earn a Navy Cross and Distinguished Service Cross to boot for his actions.

Posthumously, of course.

Other marines were desperately fighting for their lives in what was a near-encirclement, one pocket in the vicinity of Erskine, another near the bridgehead, and other small groups scattered across the field.

The 80th Company's Private Carl Brannen and a small group made it to some woods, where, peering over a bluff, they saw a "large number of the enemy."

Brannen and his pal Lewis Frillman—"Scatterbrain"—decided attacking was better than waiting for the Germans to advance on them, so they used rifle grenades and "poured it on good and proper until they were out of sight over a ridge."

On the left of the bridgehead, meanwhile, Private John Kelly and elements of the 78th Company were desperately trying to hold off an emboldened enemy. The unit's new captain, Wethered Woodworth, was shot in the leg, rose in pain, and then took a bullet in his body.

"Just my luck," he told Kelly. "No sooner get into action than I'm out again."

Woodworth was brought back of the lines, while Kelly and the rest fought for their lives for two hours, "the company steadily dwindling." Finally, Kelly and a sergeant agreed they needed to attack with what remained of the 78th's men.

Kelly took half of the men to the left, and the sergeant led the other half to the right. Before long, Kelly and sixteen men found themselves pinned behind a pile of rocks, desperately hurling grenades, firing their Chauchats, and stalling three German attacks. Before too long, only eight men remained.

Covered by a patch of bushes, Kelly fed the magazine of a Chauchat operated by a corporal. The corporal suddenly went still, and Kelly rolled him off the gun and fired it himself for fifteen minutes. During a lull, Kelly went to the wounded corporal and saw that his helmet seemed to be unusually tight.

Kelly pried it off, and found that either a bullet or a fragment of shell had dented it, pushing it into the man's head. Once it was off, the corporal stirred. As Kelly dragged him to the rear, Lieutenant James P. Adams and a mélange of men from different companies moved forward and established a strong defensive line.

Meanwhile, much of the 96th Company, under the command of Captain John Minnis, crossed the bridge and swung right to attack Hill 231.5 looming above. Minnis went down with a bullet in his chest; he would live.

Reinforcements finally arrived to save the marines from what Brannen would call "an embarrassing situation." One platoon each from the 3rd Battalion's 82nd and 83rd Companies and guns from the 81st Machine Gun Company established a perimeter from the crest of Hill 231.5 west across the Xammes–Charey road.

Those stranded for hours in the melee were able to pull back. Graves Erskine, a broken bone sticking out six inches from his shattered ankle, heard voices approaching. A big husky private named Archie Vale, of the 96th Company, grabbed him by an arm and pulled him to the rear and safety.

"I think you probably saved my life," Erskine told him. "What in the world can I ever do for you?"

Vale pointed to Erskine's sidearm and said, "I've wanted a .45-caliber pistol ever since I've been in this outfit. You can give me that gun."

Erskine obliged.

The day's action was far from over, but the bulk of the 6th Regiment's men had reached relative safety at the north edge of the Bois de la Montagne. The Germans shelled the woods through the day, and at about six p.m. and then again at dusk, they launched attacks on the marines.

"Each time his attacks were preceded by brief but violent artillery preparations," Bull Williams wrote. "Each time he was repulsed by rifle and machine gun fire, with losses to himself."

Cliff Cates, meanwhile, couldn't help but wonder at the sounds of machine-gun and artillery fire consuming the front, and fretted over his men.

When wounded men began drifting back through his road-building crew, Cates learned that Captain Minnis had been shot in the chest. He immediately felt the strong urge to be with the 96th Company in what seemed to be its hour of peril.

"When I heard that Capt. Minnis had been hit, I went up to regimental and asked Colonel Holcomb to let me go out and take command of the company," Cates wrote.

Holcomb told him not to worry: "He said everything was all right and that we would be relieved that night, so I did not go."

That, of course, didn't mean he was out of it entirely. During the afternoon, as the battle waged unseen several miles north of him, the Germans shelled the village in which Cates and the other twenty-percenters were quartered, and Cates and Second Lieutenant Sam Meek of the 82nd Company decided it was a good time to take a walk.

They headed down "one of those white chalky roads" but stopped to confer with a map "when wham, this shell exploded on our right and another on our left," Meek would remember. "We were pretty battle-wise by this time and we knew the next one was going to split the middle."

"All of a sudden I heard the whiz of one and I knew that it was coming close, so we both made a dive for a small hole and hit the dirt," Cates recalled. "I thought sure the blamed thing would land right on top of us."

The shell landed four feet away, leaving Cates—of course—unscathed. Meek was another story; he was hit by a fragment, which left "a hole in my thigh I could stick a finger in," Meek said.

Meek tried to rise and walk with a cane he'd liberated from a German officer earlier, but couldn't manage. Luckily, a Red Cross man soon appeared, hoisted Meek onto his back, and carried him back to a field hospital.

"And what about Cates?" Meek would ask years later. "That experience was typical of his World War I days. He was the luckiest man that ever was in the Marine Corps."

Because of gross negligence, ignorance, or plain old stupidity, the same couldn't be said for many of the marines of the 6th Regiment that day. Brushing off Graves Erkine's caution and advice, Bull Williams had led his men directly into an ambush.

The regiment lost 421 officers and men killed and wounded in the St. Mihiel operation—most of them, sadly, during the scattered firefights of September 15.

By that same night, the salient had been mostly reduced across the board; the 2nd Division would account for the capture of 3,000 prisoners and 118 guns of all calibers, while losing just 9 officers and 186 men killed and 34 officers and 1,007 men wounded—or just one-third of the division's appalling losses at Soissons.

On the night of September 15–September 16, the 2nd Division was relieved by the 78th Division. Cliff Cates was waiting when the 96th Company's men came back.

Twenty-three-year-old Private Homer Osborn of Kansas would remember that Cliff Cates "rustled up the best feed we ever had in France," and even brought up a barrel of "vin rouge" for the boys.

Although Cliff Cates was still just a second lieutenant, with the wounding of Minnis, they were now, finally, *his* boys, the 96th finally *his* company. He listened that night as his men—mostly new, now—talked in wonder at the day's action, and marveled that they'd made it out.

But Cliff Cates knew that what had occurred that day was more of a scrap than a fight, and he was happy to forgive those who had replaced the veterans lost at Soissons for thinking this was the worst the war could offer.

He'd been given a pass this time, but Cliff Cates, of all people, knew for certain that worse was sure to come.

Hell, it always did.

THE HILL

IT WAS NOT so much a fastball this time but a careful lob, with just five harrowing seconds from the time the object left his hand to its shattering explosion; the French grenade plopped into the blackness of the German dugout, and Cliff Cates ducked away and counted down . . . four . . . three . . . now two. . . .

Right on time, the explosion rattled the walls and roof of the hideout, sending a thick, gray cloud of earth spewing from the entrance, followed by the choking, desperate entreaties from those who had somehow not been killed within. A soiled German helmet soon appeared, as did two dirty hands held high. More faces and more gray-green uniforms soon trotted from the dark and into the arms of the waiting marines.

"You should have heard the rest of the damn rascals yell 'Kamerad!'" Cates would write. "One of my runners got six more prisoners out of there."

It was October 3, 1918.

Lucky Cliff Cates was back in action.

He stood on the southern hump of what was called Blanc Mont, or Blanc Mont Ridge. The French had tried for four long years to push the Germans off the near edge of the rolling, tabletop massif; Cliff

Cates and the 2nd Division accomplished the task over the course of one very, very bloody day.

For both sides.

But the battle was far from over.

Cliff Cates had indeed been lucky to have missed the "embarrassing" scrap above Thiaucourt eighteen days previously. It had been no Belleau Wood, no Soissons, but marines had been killed—that would never end, it seemed—during an encounter with the enemy that perhaps could have, perhaps should have, been avoided.

Whatever. On the evening of September 15, the marines of the 4th Brigade were relieved by elements of the 78th Division and began to withdraw from the St. Mihiel Salient, heading south to the area of Ansauville and Royaumeix, seven miles north of Toul. What had happened north of Thiaucourt was best forgotten.

By September 21, the 2nd Division was headquartered in the vicinity of Toul, where it received clothes and new equipment. There were other things to be had—including, for Cliff Cates, command of the 96th Company.

Though Cates was still just a lieutenant, and despite the arrival of five new captains to the 2nd Battalion, battalion commander Bull Williams turned the company over to Cates, and also put James Sellers, Cates's Quantico pal—newly returned from the hospital after being wounded at Belleau Wood—in command of the 78th Company.

Sellers would credit the battalion adjutant, Lucian Vandoren, with the move. Williams, Sellers wrote, was "a simple kind of soul who liked to leave everything up to his adjutant while he tried to get up to the front line with an automatic rifle."

Vandoren "really ran the battalion administratively," Sellers added, "so I think he made the decision to leave me and Cates in command. I never knew what Bull had the excess five captains doing."

Cates alternately drilled his men and let them rest in the vicinity of Charmes-la-Côte, a small village perched on the side of a mountain above the Moselle River, just on the edge of the Vosges, where the 2nd Division had gotten its feet wet the previous spring. Cates, now rested after being allowed to skip the St. Mihiel advance, found the village enchanting, its beauty eliciting some uncharacteristically florid prose from his pen.

"The view from this village is the prettiest that I have ever looked at," he wrote to his family. "The whole mountain side [sic] is covered with vineyards, and it is a beautiful sight to look down below at the different colored [sic] fields and the winding roads.

"In the distance there is a good sized [sic] town and two big mountains behind it. This morning the valley was filled with fog and it looked like a foamy sea; the top of the mountains were sticking out clear and they looked like islands with the surf breaking on them."

The map of the western front at that point was similarly redolent of a coastal scene; from the North Sea in the north to the Swiss border in the south, the Allies' lines were lapping against the German defenses and slowly eroding their front lines.

The German army, though beset with widespread influenza, continued to resist strongly as it slowly fell back, but the momentum was no longer with it. Any hope of victory had evaporated below Soissons in July; now the goal of the Germans was "simply to secure for the Fatherland an indurable [sic] peace," German Lieutenant Colonel Ernst Otto would write after the war.

"It was essential that our troops should be able to march back in the Fatherland with their heads proudly held high, conscious that they had remained undefeated in the field."

Even as Cliff Cates contemplated the beauty of the mountains and the Moselle River on the morning of September 25, thousands of Allied soldiers were taking their places along the line, set to throw themselves in waves once more against a desperate enemy.

Between the Meuse River on the east and the Argonne Forest on the west, the American 1st Army—nine divisions—was preparing to jump off on September 26 and push north across rugged terrain, its eventual goal to push through the Germans' successive fortified defense lines, and cut the vital supply lines running through Metz, Sedan, and Mézières.

On the Americans' left, in Champagne, the French 4th Army would also jump off on September 26, and in a two-phase offensive cover the Americans' flank and try to rout the Germans from their strong and long-held positions on high ground east of Reims, twenty miles to the west.

Knowing the difficulty the French would encounter, French General Henri-Philippe Pétain on September 16 had asked John Pershing for three American divisions to throw into the fight. Pershing at first offered the use of two divisions newly arrived in France, but then reconsidered and on September offered Pétain the bloodied 2nd Division, fresh from the St. Mihiel offensive, and the untested 36th Division, which even then was undergoing training.

Within a week, the lead elements of the 2nd were aboard trains and heading from the Toul area northwest to Châlons, fifteen miles southeast of Reims, where the French 4th Army was headquartered.

But the 2nd Division was not immediately assigned to the French 4th, though it had been entrained to its sector. Instead, it and the 36th Division were designated as part of the reserve of the Group of Armies of the Center.

However, General John Lejeune, who had assumed command of the 2nd after General James Harbord was placed at the head of the Service of Supply following Soissons, began hearing disturbing rumors to the effect that his division was to be split and sent into action by brigades in support of the French effort in Champagne.

If true, it was a repeat of the original Allied intentions that the Americans be parceled out to the French and British armies along the front—intentions Pershing had fought tooth and nail against before relenting during the spring crisis. A "much concerned" Lejeune sought out the 4th Army's General Henri Gouraud at his headquarters on September 28.

Gouraud showed Lejeune a situation map, and pointed out that while progress had been made in the first phase of the French offensive on the right, where the Americans pushing through the Argonne had made contact with the French, his left had stalled before high ground east of Reims.

"From previous sad experience the French had come to look upon the defense there as impregnable," a division history says.

Gouraud planned to flank the heights, the French 5th Army attacking just east of Reims from the west, and the 4th Army faced with the daunting task of carrying Blanc Mont Ridge above the village of Somme-Py, fifteen miles north of Châlons.

If the ridge could be breached, and the village of St. Étienne several miles north taken, the Germans would be forced to fall back to the Aisne River, thirty kilometers (eighteen miles) north. But, as Gouraud explained to Lejeune, his men were exhausted, and he held little hope they were worthy of the task.

Lejeune, faced with the real or simply rumored prospect of having his command divided, offered Gouraud a solution: If the 2nd Division was allowed to remain intact, it would take Blanc Mont "by a single assault."

Gouraud told Lejeune he would pass along his offer; by the next morning, orders had been issued, attaching the 2nd Division to the French 4th Army, and the Americans by ten a.m. on September 30 were opening new headquarters at Suippes, six miles south of Somme-Py.

(Lejeune, with a certain suspicion he may have been hoodwinked by the French, went out of his way to steel his men for the coming trial of Blanc Mont, saying in an order issued October 1 that because of its "world-wide reputation for skill and valor" the 2nd Division had been selected for the job: "The hour to move forward has now come, and I am confident that our division will pierce the enemy's line, and once more gloriously defeat the enemy.")

Cates and the 2nd Battalion had already passed through Suippes on their way to the front, and spent the night of September 29 and all of September 30 in "a big deep ditch" just to the north.

On the afternoon of October 1, the marines were ordered to relieve the French 61st Division and part of the French 21st, which were holding an old trench line north of Somme-Py at the base of Blanc Mont, which gently rose two hundred feet above the valley and crested three miles to the north.

Between the marines and that crest lay a succession of trenches that ran east and west. The 5th Regiment would take over the Essen trench on the right, which west of Somme-Py was held by the Germans; the 6th Regiment would occupy the Krefeld trench just north of the village.

Between the five thousand marines and the crest were about twelve hundred well-emplaced Germans manning well-sited machine guns, including many on the daunting "Essen Hook," an extension of the Essen trench on Helenen Hill five hundred yards west of the left of the line; it featured several concrete emplacements for machine guns, which, as the marines would discover, were easily able to enfilade the lines below.

As had become usual, twenty percent of the officers and enlisted men were left behind as Cates and the 96th Company drew hand grenades and ammunition before heading off at eight thirty p.m. for the front line, seven miles away.

The 2nd Battalion, Bull Williams would write, made good time "without a rest and over a road jammed with traffic of every description, nor did we lose a man."

The trek took the men through a scene of utter devastation, the first such ground the 2nd Division had encountered; at Belleau Wood, at Soissons, and to a lesser degree in the St. Mihiel Salient they had fought over virgin territory on which trees still had their leaves, and fields were planted and green with the promise of harvest.

Now they got a good glimpse of the ravages the Great War had wrought from Flanders to the Argonne. Years of war, of back-and-forth assaults and artillery bombardments between the French and Germans, had left the ground barren, devoid of life, its chalky lunar landscape holding bleaching bones and rotting bodies and tangles of barbed wire and dead horses downed in their traces.

Successive trench lines, now abandoned, told some of the grim story; the village of Somme-Py, a pile of lifeless ruins, told some more. Cliff Cates and the 6th Regiment now plodded through its grim, silent remains and were met by French guides, who ushered them to the north and left of town.

The 6th Regiment filtered west, and as night fell, its men were directed to the trenches they were to occupy—"merely ditches," Cates wrote. These had just recently been taken by the French in vicious fighting that pushed the Germans to a second trench line to the north.

Their contents told the story.

"The regiment that we were relieving had attacked and taken the boche front line [sic] trenches," Cates wrote. "It was dark as pitch and the ditches were full of dead boche and Frenchmen."

Three companies of the 2nd Battalion took over the Krefeld trench just north of Somme-Py. Cates and the 96th Company were sent to the left flank, where they entered a communication trench that ran through the Boyau de Bromberg and perpendicular to the Krefeld, and which at its northern end was blocked by the German-occupied Elbe trench.

The 96th Company would thus become the left flank of the 2nd Division; the numerous machine guns emplaced in the Essen Hook looming to their left were already active, sending streams of bullets into the blackness and toward Cates and company as they stumbled toward their assigned trench.

"We had a lot of trouble getting into our right position, but finally did get into our right place just before daylight; luckily, the boche artillery was not working much, but the machine guns and flares did worry us a lot, as we had to walk over open territory within fifty yards of their lines," Cates wrote.

"Every time that they would shoot up a flare, we would hit the dirt; then they would cut loose with their machine guns, but they did not damage us much."

All were in place by five a.m. Hours later, orders were sent from the 6th's headquarters to be prepared to go over the top at noon. However, that warning was soon rescinded, and the attack was postponed.

The marines, meanwhile, found in the morning light that they had spent the night in what amounted to a graveyard.

"My first sergeant and I had sat on a hump in the trench the remainder of the night only to discover with daybreak that two feet were sticking out from under the mound," the 78th Company's James Sellers would remember.

"We had been sitting all night on a dead Frenchman!"

Private John Kelly of the same company had stumbled onto a niche cut into a parapet; within sat a line of dead Frenchmen. One still held a grenade, though the top of his head had been blown away.

When a sergeant came through shouting for his men, Kelly pointed to the sad bunch of dead men within the darkened niche. "Why, there's a whole gang of them over there," Kelly told the sergeant.

"Get them for me," the sergeant said.

"Get them yourself," Kelly replied. The sergeant went over and groped into the niche; his hand landed on the exposed brain of one of the dead men.

"I laughed like hell," Kelly would say.

With the coming light of day, the men peered north over upward-sloping and mostly bald ground, which was patched with splotches of the white chalky limestone that gave the hill its name and haphazardly strewn in spots with the remnants of stubby pine trees.

The sights of an intimidating array of machine-gun emplacements and the battered, planked tops of German dugouts also greeted the marines that morning, putting lumps into the throats of even the most battle-hardened among them.

"The marine song had the words in it, 'If the army and navy ever look on heaven's scenes / they will find the streets are guarded by the United States Marines,'" the 80th Company's Carl Brannen would write. "After looking at that ridge ahead, I decided that my next duty might be helping guard the heavenly streets."

Cates, meanwhile, found the going to be nerve-racking on his end of the line. "It was a bum place," he would write.

The Germans spent much of October 2 slipping into the western end of his trench and throwing potato mashers at the men of the 96th Company, "but our men gave them just as much as we received."

The Germans three times tried to take Cates's dusty, dead-filled trench back; three times they were repulsed, in one counterattack gaining fifty more yards of it. Finally, at four thirty p.m., battalion adjutant Lucian Vandoren ordered Cates to take two of his platoons and try to capture that section of Essen trench occupied by the Germans three hundred yards away.

It was difficult for Cates to make himself heard by all 250 men lined single-file and huddling along the trench, but "I lined the men up the best that I could and instructed the two remaining platoons to get fire superiority on the boche machine gunners which were very thick on my left," Cates wrote.

At five p.m., he led one platoon over the top, ordering the other to follow thirty paces behind. "The men went over with a whoop and a hollow," he wrote. "It was a regular Indian war hoop and it sure put the fear of God into the boche."

A few machine guns opened up from the Essen Hook as Cates and his men made their move, and a flurry of potato mashers sought targets among the wild-eyed marines. Then, "they all ran like sheep," Cates crowed.

"My men went at it on the dead run. In less than two minutes we had gained our objective, so I sent up a flare signaling to that effect. We had lost only about ten men wounded, and we soon had them cleared off the field."

(The company's history lists one man killed—Private Andrew Jackson Van Cleve—on October 2 and five others wounded, among them Second Lieutenant Barney J. Kane, who had been promoted from gunnery sergeant just one week before.)

The other companies in the 2nd Battalion moved forward as well; these found that that portion of the Essen trench before them had already been evacuated by the Germans.

Cates, "who had the difficult flank," according to Bull Williams, sent this message to Williams at eight p.m.: "Attack a success. Few losses. Consolidated. Liaison with 78th on right and French on left. Everything in good shape."

Orders for an assault were meanwhile being written, but the first Bull Williams heard of them was shortly before midnight on October 2 when several artillery liaison officers showed up at his dugout behind the 2nd Battalion's lines. From them, he learned that "H hour"—the time set to attack—would be at five fifty the next morning.

Still, no official word came, leaving the men to huddle and shiver and wonder through much of the night in their frontline trenches. At three thirty a.m. Williams received word via telephone that "orders would be sent to us."

At four thirty a.m., Williams called his company commanders together and, while covered by a poncho, he used a flashlight to show them what to do. He knew the east-west boundaries of the assault by dint of the orders that had been written for the canceled Oct. 2 attack. (Along with those orders had come this from 6th Regiment commander Harry Lee: "Impress all men with the fact that musketry is still KING and they have but to sit tight and shoot straight, insuring the superiority of fire and guaranteeing success.")

In any event, there was only one direction to go: toward the Germans.

The 96th Company would advance on the left. On its right, 78th Company, 80th Company, and 79th Company would advance in line by platoons, four waves to a company.

The 2nd Battalion was to be followed in turn by the 1st Battalion and then the 3rd Battalion, also attacking in waves of platoons, a space of five hundred meters (1,640 feet) between battalions.

Once the entire regiment had cleared the forward line, the 5th Regiment would slide to its left and follow, also in a column of platoons. On the right, the 3rd Brigade was to jump off at the same time and in the same manner as Cates.

It was decided, however, that while the brigades would both advance to the north-northwest, they would not do so abreast. The 3rd Brigade's left would advance half a mile east of the 4th's, skirting the troublesome and well-fortified center of the German defenses and angling slightly more northwest than the 4th Brigade, with the intent of linking with the 4th at the crest of Blanc Mont.

Afterward, elements of both brigades would turn south and clean up the Germans left in the untouched, triangular center of the lines in the Bois de la Vipère. Meanwhile, the French would guard the flanks of the divisions' advance, the 21st Division on the left and the 167th on the right. One company of French tanks, twelve in all, was assigned to each of the two lead battalions in both brigades.

At five forty a.m., a "breathless runner" finally delivered to Williams the regiment's orders for the attack. He stuffed them into a pocket, unread; he wouldn't get a chance to actually look them over until his men were standing atop Blanc Mont.

At almost the same time, the air erupted with shellfire, the guns of the 61st French and American 2nd Divisions opening up a preparatory five-minute barrage aimed at softening the German defenses.

Looking toward the front, Cates noticed a rainbow streaking the morning sky—"one of the prettiest rainbows that I ever looked at," he would write. "It was a double rainbow and went from the eastern horizon to the western horizon.

"I told my men that it was an omen of good luck."

At five fifty a.m., whistles shrieked, and Cliff Cates led the 96th Company once more over the top, following a rolling barrage that crept one hundred meters (328 feet) every four minutes; after pulverizing each objective line, the artillery would then move forward and stand for a full thirty minutes three hundred yards beyond, the intent to block any counterattacks and allow the marines to consolidate.

Having missed St. Mihiel, Cates was back in his element, back leading men into terrible battle, back doing, it was becoming more and more clear, what he was born to do.

Follow me, Cliff Cates yelled as he raced for the German line.

Follow me!

"RAUS MITTEN!"

IT WAS ABOUT eight a.m. when Cliff Cates and his company were first espied by the Germans holding the crest of Blanc Mont. It had taken just more than two hours for Cates and those who remained to traverse the barren, scarred hills and dales below; two hours to do what the French had tried unsuccessfully for four years to accomplish, wasting 175,000 lives in the process; two hours, though, of almost unremittent hell, as the marines fell "like ten pins," as Carl Brannen would write, before the machine guns on Essen Hook and above.

"We moved forward in perfect formation, altho they were cutting us with machine guns real heavy," Cates would write. "On we went; we followed our barrage as close as possible without getting into it."

Marines quickly fell, among them the 96th Company's Private Bernola Turner, a twenty-four-year-old from Beaver, Oklahoma, who was barely fifty yards from the jump-off trench when a machine-gun bullet hit him just below his heart.

Turner managed to retrace his steps to the trench. "When one of the men asked him how he was, he said, 'Oh, I am all right; am hit pretty hard below the heart, but guess I will pull through all right,'" his bunkmate, Private Archie Vale—the same who had saved Graves Erskine's bacon on September 15—would relate.

"He was soon taken to the rear in an ambulance and died before reaching a base hospital."

For obvious reasons, the battalions waiting to advance behind the 6th Regiment watched with intense interest as the attack unfolded. "It was plain to be seen at the very start that they were being subjected to heavy artillery and machine-gun fire," Captain Gilder D. Jackson, Jr., of the 5th Regiment's 20th Company would write.

"Seeing their comrades go down under this fire made our men all the eager to be off to help them."

"Wave after wave, the 6th went forward," the 49th Company's Lieutenant John Thomason, Jr., watching with the 5th Regiment below, would write. "For a moment the sun shone through the murk, near the horizon—a smoldering red sun, banded like Saturn, and all the bayonets gleamed like blood. Then the cloud closed again."

Fog hung in the crevices and gullies they passed through, helping screen the advance. So did the creeping barrage: By the time it had passed over the German machine-gun emplacements and dugouts that populated the hill, the marines were on them.

"A few showed fight," Cates wrote, "but they were soon shot down; some ran and they all shared the same fate. If we failed getting them, then our barrage caught them, as they had to pass back through it.

"Most of them threw up their hands and yelled, 'Kamerad!' We would send them running to the rear with very light guards or none at all. They were only too glad to be alive."

"The Germans had set up their machine gun nests all over the hill so that the cross fire would cover the entire area," Cates's pal James Sellers, leading the 78th Company to the right of the 96th Company, would remember.

"But with our very precise barrage, our men would be on top of the machine gun emplacements before the Germans could come up for air. Despite this advantage, our casualties were quite heavy."

What the barrage didn't eliminate, simple heroism did as the marines advanced that morning. The 78th Company's John Kelly had promised Sellers he would be the first man of the unit to capture a machine-gun nest; as the 2nd Battalion advanced, he made good on his promise.

Held up by his own barrage as he sought to locate a machine gun behind it, Kelly, a grenade in his right hand and a .45 Colt pistol in his left, made the not necessarily bright decision to go through the rain of shells. He emerged as a lone American, and soon encountered a panicked German soldier racing his way.

The German fell to his knees in front of Kelly—he was just "a boy," Kelly would remember. Kelly debated whether to shoot the boy, and when the boy slowly turned his head to the left, Kelly glanced over as well—and saw a German machine gunner preparing to fire.

Kelly pitched the grenade into the hole, killing the gunner. Another of the crew emerged, and Kelly put a bullet in his heart. He then collected the eight remaining members of the crew and began running them down the hill, Kelly and his prisoners crouching low as the barrage once more miraculously passed over without harming either Kelly or the Germans.

"If I had killed him[,] he wouldn't have turned his head, and I wouldn't have seen the machine gun and I would have been killed," Kelly would say. "But I spared him, and he turned his head, and I saw the machine gun. I gave a break and I got a break."

Another of Sellers's men proved himself a hero that morning. Corporal John H. Pruitt, twenty-two, "a stout young fellow" from Arizona, answered Sellers's call for volunteers, charged a machine gun, "and shot the gunman right between the eyes," Sellers would write.

Later, Pruitt and another from the company rounded up forty-two

German prisoners, among them three officers. An hour later, his day, brave deeds, and life ended in the sharp explosion of an artillery round.

Sellers would successfully nominate both Kelly and Pruitt for Medals of Honor.

"The same sort of thing was going on up and down the line," Sellers remembered. "The surprising part of it was that we did not have more casualties than we did.

"The French and evidently the boches couldn't understand the American methods of attack. The French advanced very carefully and cautiously and lost many more men than we did, because the square-heads knew what to expect.

"We started over in a pretty formation but the fight soon degenerated into a sort of free for all, every man for himself and everybody right up behind the line of the barrage, which was proper."

(Sellers would recall advancing with a small group of replacements to the 78th Company—"inexperienced young men"—when a rabbit scurried from the brush. Instinctively, every man in the group took a shot at the panicked animal. One of the youngsters, almost oblivious to the battle raging around him, looked at Sellers with a guilty grin and said, "This is kind of fun.")

Others with the 96th Company distinguished themselves during the advance. Corporal Oscar Moreland, a twenty-four-year-old from Indianola, Illinois, earned a Navy Cross, being cited for remaining on duty though wounded and helping ward off German counterattacks.

Another of the 96th's corporals, Roy W. Reeves, earned a Navy Cross and a Distinguished Service Cross by grabbing a potato masher that had been thrown into a group from his company and hurling it away. It exploded just yards from him, and left him with serious wounds to his face and head.

Surely the Germans resisted, but still were not in best form that morning. Several of the German divisions reported their men to be exhausted, the assaults by the French and the unending need to improve entrenchments pushing them to the limit.

One frontline German battalion commander on the field wrote that as a result of the "mental and physical exertions, the troops have grown apathetic and indifferent to such an alarming extent that I can no longer guarantee that, during a surprise attack, they will continue to hold the positions."

The 2nd Division assault on Blanc Mont was not a huge surprise— the Germans from their observation tower on the crest had seen the marines and regulars moving into position, and had expected an attack on October 2—but it was for some German soldiers the final straw after four years of war.

But there remained fight in enough of them, particularly on the Essen Hook on the western side of the hill, from which machine guns continued to take a toll on the left flank of the advancing marines.

The French 21st, assigned the task of reducing the position, had made little or no headway, and even as Cliff Cates and the survivors of the 96th Company approached the crest of Blanc Mont, the Germans continued to rake the flank of those coming behind.

"We were just going into the second wave when a machine gun bullet hit me in the leg about 4 inches above the knee and went clear thru," the 96th Company's twenty-two-year-old Corporal Lynn Smyser of Gettysburg, Pennsylvania, would write.

"Some of the boys carried me to a shell hole and I laid in this until I was picked up by the stretcher bearers. Some of the Germans we had captured carried me into the first aid station."

Smyser would add, "All the Germans have up at this front is machine guns. It seems like a machine gun to a man."

Meanwhile, as the leading marines, Cates among them, approached the hilltop, it erupted in continuous showers of dirt and limestone as the artillery below laid a standing barrage on the trenches guarding the tree-lined crest, which hid numerous, deep dugouts, some large enough to hold a company of Germans.

It was from these that the Germans emerged at about eight a.m. to see Americans pouring toward them—the regulars of the 3rd Brigade on their left, Cates and the marines of the 2nd Battalion, 6th Regiment on the right.

"The noise of combat coming from the front lines was audible and orders were issued to occupy the positions," the 2nd Battalion of the German 74th Reserve Infantry Regiment would report.

"Hardly was the last man at his post when the enemy became visible, urging our men to surrender by waving at them. They had overrun the front lines with almost no resistance.

"Our machine-gun fire, which was launched at once in compliance with orders, brought their advance to a halt. . . . The bullets of our machine guns, easily finding their mark in the dense masses of the Americans, inflicted heavy casualties."

But Cates and his men, screened by dense brush and a depression in the hill, worked to the left and enveloped the German right, moving steadily forward and firing their Chauchats and Springfields with deadly accuracy.

"[S]trong detachments of Americans appeared on the right flank, advancing in the direction of Blanc Mont," the 74th Reserve Infantry Regiment report says. "They were immediately subjected to the fire of two heavy machine guns on the extreme right flank of the battalion.

"But now the Americans appeared also at the front, supporting their advance . . . with machine-gun fire." The desperate Germans fired "free hand" from their trench, and still the marines came on until they were close enough to use their grenades.

On the right of the battalion's advance, Cates's buddy, Second Lieutenant John West, took over when the 79th Company's commander,

Amos Shinkle, was wounded. "We picked up batches of prisoners here and there," West wrote.

"Just this side of the Blanc Mont Ridge the Germans had a trench about 200 yards in length from which they put up a good machine gun fire. We advanced on them with marching fire and took the trench and about fifty prisoners."

The 78th Company's James Sellers saw several Germans pop out of and then back into a large dugout as he approached with some of his men. Sellers led them to the dugout entrance, and yelled, *"Raus mitten!"*

"If they came up, we took them prisoner," he would write, "and if not, we threw a grenade down and continued on, leaving the dugout for the outfits coming behind to clean up.

"No one came out, so I dropped a grenade and continued on ahead. Only 40 or 50 yards beyond that was our objective, a road, where we dug in."

The 80th Company's Corporal Don Paradis made the crest "just as a bunch of German prisoners came out of a large dugout. They were about twenty-five, some looked to be not over sixteen years old.

"They were so scared that their knees actually knocked together, flapped together. To me it was a pitiful sight. They were immediately sent to the rear, carrying our wounded as well as some of theirs."

Enveloping the Germans from left to right, and also appearing "even in the rear," the men of the 2nd Division pushed on relentlessly. "Not one man of our battalion would have been able to escape capture, not even by flight. Further resistance was out of the question," the German 74th Reserve Infantry would report.

Cates led his men to the day's objective—the near crest of Blanc Mont—where he saw a German trying to escape. It was then that he stood toe-to-toe, like Wyatt Earp against Ike Clanton on the streets of old Tombstone, with the German officer who emerged from a nearby dugout.

It was then that the young marine officer from Nowheresville,

Tennessee, shot and killed one of Germany's finest who was trying to kill him, but who instead fell mortally wounded back into the black hole from whence he had come.

It was then that Cliff Cates, his blood up, cracked a grenade and tossed it into the dugout.

*You should have heard the rest of the damn rascals yell "Kamerad!"**

The marines were in the rear of the German 200th Division, part of which was also engaged on the Essen Hook. The division continued to harass and stall the battalions following Cates in line up the hill.

Some of the German division's headquarters staff was captured even as reinforcements were being ordered in to stem the marines' assault. Cates and his men went along the crest of the hill, rousting about seventy-five Germans from their dugouts.

All told, on October 3 Cates and company captured some 250 soldiers and eighteen pieces of heavy artillery. Then they began digging in and reorganizing for the counterattack they were certain would come; with the failure of the French 21st to advance in line, the marines' left was still in the air, and the situation was somewhat perilous.

"The enemy still held on our left, where no Allied advance had been made, and his machine guns, one-pounders and mortars proved particularly troublesome," Bull Williams wrote.

What's more, the Germans had expected the Americans to continue the advance north toward the village of St. Étienne several miles to the north. When they didn't, and instead consolidated their gains just to the

---

*Cates would dine out for years on his thrilling tale of going toe-to-toe with the German officer. On one occasion in 1925, while hitting the harbor-front saloons in Norfolk, he repeated it to Lemuel Shepherd, his successor as commandant, "for the hundredth time," Shepherd would later say. "I went to sleep with it still preying on my mind. Then I started to dream that I'm facing this big Prussian-looking officer. 'Put your hands up,' I yelled, 'you're my prisoner.' Well, he went for his pistol, and I went for mine. I shot the son-of-a-bitch right between the eyes. I don't know what one of those dream-analysis experts would make about that, but it never bothered me again."

north of the crest of Blanc Mont Ridge, the German artillery stationed near St. Étienne came into play "and was very annoying, particularly his pieces of .88 calibre," Williams added.

"We reached the summit of the hill, but Clif Cates'[s] 96th Company on the left flank got considerable fire," James Sellers would recall. "Clif [sic] rearranged his company and faced the left flank."

When a German battalion approached the crest from the north and west, "we slaughtered them and they did not gain an inch," Cates wrote.

But the flank continued to pose a problem, as the marines were pounded by mortars and harassed by machine guns. Toward noon, seven hundred to eight hundred Germans were seen passing around the Americans' left rear, threatening them with encirclement.

Cates raced to a group of French tanks lumbering toward the crest, and motioned for them to turn west to meet the threat.

"We could see one battalion of boche filing in behind us," Cates wrote. "Of course, this was very serious, but I succeeded in getting four big tanks over on our left and they opened up on them with their machine gun one pounders and three inch.

"They were firing at point blank and you should have heard the boche yell; it knocked them to pieces. The men were picking them off with their rifles also. Later, we found about twenty-five with holes thru their helmet and head. That soon put an end to their counterattack."

As the German artillery continued to pound their position, the trailing battalion—1st Battalion of the 5th Regiment—sent the 17th Company and a cadre of machine gunners west toward Essen Hook.

After advancing through the Essen trench, the marines went over the top and surrounded and took the position, then turned it over to the French; the French for some reason again failed to advance, and the Germans once more climbed into their dugouts and emplacements and blasted the marines with machine-gun fire.

In response, the entire 2nd Battalion of the 5th Regiment faced left, and it and the 4th Machine Gun Battalion laid protective fire as the rest of the marines streamed toward the crest.

At four thirty p.m., the 2nd Battalion of the 5th Regiment reported to Williams that it had closed the gap between the 96th Company and the French 21st Division. An hour later he received word that the French were moving up on the left, and a general advance toward St. Étienne had been ordered.

The 5th Regiment was to pass through the 6th and lead, with the 6th to re-form and advance one kilometer (half a mile) behind, protecting the ever-dangerous left flank. After Colonel Logan Feland, commander of the 5th Regiment, explained the orders at his headquarters, Gilder Jackson and other company commanders complained.

"We had had a hard enough time getting this far in the daylight, and it was easy to see with darkness coming on, and a woods to go through, that it would require infinite care to keep the companies from becoming scattered," Jackson wrote.

As well, the regiment's men were scattered along the slope, where battalion commanders sought their companies and junior officers sought their platoons. The 4th Brigade advance was called off for the time being, but the 3rd Brigade's 23rd Regiment attacked at eight p.m., aiming for a hill one kilometer (half a mile) southeast of St. Étienne.*

The 23rd's 1st Battalion made it to some old training trenches in the general area of the objective, while the 2nd Battalion advanced a short distance and placed its left on the Somme-Py–St. Étienne road; the

---

*The 3rd Brigade had only just managed to jump off on time on the right—it started its march on the night of October 2–October 3 from Navarin Farm, four kilometers (two and a half miles) south of Somme-Py, and became lost. When French guides finally located the wandering brigade and led it to what was supposed to be its assigned jump-off trenches, it was discovered the Germans still occupied them. Thus the 23rd and 9th Regiments first had to assault their own trenches before launching themselves successfully up Blanc Mont.

3rd Battalion moved up and protected the 1st's right rear. The result was a sharp wedge cut into the German line.

While this went on, the marines remained on the crest of the hill. There, the lucky ones took advantage of four years of German construction. They found officers' dining halls, and huge dugouts, fifteen feet deep, ninety feet long, and eight feet wide, lined with bunks and strung with electric wires.

Cates that night took refuge in "a hole with a big dutch [sic] dog as a bed fellow. [sic] He sure helped keep me warm. He was a dirty, flea-bitten rascal, but I could not mind a little thing like that."

James Sellers's orderly—"just a young kid"—asked permission to revisit the German dugout into which Sellers had tossed a grenade on the way up. Sellers agreed, and the lad and a friend retraced their steps down the hill, planning on spending the night out of the elements.

They had climbed halfway down the steps into the dugout when "they heard this guttural German talking," Sellers wrote. "They scrambled back up to the top and yelled, *'Raus mitten!'*"

To everyone's surprise, Germans began pouring out of the shelter—forty-two, to be exact. One of Sellers's men who had suffered a "bonne blesse"—a non-life-threatening wound—marched them to the back lines.

Sellers decided to use the dugout for his command post, and upon inspection was amazed at its size—"a space which could have housed a few hundred men. It had two entrances and was concrete lined with electric lights, run by a broken down generator housed in a small, separate building."

He would quickly find that the space housed a more unwelcome amenity—lice. "The boche blankets were full of cooties," Sellers wrote. "My wrists and arms were all chewed up."

Below his little haven, stretcher bearers—Americans and captured Germans alike—were crisscrossing the scarred fields and blasted thickets, looking for wounded and dead. It had been a hell of a day once again for the regiment's 2nd Battalion, and another hell of a day for the 96th Company.

Its history says twenty-one men were killed in action on that day, while scores more were wounded—among them Second Lieutenant John D. Bowling for a second time. Four more enlisted men would die of their wounds in the next few days.

Second Lieutenant Walter Strand, promoted from gunnery sergeant just eight days before, was mortally wounded on October 3 and lingered until October 17.

Also among the other dead was Private James F. Boylan of Troy, New York. "The fighting was fierce and the machine gun fire killed a good many men," Corporal Thomas Mack would tell Bolan's father in a letter. "Jimmie was hit in the head and died instantly while attacking a strong machine gun position and is buried at the spot he fell with three other comrades."

Others who died that day from the 96th Company were Private Samuel Henry Shunk of Scottville, Michigan; Corporal Arthur Roland Ballard of Milner, Georgia; Private George Cleveland Bates of Marietta, South Carolina; Private Perry Franklin Bowers of Montfort, Wisconsin; Private Joseph Aloysius Stanton of New Orleans, Louisiana; Corporal John Lee Dorrell of Heyworth, Illinois; Corporal Alfred Erlandson from Calumet, Michigan; and Private Andrew Jackson Van Cleve of Crystal City, Texas.

There were others—plenty of others. And even more would join the above in the Honor Roll in the coming days.

But not Lucky Cliff Cates, who would manage just an hour's sleep with his flea-bitten canine companion that evening. Sleep was difficult even after the day's exertions, and all on that hill were on edge with an enemy somewhere out there in the night, and the situation on the left flank still unknown.

"We were cold and hungry, and there was a feeling of uneasiness that we were more or less 'out on a limb,'" Gilder Jackson wrote.

"The French had not, as yet, come up on our left. . . . It looked like a simple matter, if the Germans had reserves to throw in, for them to come on our left and capture the whole Marine Brigade."

ZOMBIES

IT WAS A week before he left the hill; a week of advances, retreats, of taking refuge in the Germans' dugouts and then moving forward again. By October 10, Cliff Cates appeared as if he'd been rolled in white flour and then showered in dirt—"the dirtiest, flea bitten, cootie ridden [sic] rascal that you ever looked at," he would write.

By then he could once more say he and his company had done their part. "We had more than done our share and truly deserved to have a little rest," he wrote. "We had gone over the top three times within four days—something very unusual."

The attack originally ordered for the evening of October 3 had instead gone off at first light the following morning. The 5th Regiment—3rd Battalion leading, then the 1st with the 2nd in support—passed through the sparse lines of the 6th and headed over bare, rolling ground for a line of German trenches about six hundred yards south of St. Étienne.

Although the rolling barrages had played such an important role in the successes of the previous day, the French and American artillery were strangely silent on October 4; the marines jumped off with no artillery preparation or even a barrage to follow; caught in the open, they soon faced annihilation.

The French, yet again, had failed to push beyond Essen Hook to cover the marines' left flank, leaving the Germans on the western portion of Blanc Mont to enjoy what amounted to a turkey shoot.

"The order was ridiculous, shooting at the Germans with no artillery preparation," James Sellers would write, adding, "This lunatic action had no chance of gaining ground."

The 3rd Battalion managed to cover almost two kilometers (about one and a quarter miles) in the face of furious machine-gun fire coming from its left and artillery fire from its front just south of St. Étienne. As well, German planes scoured the skies above uncontested, helping the artillery find the scattered companies of the 5th.

The 20th Company's Captain Gilder Jackson ordered two of his machine gunners to attempt to bring down one of the birds. They did so—but, he noted, the action "nearly proved fatal for me, and did prove so for a number of the machine-gunners attached to my company."

The attempt to bring down the plane brought the attention of a concealed German .77. It fired point-blank into Gilder's men, "and scored direct hits on our guns, killing and wounding 22 men," he would write, adding, "Had we been given an artillery barrage prior to our 'jumping off,' things would have been a great deal easier. . . . I have never yet had it explained to me why we were forced to 'jump off' into such a strong German positon with no artillery preparation."

Desperate messages from the 3rd Battalion's Major Harry Larsen brought up the regiment's other two battalions, the second taking a position on Larsen's left. With the flank still in the air because of the long gap along the hill's western side, the marine ranks continued to be torn apart, suffering sixty percent casualties.

Major George Hamilton, his own 1st Battalion having also taken heavy casualties, moved left and took position in support of the 2nd and 3rd Battalions. What remained of the 5th stabilized in a line spread east to west across the Somme-Py–St. Étienne road.

The regiment again tried to advance at about one thirty p.m., but again fierce fire from an elevation on the left flank took its toll. Hamilton would later report that elements of the 2nd Battalion, including company commanders and even battalion commander Major Robert Messersmith, late of the 78th Company, "were leading in what appeared to be a grand rout."

"Major Messersmith explained that he had lost all his officers, but didn't show any initiative or leadership," Hamilton complained in writing. Hamilton and his officers stopped the rout at pistol-point, reorganized the men, and had them dig in.

With no way to retreat, Hamilton led his battalion forward into the world of hurt being thrown out by the Germans, heading toward a sparsely wooded rise directly south of St. Étienne that the Germans called Ludwigs-Rucken.

A German trench loomed at its southern base, and all expected to encounter stiff resistance there. But the sheer audacity of the marine attack had led the Germans to flee; the marines leaped over the ditch and continued up the rise, until finally the thin line ran into a last line of resistance formed among the artillery parked south in a grove of St. Étienne.

"Scarcely pausing, they shot the gunners down amidst their pieces and chased the survivors into the cover of the patch of wood beyond," Private Elton Mackin of the 1st Battalion's 67th Company would write.

"They were in their element—the Yankee style of fighting amid the trees. The line broke into scattered groups, all pressing forward. Working so, in vicious little deadly packs, they kept going. While the fever of the attack lasted, discipline was forgotten in the urge to hunt and kill."

The marines fell in among the Germans, swinging rifle butts and thrusting bayonets almost with glee, although they left a trail of brown-clad American bodies behind them.

The 49th Company's Lieutenant John Thomason, Jr., watched as one German soldier—"a big feldwebel"—went after one of the company's noncoms. The sergeant, ducking under the German's lunging bayonet, came up under him and thrust his own long knife into his throat.

"And as his point touched, he pulled the trigger. The feldwebel's helmet flew straight into the air, and the top of his head went with it," Thomason wrote.

But the battalion had run itself into what Mackin would call "the Box"; the advance lashed up against a semicircle of German machine guns. "The separate and isolated groups, coming in carelessly at first, were at once subjected to a withering concentrated fire of light and heavy machine guns," a German report would say.

"Everywhere good results were observed. Gaping holes were torn in the lines of riflemen, entire columns being mowed down. Much to our advantage were the light yellow-brown uniforms of the Americans, altogether impractical for this terrain."

The marines wavered. "The unrest in his ranks grew every minute. Lone individuals, and frequently entire detachments, ran aimlessly about."

The Germans grouped for a counterattack as the 1st Battalion, "a very small battalion now, little more than a hundred men, lay along the crest they had stormed, with their dead and wounded and the Boche dead and wounded around them," Thomason wrote.

At seven hundred yards, the German attack faltered under the accurate fire of the marines. But the position was beyond perilous; two regiments of Germans were now re-forming to get after the marines.

It was time to declare victory and get the hell out.

Hamilton and his remaining few officers ordered a retreat to their starting position, and the survivors scurried "through a hail of machine-gun fire and an inferno of shelling," Thomason wrote.

Finally reaching their original position around the Somme-Py–St. Étienne road, Hamilton counted heads that night and found he had but 12 officers and 156 enlisted men left unscathed.

When one company's ration cart was brought up, it had 230 rations of tinned meat. With but twenty-odd men left, the marines ate what they could and used the rest of the cans to build breastworks.

On the right, the 3rd Brigade had also advanced on the east side of the Somme-Py–St. Étienne road, the objective a heavily fortified position on Blodnitz Hill southeast of St. Étienne. The 23rd Regiment led with the 9th in support, both flanks in the air.

The attack took the Germans by surprise, but they quickly gathered their wits about them. As the American regulars stormed across the crest of the hill and then down the slope, "our machine guns here, too, found their targets and began to cut down the attacking files, for in this open terrain they could find no suitable protection," the Germans reported.

What was left of the 3rd Brigade, too, hustled back to its starting point.

The 6th Regiment, meanwhile, remained in the foxholes, trenches, and dugouts on the southern ridge of the Blanc Mont massif. It, too, was under fire from the western edge of the mountain. A new French force, the 22nd Division, had relieved the hapless 21st and was moving north of Essen Hook—but, as ordered, was trending west of the marine flank.

The 6th Regiment nonetheless was ordered to attack west and help relieve the pressure on the marines ahead of it. However, a chagrined Bull Williams was forced to report that he had erred the previous day in not pushing his battalion's advance 450 meters (1,476 feet) to the west—the actual western end of the massif.

The Germans held the higher ground there in strength, peppering the 6th's men with machine-gun and sniper fire, and the low ground in between was also strongly held, making an advance "impossible without heavy artillery preparation on his [the Germans'] position on our left or until the French advance on our left," Williams reported.

The 97th Company was sent forward nonetheless and managed to reduce several machine-gun nests before falling back to the ridgeline. While the remains of the 5th Regiment lay nearly surrounded all night south of St. Étienne, the 6th remained in its places, awaiting help from the artillery.

Other help, fortunately, was on the way. The commander of the French 22nd Division had corrected its march somewhat, and sent its easternmost regiment on a northerly course.

The movement threatened the rear of the Germans holding the western portion of the massif, and the threat to the marines was entirely removed after an hour-long artillery barrage from French 155s and 75s was laid on the German positions.

The French then advanced along the western side of the hill while the 6th Regiment also attacked at six fifteen a.m. on October 5, Major George Shuler's 3rd Battalion in the lead.

Without taking a single casualty, the battalion swept the Germans away, capturing nearly three hundred Germans, an astounding eighty machine guns, "and a number of trench mortars" and other materiel, a divisional history says.

The 6th was now ordered to advance and relieve the 5th Marines. After drawing ammunition, it moved forward at three p.m. with the 2nd Battalion in the lead, followed by the 3rd Battalion and the 1st in support.

The battalion moved in two waves, the 78th Company in the lead on the left and the 79th on the right. The 80th Company formed behind the 78th Company, while Cliff Cates placed his men behind the 79th; the formation spread for nearly one mile across the rolling plain.

It would have been even longer, but the previous day had taken its toll; Williams could count just 305 men out of the thousand that had gone over the top on October 3.

The rest weren't all dead or wounded, though the casualties had been severe; in the advance up Blanc Mont, many men had become separated from their units in the confusion of battle, and even as the 2nd Battalion jumped off, scores more of its men remained scattered.

Colonel Harry Lee set the objective for the attack at St. Étienne, but shortly before the regiment set off, his adjutant, Thomas Holcomb—perhaps realizing that objective was a bit lofty, considering what had happened to the 5th Regiment—modified the orders. Holcomb set the new goal as the ridge southeast of the village—Blodnitz Hill, where the dead of the 3rd Brigade still littered the slopes.

Once again, the marines would go over with no help from the artillery.

Once again, the lack of help from the big guns would doom the assault.

Cliff Cates lined up what remained of his 96th Company. After two nights of sleeping on the chalky soil and in the grimy dugouts, the men—Cates included—looked like ghouls, a pasty-white army of dust-caked zombies ready to scare the bejeezus out of the Germans.

Over they went—yet again.

"We advanced without a barrage this time and naturally, we ran into stiff opposition," Cates would write with characteristic nonchalance. "We were shelled slightly and they threw a few gas shells into us."

Cates's friend John West, still in command of the 79th Company and in the lead, would write that his superiors "supposed" that the wooded Blodnitz Hill was lightly held.

"This, however, proved wrong as a heavy fire was directed at us from the woods as soon as we stepped from our holes on Blanc Mont Ridge."

About halfway to the objective, and after crossing a kilometer (half a mile) of open ground, a runner from the 23rd Regiment approached West with a message from one of the 23rd Regiment's battalion commanders. In it, the major told West to stop "until further orders."

"This conflicted with the orders I had and I sent the runner back with the message that my orders were to take a position in the woods and any further word from him would find me in the woods," West wrote.

The 23rd's major certainly would have known what he was talking about—his regiment had attacked the hill and taken appalling casualties just twenty-four hours beforehand. Bull Williams, for his part, would later say the warning had included the mention of "strong machine gun nests" that needed to be reduced with artillery before any further attempt could, or should, be made.

"The preceding day his command had been badly cut up in attempting to take the position," Williams noted.

West brushed aside the warnings and attacked the hill's wooded southern slope. "We continued on and routed some Germans just outside of the woods," West wrote.

"On reaching the woods our line was very thin—at least a 50 yard interval between men. It was impossible in the heavy undergrowth to keep any line in the woods, so it was more a case of each man for himself."

West was trying to locate the members of his scattered command when a single rifle shot rang out and he fell, severely wounded in the head. He managed to dictate a message for Cliff Cates, turning over what remained of his company to him.

Cates himself had been circumspect about the chance of carrying the position. "We ran into the largest machine gun nest that I have ever seen, and naturally, we were held up," he wrote.

He agreed with the battalion commander of the 23rd and Bull Williams: "It takes heavy artillery to put them out of business." With the 79th Company repulsed and West out of action, he consolidated West's men with his own and "dropped back to an old ditch a few yards back and held it."

The endless casualty lists from Belleau Wood, Soissons, and now Blanc Mont had finally taught Cliff Cates, if not the ever-driving marine command, a lesson. From his "ditch," he sent a message to Lee at seven fifteen p.m. acknowledging what he had learned:

"[I]t is a needless sacrifice of men to try and take this nest. . . . It will take a good heavy barrage to get the guns out—at least eight in the nest."

The usually impetuous Williams, too, was thinking rationally, telling Lee in a message sent half an hour after Cates's that his battalion was taking heavy fire from the machine-gun position to its right front, and Germans carrying even more machine guns could be seen heading from St. Étienne toward his men.

He, too, asked for more artillery fire to be placed on the position.

Williams was ordered to hold his battalion in place. At midnight, the artillery finally became active—too active. Cates would report at midnight that the division's artillery was shelling the 23rd Regiment to his right: "They are dropping back and we are also."

At about the same time, Lee and Colonel E. R. Stone, commander of the 23rd Regiment's 2nd Battalion, agreed to attack the position the next morning together. George Shuler's 3rd Battalion and Stone's men would attack at six thirty a.m. on October 6 following a one-hour artillery preparation.

Lee, it seems, had finally learned that the rifle was not "still king."

The Americans quickly ran into fire coming from the largest machine-gun nest that Cliff Cates had ever seen, but after losing thirty percent of their men, both battalions reached their objective, a German trench line east of St. Étienne.

By then, the French 22nd Division was reporting it was on Shuler's left flank, and though it had not quite taken the village, the French and Americans were closer than ever to forcing its evacuation by the Germans.*

---

*In fact, the former German Lieutenant Colonel Ernst Otto would claim that the forces facing the Americans were so depleted by the afternoon of October 6 that had John Lejeune ordered an attack by the entire 2nd Division, St. Étienne would

Better news was on its way to the hard-pressed men of the 2nd Division: It was to be reinforced, and ultimately relieved, by the un-bloodied Texans and Oklahomans of the 36th Division, which had only arrived in France the previous July and August.

On the night of October 6–October 7, the 142nd Regiment began filtering in among the men of the 6th Regiment. "They came up and their troops moved right into the trenches with us," the 78th Company's James Sellers remembered. "Our battle-weary marines scared them to death with the gory tales of our experiences.*

"When the order came for the 36th to advance, their lieutenant colonel, a West Pointer, had a very difficult time trying to rout these inexperienced men out of their trenches and dugouts."

Most of the 2nd Division was to "stand fast" and hold its positions along with the regulars; the 1st and 3rd Battalions of the 6th Regiment would find themselves still in action until October 9.

That was not the case with a happy Cliff Cates. After being relieved by the 3rd Battalion on the morning of October 6, Cates and the 2nd Battalion were placed in reserve, and had pulled back to the hard-won positions of October 3.

This time, Cates had no problem with being left out of the action. "We had more than done our share and truly deserved to have a little rest," he would write.

That day, Cates sent out salvage details, which came back loaded with German blankets and other creature comforts to help ward off the cold of the French nights. Hot food arrived in large thermos cans, as did water.

---

have fallen. But, Otto would allow, such an undertaking would have been "costly" for the Americans; clearly, the depleted state of both brigades at that point precluded more wholesale sacrifice on the 2nd Division's part.

*The marines also helped relieve their burdens, talking the greenhorns out of as many shiny new trench knives, automatic rifles, and other equipment as they could carry off.

"Oh, how we did enjoy both," Cates would write.

At night, Cliff Cates descended into one of the majestic German dugouts, built a fire, and shaved and washed up as best he could.

"We had gone ten days without either and without having my equipment off," he wrote. "The night of the sixth, I went to sleep and put in the best sleep that I have ever had."

THE VALLEY OF DEATH

THERE WAS BUT a lone French grave, simple yet somehow beautiful, that caught Cliff Cates's eye that morning. He'd buried plenty of his own men, seen more dead men than he cared to think about over the past four months; but somehow this lonely mound that held the body of a French *poilu* churned his soul. It seemed somehow so incongruous to its surroundings, its rude and rugged cross, topped by a battered helmet, speaking at once of the beauty and sadness and sacrifice of war. This one French grave, forlorn and lost in a sea of destruction and desolation yet lovingly prepared, seemed a small and hopeful beacon for a world gone mad.

The sheer devastation surrounding the grave, encountered as Cates and his men plodded from Blanc Mont to the back lines on October 10, painted a picture Cates would never forget.

"As we marched back from the line, we had to cross over a stretch of ground that had been no man's land since the beginning of the war until this last scrap," he would write. "It had been nip and tuck; first one advancing a little and then the other, but neither side gained any ground to amount to anything.

"The ground is perfect white chalk dust. In the center is a big valley and the dutch [sic] lines had been on a high chalk hill on the north side while the French held a similar hill on the south side. In the valley there used to be a forest, but now the only thing remaining is a few stumps. The land is torn with shell holes; here and there, you can see a big shell that failed to explode (we call them duds). Some are as big as fourteen inch.

"What used to be trenches are now torn to pieces and caved. What used to be miles and miles of barb wire is torn up and all tangled up in one big mass. The big iron saw-horses covered with wire are all scattered and torn by shell fragments. Here and there in the boche lines, you can see what used to be a concrete pill box machine gun emplacement, but even they too had been destroyed by the terrific artillery fire of the French.

"Laying around in every trench and out on the field, you can see many dead boche that had been killed days before; some of them were literally torn to pieces. In one place, I saw a boche machine gunner dead with his gun chained to him—poor devil, I feel sorry for him. It was a ghastly sight to see the dead, but a man gets used to that over here."

And amid the carnage, amid the unburied, splayed, rotting bodies, that simple grave was a sign, perhaps, of civilization, or of man's better nature striving to return. Like an island cast onto this sea of impersonal violence, it was a sign that someone had cared that someone else had lived, and died.

Perhaps there was hope after all. . . .

That Cliff Cates noted the scene and was so affected by it was also a sign—a sign that, even for him, he who had been so lucky and taken to battle and leading men into combat with so much natural enthusiasm, this war and its wanton destruction and waste of human lives was perhaps becoming old.

He was optimistic, though, that it would end soon. "I believe the whole German army is disorganized and in a pitiful plight," he would write home on October 13, 1918. "It truly is a question of time until it is over. I expect peace within two weeks."

He had reason to be optimistic. Across the western front, the Germans were under pressure and exercising a slow retreat, employing well-planned extractions from previous strongholds, their hopes no longer focused on ultimate victory but on a future conditional surrender.

In fact, on October 5, Germany's ruler, Kaiser Wilhelm II, had issued an order that praised his forces on sea and land, and wrote that in "agreement with our Allies," he was offering terms of peace to "the enemy." However, he added: "But only to an honorable peace will we consent. This we owe to our dead heroes who have sacrificed their lives for us; this we owe to our children. Whether arms will rest is still undecided. Until then we must not cease in our efforts; we must, as heretofore, give all our efforts tirelessly to withstanding the onslaught of the enemy."

The Allied onslaught would continue, and for Cliff Cates, and for the men of the 96th Company, the sacrifice would continue as well. More names, more numbers, would be added to the rolls of the marines fallen, which, by the time the battle at Blanc Mont ended, would total 940 6th Regiment men dead or wounded—the equivalent of an entire battalion—and in the 4th Brigade overall, 292 men killed and 1,893 wounded.*

Cates certainly knew the numbers, and he saw the toll yet again in the decimated ranks of the 96th Company. Now it was someone else's turn to bleed, and Cates and his surviving men took three days to rest while the 71st Brigade of the 36th Division with French divisions on either flank attacked St. Étienne and the machine-gun-filled environs to east and west.

---

*The 2nd Division, as a whole, lost 41 officers and 665 enlisted men killed and 3,453 wounded while taking 1,963 German prisoners, 25 pieces of artillery, 332 machine guns, and other materiel. Division commander John Lejeune extolled the performances and sacrifices of his men thus: "To be able to say when this war is finished, 'I belonged to the 2nd Division, I fought with it at the Battle of Blanc Mont Ridge,' will be the highest honor that can come to any man."

The 1st and 3rd Battalions of the 6th Regiment had been pulled into the fray once more as well, and by October 10—when the 36th Division took over the 2nd Division's sector once and for all—St. Étienne and the ground north of it had been well cleared of Germans, who were now in full retreat toward a new line before the Aisne River, fifteen miles north.

A retreat to the fortified Hindenburg Line above the Meuse-Argonne region to the east was also under way, the second phase of the all-American attack proving costly but effective.

As Cates and his men trekked south across the devastated, lunar landscape around and below Somme-Py, headed for Navarin Farm several kilometers (a few miles) south, the American 1st Division was on the cusp of being relieved just shy of the Kriemehild Stellung, a "switch" of the Hindenburg Line that crossed high ground just north of the Romagne Hills.

There, none other than Douglas MacArthur and his brigade of the 42nd Division would in coming days relieve the 1st, carrying the fight to the well-fortified Côte de Châtillon and breaking through it in bitter fighting.

Just above there, none other than Cliff Cates would find himself carrying the fight even further as the war's momentum switched ever more into the Allies' hands.

But first, there would be a rest.

Hell, even God rested once in a while.

The survivors of the 6th Regiment marched back down the hill on October 10, many in a daze and wondering how they had made it through a German defense "composed of nothing but machine guns," as one 96th Company private and recent replacement, Everett Williams of Iowa City, Iowa, would write.

"When a fellow comes back from a front where so many of your pals were either wounded or bumped [off], it makes a fellow wonder, think and feel as though he has never felt."

They hadn't gotten far when they were stopped and, "to our great disappointment, made to give up all the beautiful Browning automatics, trench knives and other new supplies which our marines had liberated from the newly equipped 36th Division," James Sellers would complain.*

The regiment made Suippes and fell out. The usual resting and refitting ensued; Cates needed it, writing home that he had spent October 12 in bed with "influenza." It couldn't have been the same strain then ravaging the western front and the training camps in the United States—by the next day, he felt fine.

As usual, more replacements arrived—fifteen hundred to the marines alone—but not enough to bring the 96th Company to its prescribed size of two hundred fifty men. Whereas he had gone into action at Blanc Mont with a slightly oversized company, even with replacements the unit would be nowhere near as large.

"I now have a decent sized [sic] company again," Cates would write, "about 180 men. They are naturally green and inexperienced, but they will soon learn, as they will be mixed up with old men."

And how he loved the "old men," most of whom were only in their early twenties, if that.

"Mother," he would add, "you cannot imagine how proud I am of my men. They are sure one good bunch and will follow me thru everything. That is all I can ask."

---

*Sellers, out of action after being severely wounded at Belleau Wood on June 6, was perhaps not used to seeing marines performing their by-now routine heroics. Kelly and Pruitt received their Medals of Honor [Pruitt posthumously], but Sellers also managed to get Distinguished Service Crosses for eight more of his men; Sellers himself earned a Croix de Guerre and Silver Star. "I do not know who wrote the citation to back mine up," he would write, adding, "I did not mind. I thought I rated a little something since I had done my part." By comparison, only ten men in the 96th Company earned a DCS during the entire war, and just one—Fred Stockham—would eventually receive a Medal of Honor, although Thomas Holcomb would unsuccessfully nominate Cates for an MOH.

October 19 found the 6th Regiment camped five miles north of Châlons; on that same day, the French 4th Army, under whose control the 2nd Division still remained, asked for a brigade to relieve its 73rd Division, which was holding the line below the Aisne River.

Division commander John Lejeune offered his marines; they were closer to combat strength than the regulars of the 3rd Brigade, though he was reluctant to split his division. It was the same threatened circumstance that had led him to offer the division for the capture of Blanc Mont—but this time, with no choice, he went along. But he made sure that Pershing and the American command then overseeing the fighting in the Meuse-Argonne knew about the situation.

It didn't matter: Cliff Cates and the marine brigade once more hit the road. Midnight on October 20 found them marching through cold rain back to the Nantivet Barracks near Suippes, where they spent the night and then headed north the next day toward Leffincourt, northeast of their old objective of St. Étienne.

It was about twenty miles to Leffincourt, and Cates would call the trek "the hardest hike of my career. I will never forget it as long as I live. . . . We had not been out of the Champagne fight for over a week, and we were good and tired.

"I have been tired on some other hikes, but I was never as near gone as I was on this hike. Hour after hour, mile after mile, and still we marched on. Man after man fell out until there was only about one good platoon out of a company.

"Our feet ached and our limbs were dead, but still we kept on; became automatic."

Finally, after seventeen hours on the road, the brigade—or, once again, what remained of it—reached Leffincourt at ten p.m. The Germans greeted the marines with some desultory shelling; the chow wagons were far behind; all in all it was going to be another hell of a night.

What was bad became worse, however, when Bull Williams sent for the four company commanders in the 2nd Battalion and told them to reconnoiter the forward lines for the next day's relief of the French 73rd.

It meant pushing on another twelve kilometers—seven miles—and back again.

For Cates, at least, it was the last straw.

"I was ready to quit then," he would write. "I know that I could never have made that twenty-four kilos."

Lucky Cates: Just before he and his grumbling companions were about to set off, orders arrived, canceling the reconnaissance.

"Gee, but I was a happy man," he would write. "I then hit the hay and slept the best sleep ever."

As it turned out, there would be no reconnaissance, and no relief of the French for the marines. At eight forty-five p.m. on October 21, the French 4th Army notified Lejeune that the 36th Division, which had finally pushed the Germans out of and well beyond St. Étienne to the Aisne River, would extend its lines to cover the 73rd's front.

The marines would never really know what the fuss had been about, why they'd had to endure the forced march to nowhere. Cates could only guess.

"It seems as if the French had a bridge head on the river and they were having some difficulty taking it," he would write. "Gee, but we were sore. I think that someone put in a protest to G.H.Q., so they ordered us back."

On October 22, the marines were ordered to rejoin the 3rd Brigade, which, unfortunately for their tired feet and aching bones, had moved even farther away and was now on the march into the Argonne, encamped between Valmy and Ste. Menehould. Here, the 2nd Division was put back under the jurisdiction of the American 1st Army.

The marines remained in the area of Leffincourt until October 25, when they hiked back to Suippes, a cross-country hike over and through old trenches that only exhausted the men further. All of the movement, the 6th Regiment's history notes, "taxed the endurance of the troops to the utmost."

Twenty percent of the regiment was marching "with difficulty," mainly because of new English boots that had been issued following the Blanc Mont fight. Remarkably, it was the newly soled veterans, and not the replacements, who suffered more; their American-made footwear was superior.

Reaching Suippes, the marines found the dreaded *camions* once more waiting for them.

"We knew that there was trouble the minute we saw the trucks," Cates would write. "Any time that you get a ride is when they need you real badly; otherwise, you walk."

Trouble. Who you gonna call?

The 2nd Division, of course.

BEGINNING OF THE END

FROZEN. DRENCHED. SICK.

Sick of war now, sick of death; just sick.

The war was damned near over, but there was one more thing to do, one more river to cross, more men to be slaughtered; but there was no spring in the step now, and no novelty. The war was old, and Cliff Cates was sick of it.

Cliff Cates was just sick, period.

His men dropped one by one; they dropped in bunches. Not from German bullets or shells, but from disease, from the elements. And Cliff Cates was ready to drop as well.

The 4th Brigade on October 25 had hopped aboard the *camions* once more, and were trucked to Ste. Menehould on the western edge of the great Argonne Forest.

They encamped in the woods that night, and on the next day hiked thirty kilometers (eighteen miles) to the vicinity of Exermont, at the southern base of the Romagne Hills, which had been the scene of a costly fighting by the American 35th and 1st Divisions weeks before.

They were following in the footsteps of dead men, following in the footsteps of a great tragic play, following in the footsteps of the remnants of a German army that continued to lash out like a wounded and cornered animal that would not give in.

The 35th Division, former Missouri and Kansas national guardsmen, had jumped off on September 26, one of nine American divisions the American 1st Army sent howling north between the heights of the Meuse River on the east and the western edge of the Argonne on the west.

The goal of the huge, all-American offensive was generally the key cities of Sedan and Mézières, through which railways supplied the German effort on the far left of the western front. But the terrain was beyond formidable, consisting of rocky wooded ridges running east and west that provided a natural defense.

The Germans in addition had had four years to build pillboxes and artillery emplacements on the heights, which now formed a southern switch of the Hindenburg Line. Contesting them would be some two hundred thousand Americans, most of whom had seen little or no combat.

The 35th, which had been in reserve at St. Mihiel, had on its left the Aire River; two divisions, the 77th and the 28th, were on its left across the river, the 91st Division on its right.

The Midwesterners made good progress the first day, taking Varennes and Cheppy, and over the next few days they took Charpentry and by September 28 were on the northern edge of the Montrebeau Wood just below Exermont.

Though by now exhausted and its ranks depleted, the 35th was ordered personally by AEF commander General John Pershing to continue its advance on September 29. That morning, the remnants of three of the division's four regiments advanced without the cover of artillery, and Exermont was taken and some ground gained beyond.

But the Germans, inserting fresh troops, infiltrated the woods to the east and west, encircling the pitiful survivors clinging to the ground in full view of enemy machine guns and artillery.

As the encirclement continued even to the southern edge of the

Montrebeau Wood behind them, those who could broke and ran for the rear. Only a hastily gathered line of engineers and the 128th Machine Gun Battalion stood between the Germans and complete disaster—but the Germans, by now disorganized, remained in the woods.

The results of what would be called the First Phase of the Meuse-Argonne battle were similar all along the line. The Germans had expected a continuance of the Americans' St. Mihiel campaign toward Metz, and had just ten divisions in line on the morning of September 26.

However, once the Americans' plan of attack became known, the Germans rushed reinforcements from the area of Metz. These, plus the strong defenses on the Hindenburg Line, from which artillery and machine-gun fire caught the Americans in a cross fire, caused the attack of the 1st American Army to stall by September 29—as witnessed by the nearly destroyed 35th Division on the left.

The advance was paused; new divisions were ordered in. The 1st Division, well-blooded at Cantigny and Soissons, followed the trail of tears left by the 35th Division in its sector, and on October 4—even as the 2nd Division was attempting to take St. Étienne—began a fresh push below Exermont, the Wisconsin and Michigan men of the 32nd Division on its right.

The 1st overran Exermont and Hill 240 above it, but paused, too, after several days as it came under artillery fire from the heights on the western side of the Aire River, which the 28th Division had been unable to gain, and heavy fire spewing from the series of hills—272, 269, and 263—to its front.

In a bold step, two regiments from the untested 82nd Division were sent behind the 1st's lines and across the Aire River on October 7, with the intent of taking the heights from which the Americans were being pounded. At the same time, the 28th Division would again attempt its advance.

The next day, Corporal Alvin C. York of the 328th Regiment made his name, calmly killing 28 Germans and then taking prisoner another 132. With some of the pressure on the left eased, the 1st Division on October 9 moved at first light through a heavy fog toward the offending hills to its front.

By the end of that bloody day, the hills were taken, and the way was clear toward another portion of the Hindenburg Line that lay strung across the Côte de Châtillon just south of Landres-et-St. Georges.

On October 10, an attempt was made against that line, an attack spilling from the north edge of the Bois de Romagne and across open ground. It was quickly brought low by German machine-gun fire.

The 1st had done its job, though. Now it was time for someone else to step in and continue the hard and soul-numbing slog against the German defenses.

Another veteran division, the 42nd, moved up and through Exermont and on October 12 relieved the 1st. On October 14, the 83rd Brigade and the 84th Brigade, under the command of General Douglas MacArthur, began an arduous three-day effort to take the Côte de Châtillon on the right of the division boundary, with the villages of St. Georges and Landres-et-St. Georges on the left.

MacArthur's men managed to take the southern base of the hill on October 14, though the casualties were horrific. The 83rd, attacking across open ground, was stymied by heavy resistance coming from the villages and the Côte de Châtillon on the right. There was one bright spot to an otherwise bleak and costly day: The 32nd Division, attacking on the right of the 42nd, took the Côte Dame Marie, another key part of the German defenses.

The 42nd's attack was resumed the next day; again, the 84th made some progress against the hill, but on the left, the 83rd Brigade was held up by wire, and German machine-gun and artillery fire once again made short work of the attackers.

That evening, a furious General Charles P. Summerall, commander of the V Corps, relieved 83rd Brigade commander General Michael

Lenihan and some junior officers. He also called MacArthur, and told him, "Give me Châtillon, MacArthur, or a list of five thousand casualties."

The flamboyant MacArthur didn't miss a beat in reply. "All right, General," he told Summerall. "We'll take it, or my name will head the list."

That night, MacArthur personally led a patrol to investigate a gap in the German wire that had been reported by an aviator. After indeed finding the hole, they devised a plan to take the Côte de Châtillon.

Following a barrage of artillery and machine-gun fire, battalion commander Major Ravee Norris and one hundred men would storm the gap and take a position on the German left flank. When the general advance began on the southern face of the hill, they would pour fire into the Germans.

It worked; by afternoon, the hill was in American hands.

But that was as far as the 42nd Division would get; the villages of Georges and Landres-et-St. Georges remained in German hands, and the Rainbow Division of Iowans, Alabamans, Ohioans, New Yorkers, and men from twenty-two other states were in no shape to continue the advance.

Nor were those of the other American divisions, which had punctured the Hindenburg Line in several places, but at great cost. Another pause was ordered; once more, fresh, or so-called fresh, divisions would take up the third and final phase of the push, this one having the grand ambition of rolling north and east all the way to the Meuse River.

Who you gonna call?

Cliff Cates had only just come out of Blanc Mont when the second phase of the Meuse-Argonne fight was winding down. He'd marched, marched, and marched some more in the intervening days—one hundred kilometers (sixty-two miles), he guessed—and now here he was on

October 26 crossing the dead-strewn Montrebeau Wood, kicking and picking his way another thirty kilometers (eighteen miles) through mud and corpses and abandoned materiel and toward the village of Exermont, above which rose the hills taken three weeks before by the 1st Division.

By October 30, the marines and regulars of the 2nd Division were approaching Exermont, and they began preparing to relieve the 42nd. On October 31, with the relief accomplished and men situated in the vicinity of the hard-won Côte de Châtillon, hand grenades, ammunition, and other equipment were disbursed among the men, and the plans of an attack to begin the next day were reviewed.

"It was a wonderful planned attack," Cates would write. Best of all, "we had wonderful artillery support. The batteries were jammed in hub to hub. I have never seen as much as we had."

After dark, Cates and the 96th Company moved into their jumping-off place in a small ravine and he told his men to dig in, "as I knew that when we opened up with our barrage, that old heinie would come back heavy."

Private Robert Rhodes, his trusty orderly, spread some blankets on the ground, and Cates and he "hit the dirt to try and get a little sleep before we jumped off." An hour later, Cates's slumber was ruined by a "continuous roar" of the 2nd Division's artillery and machine guns pouring it onto the German lines.

It was three thirty a.m. on November 1, 1918.

The third phase of the Meuse-Argonne offensive had begun.

In exactly two hours, Cliff Cates would take his men over the top yet again.

But this would not be Bouresches, or Soissons, or Blanc Mont. It would not be a cakewalk, either, but over the next ten days the 2nd Division would pursue more than truly attack, as the Germans would put up only a token resistance, throwing a right jab here and a weak left there like a woozy prizefighter just about to go down for the count.

The 2nd, with the 89th Division on its right, comprised the new V Corps, and would carry roughly the same line of the fight as did the 35th, 1st, and 42nd Divisions before it. The division, though, would face a tougher task than its neighbor: While the 89th would jump off beyond the Hindenburg Line, the 2nd would have to crack through it on its front.

Lejeune would write that on a visit to 1st Army headquarters, General Hugh Drum, 1st Army commander Lieutenant General Hunter Liggett's Chief of Staff, told him that the 2nd Division "had been assigned the post of honor and the whole army relied on it to bring the stalemate to an end by breaking through the center of the German army and thereby forcing it to retreat to the east bank of the Meuse."

General Charles Summerall, V Corps commander, the same who was quite willing to sacrifice Douglas MacArthur on the slopes of the Côte de Châtillon, took a special interest in the marines. Prior to their attack afternoon, he called the men of the 6th Regiment's 2nd Battalion together, slapped a map on the side of a barn, and explained the importance of the marine mission.

"He showed us marines where we were going to attack and explained exactly what the purpose of the offensive was," the 78th Company's James Sellers would write.

"He said that if we captured our objective, we would cut off the whole German army between there and the coast, and that ours was a place of honor in the impending American drive since we had already qualified as the 'shock troops' of the American army.

"Then," Sellers would add bitterly, "he spoiled it all by saying that if we did not do our jobs well, heads would roll. We considered that an insult to our outfit!"

The first day's objectives were ambitious, and would involve seizing three east-west ridges that ran across the division's front. Lejeune had assured Summerall that his men could make six miles on the first day, at the end of which they would puncture the Freya Line, a last, fortified switch of the Hindenburg Line that traced over the wooded slopes of Barricourt Ridge.

The 6th Marines, with the 1st Battalion in the lead, the 3rd behind it, and the 2nd Battalion in support, would advance in waves one thousand yards apart. On their right were the 5th Marines, and on the 4th Brigade's right was the 23rd Regiment, nudged into the line with the aim of clearing the Bois de Hazois, which was initially in the 89th's sector.

Some three hundred light and heavy artillery pieces, parked hub to hub as Cates had noted, would lay a barrage for two hours, giving the division an unprecedented amount of firepower.

As well, the artillery would lead the advance, laying barrages at the easy rate of one hundred yards every four minutes on "favorable" ground, and one hundred yards every eight minutes as it passed through more difficult terrain.

In previous attacks on the front, the Germans had taken note of where the preparation fire was landing, and pushed machine gunners forward where the fire couldn't touch them.

However, on this day, as soon as the preparation fire began, the forward American troops were withdrawn five hundred yards, and the nearest limit of the barrage would fall on a line two hundred yards short of the American forward line to pulverize the machine gunners who might have infiltrated. To further aid the advance, fifteen tanks and a squadron and a half of airplanes would join the battle.

As Cates and his men huddled just ahead of the row of artillery—too close for comfort, Cates would write—the Germans went to work with their counterbatteries. Shells began coming in among them, and Robert Rhodes, Cates's orderly, was hit.

"I made one long leap for the trench, as I heard some more shells coming," Cates wrote. "Rhodes came hot footing it in right behind me yelling, 'They have got me.'"

A piece of shrapnel had entered Rhodes's thigh; it was "not a fatal wound, but real serious," Cates wrote. Cates bandaged Rhodes and rolled him up in the blankets. He stayed with Rhodes until five fifty a.m., when the dreaded whistles blew, the barrage leaped forward, and Cliff Cates once more led the 96th Company over the top.

Rhodes, he would write, "sure did hate to see me go off and leave him."

TO THE RIVER

THIRTEEN AND A half hours. He has thirteen and a half hours, just thirteen and a half goddamned hours until this is over. Thirteen and a half hours is half a day is just eight percent of a week is nothing more than a really nice night's sleep is really hardly any time at all; and yet with just thirteen and a half hours left in a four-year war in which millions have died, they want to stick men on wobbly, rocking bridges and send them across a river in the face of arrayed German artillery, German machine guns, and German snipers.

Just thirteen and a half hours. Can Lucky Cliff Cates live thirteen and half more hours?

Rumors of an armistice are on everyone's lips. Rumors that the war might end, rumors of peace, life-giving rumors that give men hope, too much hope, that they might outlive this war.

But orders are orders, and on this day, November 10, 1918, orders have come from on high that the marines must cross the Meuse River, and to hell with the rumors.

"Get into action and get across," their corps commander, Charles Summerall, has told them. "I don't expect to see any of you again, but that doesn't matter. You have the honor of a definitive success—give yourself to that."

And so it has come to this: thirteen hours.

He really doesn't want to cross that river.

Cliff Cates, in fact, is a mess. Nine days before, as he jumped off with his men, he was right as rain. By November 10, he's barely able to stand, and has watched as his men have fallen away day by day—not from bullets, nor shells, but flu, grippe, the creeping crud, or whatever else you might want to call it.

The advance went beautifully from the start on November 1. The day was cloudy, foggy, cold; but the air was wonderfully alive with shells, American, and their good work had indeed mostly removed the obstacle of German machine guns in the 2nd Division's immediate front.

The country was open, rolling, pocked by small woods and crinkled with gradual rises. Good country for tanks; good country for advancing artillery.

Where the 83rd Brigade of the 42nd Division had faltered on the left in front of Georges and Landres-et-St. Georges, the marines worked their way past the villages after facing little opposition, while the 23rd Regiment on the right made quick work of the Bois de Hazois.

In a blink, Americans were pinching in on Landreville, two miles north of the jump-off. The German opposition was mostly halfhearted, spiritless, resigned; the artillery, following on the heels of the advance, kept the enemy off-balance and moving, always moving, toward the Meuse, some thirteen miles to the north.

"Our barrage was so heavy that the boche could not put up much of a fight," Cates would write. "At first, he put up a lot of artillery on us, but luckily, it was hitting in soft dirt, and it did not do much damage."

After advancing one mile, the 1st Battalion paused at an eminence known as Hill 253, and the 3rd passed through and continued in the lead.

At three p.m., the 3rd Battalion reached its objective, and Bull

Williams's 2nd Battalion took the lead. The creeping barrage continued to roust the opposing Germans as Cates and his company trudged over the open ground.

"We had about four kilometers to go to make it a good day's work," Cates wrote. "By this time, old heinie was beating it out as fast as he could get out, so we did not strike any opposition, and we could have gone much faster, but we had to stay behind our barrage."

The barrage, as it had been at Blanc Mont, was a godsend. "Our barrage caught lots of them and left them dead and wounded on the field," Cates wrote. "All along the road were dead horses, men, big guns and a lot of other junk that they had to desert in their hasty retreat."

As well, the tanks proved more effective than in any previous drive, reducing machine-gun nests and other emplacements and limiting casualties to almost unheard-of levels, at least for the marines.

There were some hiccups. On the far left, James Sellers led the 78th Company out of its zone and away from what was supposed to be a northeastward advance. He eventually came to a drop-off in the terrain, and encountered "a town which was not supposed to be there."

He passed the word back to the trailing Bull Williams, and the men shifted to the right "where we were supposed to be." But before the battalion could fully execute the movement, tragedy struck the 80th Company.

Its new captain, Kirt Green, had been one of those many captains briefly assigned to the 96th Company in September, but took over the 80th Company after its captain, Walter Powers, was accused of cowardice at Blanc Mont and relieved of command.

Green's surname, unfortunately, mirrored his experience with modern combat. While there was some milling about as the course of advance was corrected, Green called his platoon leaders to a meeting in a shell hole to discuss how to handle a German .37 mm that was harassing his company.

Though the officers wore no insignia denoting their ranks, the observant Germans couldn't help but note the importance of the pow-wow. As Green and his lieutenants discussed sending a platoon around to take the piece from the rear, the German gun fired once more, and "wiped out all the officers of the 80th Company," Sellers would write.

"They laid in and around his shell hole when a direct hit, probably from that same cannon, hit their shell hole," the company's Sergeant Don Paradis would write.

"Men near them said that Captain Green's helmet went fifty feet in the air. He was killed instantly." Also severely wounded was Lieutenant John G. Schneider, Jr., a graduate of the Culver Military Academy. He would die on November 3.

Nor had the blast spared enlisted men; two of Green's runners would be buried with him in a battlefield grave.

Dead officers or no, the advance continued on, as the battalion now followed the blessed barrage up and over the Freya position on Barricourt Ridge. At three fifteen p.m., Bull Williams was able to send a message saying the day's third and last objective had been taken, and that contact had been made with the 5th Marines on the right and a special party of marines whose job it was to maintain liaison with the 80th Division on the left.

They were now in the southern edge of the thick, deep Bois de la Folie, having advanced an astounding five miles. Cates had his men form a defensive line and dig in, and established outposts farther ahead in the wood. He expected the Germans to launch a counterattack at any moment, but none came.

Compared to any other battle—and there had been plenty to which to compare November 1—the day had gone swimmingly. The 96th Company, by Cates's count, had had only about a dozen men wounded, and none killed.

As rain pelted his men and an ominous fog enveloped their positions, he wondered if his luck could hold.

The next morning, Bull Williams pushed the 79th and 96th Companies to the northern edge of the Bois de la Folie. The 79th, on the right, made decent progress, but Cates's men were held up by severe fire coming from Masmes Farm on the left. Across the line, the advance was held up while Summerall and his staff decided what to do.

After dickering with the idea of sending the 3rd Brigade to attack Buzancy, on the left and in the zone of the 80th Division, which was just short of the village, a bolder plan was adopted: The line would be pushed north by a night march by the 3rd Brigade right along the Bayonville–Fosse road and through the dark, heavy woods of the Bois de la Folie.

Early on the morning of November 3, the 2nd Battalion of the 23rd Regiment, marching in column, appeared out of the darkness, startling Williams.

"They halted when they came to our line, so Bull Williams went over, and Bull asked what was going on," James Sellers remembered. "Their regimental commander said, 'I have orders to advance in a column of squads. What about it?'"

Williams looked at the major, and told him, "Well it's as good a way to commit suicide as any I know of."

But the major had his orders. "Risk there was, of course," the 2nd Division's history would report, "but the bold course seemed the safer."

The 23rd Regiment proceeded northeast on the road to Fosse, the 9th Regiment to the northwest along the road to Nouart. The 4th Brigade, now in reserve, followed one kilometer (just over half a mile) behind.

"From then on," Cates would write, "it was a case of fighting the weather and not heinie. It had been raining for about twelve hours, and it was beginning to get cold. The men that did bring blankets soon had them soaking wet."

During the advance of November 3, "one of the strangest moments of our months in France" occurred, James Sellers would write. "A Y.M.C.A. man, riding in a motorcycle sidecar, travelled up a road looking for a suitable site for his headquarters. . . . He found a house which he thought would be a good place to set up shop."

The Y.M.C.A. man went inside—and found himself in the midst of a German regiment's headquarters group. Luckily, they were all out of fight.

"They all surrendered to him!" Sellers wrote.

By noon, the 3rd Brigade had passed through Fosse and Nouart and was perched at the southern edge of the Bois Belval, two miles north of the Bois de la Folie.

From the front line to the rear, all smelled that the end was near. The Germans, too, had finally recognized the hopelessness of trying to hold below the Meuse, and the German army's Imperial Headquarters at eight thirty p.m. ordered the defenders to cross "at once" to the north bank of the Meuse, employing a curiously named movement it called "War March."

The Americans, meanwhile, kept coming.

The regulars were ordered forward, their objective the northern edge of the Bois du Port Gerache just below the heights on which the village of Beaumont sat, less than one mile from the Meuse.

The artillery was brought up. At two thirty p.m., it began laying barrages on the north end of the Bois de Belval, then swept back, tearing up the woods on either side of the Belval–Beaumont road.

At four thirty p.m., the 9th Regiment began the march. The 2nd Battalion of the 5th Regiment fell in behind, trailed by the 23rd Regiment following in support. A small cadre of German-speaking soldiers led the way, with the purpose of convincing any Germans encountered to surrender.

There was some resistance, quickly quelled by holding the column in place on the road while others worked around the flanks. By eleven thirty p.m., the head of the leading regiments spilled out onto the plains north of La Tuilerie Farm. The thoughts of most—Americans *and* Germans—now turned to crossing the Meuse.

Not so much the thoughts of Cliff Cates.

He, like many of the 2nd Division's men, was miserable. The weather—the cold, the incessant, frigid rain—was taking its toll on the ranks, even as the division was poised to cross the Meuse and end this thing.

"We were soon soaking wet and it was impossible to get dry," he would complain afterward. "It was go, go, go and everyone was freezing. They could not get food up to us, much less dry clothing."

"The nights were very cold, and continuous rains made the ground like a saturated sponge," the anonymous authors of the 78th Company's history would write. "It was useless to 'dig in,' for the slightest depression made in the ground would immediately fill with water.

"We had no shelter, and when we would lie down, our blankets would soak up water like a burning wick drawing oil. . . . A number of Seventy-Eighth Company [men] were evacuated with wounds, but a great many more were sent to hospitals on account of sickness, due to exposure."

All across the front, the Americans were reaching the proximity of the Meuse. The Germans, meanwhile, continued shelling the Bois de Belval and other areas of concentration from across the river as crossing spots were reconnoitered.

Cates and the 2nd Battalion remained in support of the 5th Regiment in the Bois de Belval, enduring the cold and rain while the 5th's marines sought a safe place to cross below Mouzon. On November 5, Beaumont was taken by the 23rd Regiment, and that night the German 236th Division facing them retreated across the river.

On November 7, the 6th Marines left the Bois de Belval and moved toward Beaumont, camping below it in the Bois de Four. On the same day, a German delegation left Berlin with the intent of forging an armistice—and "all front line troops were directed to be on the watch for their approach," according to the 2nd Division's history.

On November 9, the 6th Marines' 2nd Battalion hit the road once more, passing west of Beaumont and marching two miles due north to the southwest corner of the Bois du Fond du Limon, just one mile southwest of the Meuse River village of Villemontry.

Already, engineers were building bridges. And already, the 4th Brigade had been ordered to cross the river at Mouzon and Letanne, four air miles to the south, that night.

This they were ordered to do even though peace was in the air.

As were plenty of German shells.

ELEVENTH DAY

SLIPPING AND SLIDING and cursing and hating, the marines passed the bodies of the dead engineers at the river's edge and hit the bridges at the first sad light of dawn, splashing through ankle-deep and frigid water as the flimsy, rickety contraptions disappeared below their feet.

Then dark geysers of water erupted left and right; blinking flashes of light across the river sent lines of machine-gun bullets through the fog, careering off wood and bodies—helpless bodies, dead bodies, bodies floundering and panicking and succumbing under the black, fluid current.

"You watched men die ahead of you," one of these marines, Elton Mackin, would write. "The second man ahead met the bullets as he stepped across a length of the raft, sank to his knees, twisting, and slid face first into the river, vanishing quietly. He left an empty place against the fog."

Rickety affairs, those so-called bridges were, nothing more than a few planks strung across pontoons and floated to this hell, this watery kill zone, this ridiculous place below Villemontry and just outside a patch of woods called the Bois de l'Hospice.

It was nine thirty p.m., November 10, 1918.

Only thirteen and a half hours to go.

So close now they could taste it, but for many it would be their last sensation before the thud of a machine-gun bullet cut short all hopes, all dreams.

Poor marines.

Poor 5th Regiment.

Lucky Cliff Cates.

He was set to cross, and hell, he surely would have tried had he finally been ordered to. But for once the luck of Cliff Cates shone on what was left of the 6th Marines.

"I was very glad not to cross the river, I can tell you that," Cates would admit years later.

By midnight on November 10, Cates had just fifty men still with him out of the more than two hundred who'd jumped off almost ten days before.

"All of my lieutenants had been evacuated with grip [grippe (influenza)]," he would write. "Only twenty-eight men had been wounded and only one killed, and the rest had been evacuated with grip."

It was the same across the 6th Regiment, in which sickness was so rampant over the course of the advance to the Meuse that its fighting strength had been reduced by two-thirds; by November 11, it was the size of just a battalion.

Bull Williams, who had but three hundred men under him by now, was also a victim, and had evacuated himself as a sick case after the 2nd Battalion had reached the Bois du Fond du Limon on November 9.

He was replaced two days short of the last day of the war by Major Clyde Metcalf, who would become a primary historian of the Corps postwar.

It was Metcalf who would have to relay the bad news that had come out of a November 9 conference between V Corps commander Charles Summerall and his staff and divisional commanders—a meeting in which John Lejeune had tried to forestall the hard-charging Summerall from needlessly sacrificing his troops.

Summerall had already called for the 4th Brigade to make crossings that day, but the bridges needed had been sent to the 89th Division. Lejeune asked for, and got, a delay to November 10—but at the meeting with Summerall, he asked that the movements be postponed once more.

His argument: The 90th Division was already across the Meuse to the south, so why not wait until it could drive north along the east bank and clear the guns that would oppose the 89th and 2nd Divisions' crossings? The 89th, once across, could follow suit and move north to cover the 2nd's crossing, and the 2nd Division could then clear the crossings for the 77th Division to the north.

Summerall told Lejeune he'd think about it . . . which took all of twenty minutes.

The crossing of the Meuse by the 4th Brigade, Lejeune learned when he returned to his headquarters, would take place on the night of November 10–11.

Two battalions of the 5th Regiment, plus one from the 89th Division, would cross just above Letanne. The 6th Regiment and the 3rd Battalion of the 5th would cross farther north, just above Mouzon. The 6th's 3rd Battalion would lead, while the 2nd would follow.

The attempts by both regiments were to be made at nine thirty p.m., following a two-hour artillery preparation. Once across, the marines were to follow a barrage and quickly seize the machine guns and artillery infesting the heights that towered more than three hundred meters (nearly a thousand feet) above the river.

The crossing would be fiercely contested, no matter what was happening with the peace talks. The Germans "were on their last line," the 2nd Division's history says. "It was unfortified, and depended entirely upon the obstacle of the Meuse. They were down, also, about to their last man."

But it doesn't take too many men to man a machine gun, and the artillery on the far bank remained active, probing the expected crossing sites and harassing the engineers who were attempting the herculean task of emplacing the hastily crafted footbridges across the river.

The Germans had more than a thousand men left to contest the crossing, and thirty-six machine guns. They knew they were through, but had enough fight in them to make crossing the Meuse a daunting, and deadly, task.

As George Clark wrote, "They were a tough bunch and would remain so."

They also had the cover of the wooded and bramble-strewn east bank, while each marine would have only a little artillery cover and the man ahead to offer protection.

Like condemned criminals, the men of the 6th Regiment were served a last, hot meal during the day on November 10. The companies' rolling kitchens arrived at their sodden, miserable encampment in the Bois du Fond de Limon with buckets of steaming coffee, steak, potatoes, and fresh bread.

"The boys hadn't seen a galley for a week," the 78th Company's Sergeant Melvin Krulewitch would write. Some thought the feast marked the end of their ordeal.

"Then the rumors started up again about an armistice, adding to the sense of well-being induced by the food, and the wet night was forgotten. The sun even started to come out, its sickly rays piercing the haze."

Soon enough, reality struck. The marines were told to grab grenades and bandoliers of ammunition and stand by.

"For veterans of months of fighting," Krulewitch wrote, "the routine was familiar—hot chow, then extra ammunition and hand grenades. This was another attack. No armistice for us."

At dark, the 6th hit the road, having three miles to go to make the crossing above Mouzon. But they would be late to the crossing, having to take a detour in order to remain out of the Germans' line of sight.

At ten fifteen p.m., they reached a railway embankment that followed the west side of the Meuse, and waited while the engineers struggled to place two footbridges in place across the river.

Major George Shuler, 3rd Battalion commander, whose men would lead the way across the river, met with an engineer, who told him that only one bridge was ready. The engineer suggested that the span be quickly thrown across the river and the crossing forced.

But Shuler demurred. German artillery was already playing near the crossing, the Germans by the light of flares having seen the bridge being brought to the water's edge. Shuler wanted to wait until a second span was ready; moving along one single bridge would be suicidal.

Meanwhile, the men whose job it would be to commit suicide waited and grumbled in the dark. The 80th Company's Private Thomas McQuain would write that for "the majority of the men," all of whom were aware of the impending armistice, the task seemed beyond insane.

"We had begun to believe the Armistice rumors by now," he would write. "We could not see the advantage of trying to cross the Meuse tonight. Why not wait and see what happened to the Armistice the next day, and then attack, if necessary?"

But, as usual, "we were to find that we were not getting paid for thinking," McQuain would add wryly.

Division commander John Lejeune continued to have the same thoughts. But all he could do now was fret for his men.

"The night of this last battle of the war was the most trying night I have ever experienced," he would write. "The knowledge that in all probability the Armistice was about to be signed caused the mental anguish."

He had hoped vainly that the armistice could be signed before the crossings were attempted, "but it was not to be, and many a brave man made the supreme sacrifice for his country in the last hours of the war."

But few, if any, from the 6th Regiment would make that last-minute supreme sacrifice; the work on the second bridge went at a glacial pace as the engineers struggled with the strong current and incessant machine-gun and artillery fire to tie the bridge sections together and reach the far bank.

Some would claim the work was ultimately successful, and that a crossing was made or at least attempted. Others say not one marine from the 6th got his feet wet during that long night.

The latter scenario seems to be accurate.

Bull Williams, who was not on the scene, would write that the Germans "destroyed the footbridge upon which we were to effect a crossing," and it could not be repaired.

The 78th Company's James Sellers also wrote that by the time his battalion made it to the crossing, "the bridge had been blown up." However, he notes, he was also not there, having been evacuated the morning of November 10 with "the bowel trouble that was prevalent in the Division."

Others, however, claim the 6th attempted a crossing at some point. Krulewitch would claim the first bridge was swept away by the current and artillery fire, but claimed some of the regiment's marines reached the east bank and fought off a "desperate counterattack."

The 2nd Division's history says simply, "The Mouzon crossing failed," adding that because of heavy machine-gun and artillery fire, "all efforts were fruitless."

As author Peter F. Owen has written, it seems most likely that the battalion commanders involved—with their hearts not in the operation, daylight approaching, and all fully aware that an armistice was even then being negotiated—decided on their own to forgo any attempt and spare their men.

The regiment's history says almost as much, albeit in read-between-the-lines fashion: "Major George K. Shuler, of the 3rd Battalion, after a conference with the other battalion commanders, detailed forty men to help the engineers. . . .

"Battalion commanders waited until 4:00 a.m. of November 11th and as the second bridge was not ready at that time[,] the troops were marched back to the Bois du Fond de Limon as the day was breaking and there was no suitable cover for the troops in the vicinity of the bridge."

The truth is, nobody in the 6th Marines really wanted to try to cross that goddamned river that night. And who could blame them?

The marines had gone forward into bloody combat at Belleau Wood, Soissons, St. Mihiel, and Blanc Mont, and now the Argonne, and, as Cates would write, they had endured "a living hell" of endless moving while hungry, sick, tired, and soaked through the past eleven days.

As the 97th Company's Havelock Nelson would write, "Crossing in darkness would have been bad enough . . . but sending us over in daylight would have been nothing but murder."

Shuler knew as much, too, but still offered to fall on his sword over the failed crossing if anyone wanted him to. According to rumor, Schuler went to Colonel Harry Lee, set his major's insignia on his desk, and offered to resign or face "whatever charges the Colonel might prefer against him" for not being able to cross the river, Nelson wrote.

Smiling, Lee handed Schuler back his major's leaves.

"Forget it," Lee told him. "The war is almost over!"

Let it go. . . . At four a.m., the men of the 6th Regiment turned about-face and fairly floated on air toward their camp.

Eleventh day . . . eleventh month . . . Could they make it to the eleventh hour?

"You will never realize what those boys went thru in that two weeks," Cates would write. "We had gone thru the worst fight of our lives. It was not the fighting, but it was the cold, rainy, muddy weather.

"It rained every day and was bitter cold. We were drenched to the skin and our blankets were soaked. . . . We went for hours without food. No shelter of any kind and we couldn't have fires at night. . . . God only knows how we existed."

God only knows how Lucky Cliff Cates had managed to make it this far. Bouresches . . . Belleau Wood . . . Soissons . . . St. Mihiel . . . Blanc Mont . . . now the Argonne.

Between April and November 11, the 96th Company suffered more casualties than any other company in the AEF. More than 600 members of the company had fallen, 131 of them to never rise again—a casualty rate of 250 percent.

Of the 250 men that trained at Quantico, 52 had been killed, and another 188 wounded—50 of those more than once.

Only a handful came through somehow unscathed . . . among them, Lucky Cates.

Now, offered a final reprieve, he could only revel in the delicious feeling of simply breathing, and begin to think about living once more. He began to believe he might make it through this war after all.

His marine brethren in the 5th Regiment, however, would have no such comfort.

"They lied to us that night," Elton Mackin, of the 67th Company, would write bitterly. "It was a patent, flimsy lie."

Told to carry ammunition to the 89th Division on the right, Mackin and the men of the 1st Battalion, 5th Regiment, soon saw the dark waters of the Meuse nearing.

German shells greeted them as they got their first look at the barely floating death traps they were to cross. Some turned and ran; a guide meant to lead them to the crossing turned and ran and was stopped by the regimental adjutant, pistol-whipped, and ordered at gunpoint to lead the battalion to the river.

When the adjutant stumbled, the guide took off, the major shooting at him through the dark.

The marines continued on.

Knees knocking, they carefully stepped onto the slick planks of the bridge, and sank to their ankles as the span swayed and bobbed. Bullets "ripped a seam along the water, then swung back," Mackin wrote. "They changed their tone abruptly to the *sock, sock, sock* sound bullets make when they hit flesh.

"The night belonged to bitter men who didn't seem to care, who long before had known there was no hope. Because of that, they thought they had conquered fear."

One hundred men of the 1st Battalion of the 5th made it across, followed by what remained of the 2nd Battalion and, at four a.m., a battalion of the 89th Division.

Some 435 men did not make it that night, having been killed, wounded, or drowned.

The 1st Battalion organized itself into one company, and the marines began clearing the heights above them. As they did, the bridge on which they had crossed at such peril heaved a sigh and was gone, carried away by the current.

They were alone now, and trapped in enemy territory.

"So many died that night, short hours away from the Armistice," Mackin wrote. "They had held on to hope in spite of everything."

More in the 5th Regiment died that morning as the paltry remainders of the 1st and 2nd Battalions worked the riverfront and slopes. Shortly before eleven a.m., a breathless runner raced up and told the marines to stop where they were.

"Armistice—at eleven o'clock," he said. "Just wait for orders here."

The 6th Regiment, too, was alerted of the pending armistice. After gathering what remained of the men together, an officer tersely read the news to them.

Men stood in wonder as the continuous shelling quietly ebbed and grew sporadic across the front. The chatter of machine guns was replaced with the sounds of birds singing and the whooshing of the Meuse River.

"It must be a terrible hoax," Nelson would write. "We spoke to each other in awed tones, as though fearing that fully releasing our repressed feelings of thankfulness and joy would bring down upon us once more the full fury of the war-gods' wrath."

The sudden quiet, when it came, was shocking . . . even ominous.

"It was the eleventh hour of the eleventh day of the eleventh month that the last boche shell came whistling into our lines and exploded with a terrific crash," Cliff Cates would write. "Luckily, it did not get anyone.

"Then there was a death like stillness along the whole front. Could it be that it was all over? We could not believe it possible. Each man would look at the others in doubt. Finally, word came that the armistice had been signed.

"Not a cheer did I hear, but there was not a man in the regiment that did not thank God that rainy, muddy, cold morning that it was all over and that he was safe."

"O, boy! Maybe you think there wasn't some happy and scared boys. We were scared that we would be bumped off before 11 o'clock," Second Lieutenant Harold D. Powell, formerly a corporal with the 96th Company and now with the 80th Company, would write.

"If I live to be a thousand years old[,] I'll never forget the 11th hour, 11th day, the 11th month of 1918. All that morning there was a constant roar of artillery, each side trying to get the last shot. The Germans were shooting into a field where no one had been for a week, but one of my boys was killed at 2 minutes before 11."

Cliff Cates was as dazed and unbelieving as the others—and just as sick, cold, wet, tired, just plain miserable, and . . . alive. *The war is over.* He repeated the words to himself over and over, like a mantra.

"It didn't seem possible that it was all over, and could stop so suddenly," he would write home on November 27. "Although there was no outburst of joy at the good news, there was that feeling way down in every heart of thankfulness; and only a man that has been thru such hell, as we have had for the last two months, can realize how happy we all were."

He was certainly such a man, though his own hell had extended back five months.

Lucky Cates.

Lucky, lucky, lucky Cliff Cates.

PRETTY WELL SHOT

ON BOTH SIDES of the Meuse, in and on which hundreds had perished just hours before, gray plumes arose from a thousand smoky campfires.

On both sides of the Meuse, men in sodden, filthy uniforms stood, their hands hovering over the choking yellow flames, drying skin and clothing and trying to understand what had suddenly happened.

On both sides of the Meuse, flares soared into the air in celebration, automatic weapons were fired into the colorless sky, and tired men sick of war finally found the strength to laugh, if quietly.

More than thirteen hundred marines had not made it this far; more than eight thousand had been wounded to various degrees, perhaps a few to return by November 11. Only a very few had made it all the way through.

Cliff Cates would take a count of the "old men" of the 96th Company who had trained at Quantico and were still with him, and find only twenty-one—"and they are men who have returned from the hospital lately."

He would note that he was the "only old officer and the only company commander to come out in command.

"A list of officers that have been in this company that have been killed or wounded: Capt. Duncan, Capt. Greene, Lieut. Kilduff, Lieut.

Brailsford, Lieut. Johnson and Lieut. Capps were killed; Lieut. Robinson (2), Lieut. Bowling (2), Lieut. Lockhart, Lieut. Page, Lieut. Duane, Lieut. Fritz, Lieut. Taylor, Capt. Woodsworth [sic], Capt. Minnis, Lieut. Kane., Lieut. Strand, Lieut. Grayson and Lieut. Barnett were wounded, and I have been wounded twice."

So much time had passed, so many fights endured, that he couldn't even correctly remember James Robertson's last name. After so much, faces blurred and names faded as he warmed himself by a fire on the evening of November 11.

"It was a beautiful sight, I can tell you that," he would write.

War was done, for the moment. A new push—that of enforcing the terms of the armistice and guarding the peace—would now begin.

Once more, Cliff Cates and his men saddled up and on November 18 began a long march—this one 150 miles toward Coblenz on the Rhine River, where the 2nd Division would be one of what would eventually be nine American divisions to maintain a presence until a final treaty was hammered out and signed.

"It was a bum bunch of soldiers that started out that morning," he would write. "We were just naturally played out, but we hadn't gone but a few kilometers when we forgot all about that."

Their route took them to Belgium, overrun and occupied by the Germans since August 1914, "and you cannot imagine how glad the people were to see us," he wrote. "It was truly a royal welcome. It was one huge cry of 'Viva la Amerique.'

"Old women stood weeping as we went by. Soon the word passed back that Americans were coming, and the people soon had the towns decorated with allied [sic] flags; cedar trees set up in the streets and covered with flags and other decorations. My company was the leading company of the division, so you see that I got a little more than my share of the honor."

He didn't mention it in letters home, but in fact Cliff Cates was in bad shape.

Such bad shape, in fact, that even as he proudly marched at the head of the 2nd Division, he worried with each step that he would never see Germany, much less the United States.

And wasn't that a terrible irony for one who'd come through so much.

"I was pretty well shot," Cates would admit years later. "I'd been sick with dysentery and a kind of flu and I didn't know whether I could make it or not."

While his men had remained camped near the Meuse, Cates had admitted himself into a field hospital for a few nights prior to setting out.

Only the kindness of his new battalion commander, Clyde Metcalf, kept him going. The thirty-two-year-old Metcalf, seeing Cates struggle on the long march, offered him the use of his horse. They alternated, Cates riding for half an hour, then Metcalf.

"I always appreciated a thing like that because I couldn't have made it otherwise," Cates would say.

On they marched; La Ferté and Tintigny; then through Luxembourg and into Ettelbruck, from which the Germans were "beating it out real fast." So fast, in fact, that the marines sent ahead to arrange billets ran into a group of their once and future enemy, "and talked with a German captain."

As the marines entered Ettelbruck, "all these people met us with high silk hats on and one greeted me as a I went in. A bartender opened the door and said, 'Where have you been? We've been waiting for you for the last five years,'" Cates recalled.

"I said, 'Where are you from—Chicago?'

"And he said, 'No—Newark.' He was so happy that he nearly cried."

The marines took a turn in the village square, while a brass band played and young girls, dressed in red, white, and blue, covered them with flowers.

The procession ended up at city hall, where endless toasts were offered. After plenty of Champagne, the officers were put up in the best hotels in town and then fed.

Bull Williams—"who doesn't have too good a head," Cates would recall—downed two bottles of Champagne on his own. After locating billets around town for the 2nd Battalion's men, Cates and a small group—Williams, battalion intelligence officer Lucian Vandoren, and James Sellers—returned to the small café where they were to spend the night.

"Williams by that time was feeling no pain," Cates would remember. Still, Williams told them it was time for a nightcap, and so they gathered around a table in the café.

As they were knocking back their brandies, the door opened and an imperious American major general walked in. He espied the group of hard-drinking marines, anathema to the regular army since Floyd Gibbons's famous dispatch from Belleau Wood.

That's when the trouble started.

After the Meuse-Argonne campaign, the 2nd Division had been transferred to the III Corps for the occupation. Standing over the table in that small café now was corps commander Major General John Hines, who had commanded the 1st Division's 1st Brigade at Soissons and the 4th Division in the Argonne before his latest promotion.

"Who's in command here?" Hines demanded.

Williams looked up and told him, "I am," but didn't rise.

Hines asked him, "Have you seen that all your men are billeted?"

"Nope," Williams replied.

"Why not?"

"I just got in."

"Did you start washing your rolling stock?"

"Nope," Williams replied once more.

"Well, why haven't you?"

"Just got in," Williams said.

Then Bull Williams made a fatal mistake. He finally rose, pointed to the stars on Hines's shoulders, and told him: "I can see that you're a major general but who in the hell are you anyway?"

Replied Hines, "Young man, I'm Major General Hines, your corps commander."

Hines would add, "You're under arrest. You're relieved."

Cates and the others by that time wanted no part of Hines. "We made a beeline out the door and that's the last I've seen of Williams," Cates would laugh years later. Major Franklin Garrett took over for the Bull.

The march toward Germany resumed the next day. By November 27, Cates would write home that he was in a small village "just across the river from that country called Prussia.

"We have waited many months to get to go into it, but I never thought that we would be able to march into it without a fight, but now we are on our way, and it will not be many days before we reach our destination."

After resting and training for a few days, the 2nd Division finally crossed into Germany on December 1. On December 13, the division crossed the Rhine.

Cates and some of his fellow officers celebrated in a local café, in which someone remembered they had "always said we were going to celebrate the day when we could urinate in the Rhine."

As would Winston Churchill twenty-seven years hence, Cates and his friends went down to the Rhine and had their fun. "And it was quite a cold day," Cates would recall.

Thinking the advance would continue farther into Germany, Cates had neglected to have his billeting sergeant find suitable living quarters in the village of Rheinbrohl. By the time Cates sent him out to look, "the other companies had gotten practically all the billets," Cates remembered. Cates finally located a place to stay next to a pontoon factory right on the river's edge.

"We have a nice club to live in," he wrote. "It has a good café, piano, billiard table, bowling alley, and it has the most wonderful view ever. It is right on the river, and it used to be a private tavern and club, but now only a few Germans come in to get their beer."

The 96th Company would call the environs its own for the next six months; when the higher-ups learned of the sweet locale and tried to requisition it for themselves, Cates held fast.

"About half a dozen generals tried to kick me out of that billet," he would laugh. "But they never did. I had squatter's rights."

By then, Cliff Cates had finally and officially been promoted to captain, even though he'd been commanding the 96th Company on and off since June, and had led it through most of that awful July 19 at Soissons, and at Blanc Mont and the Argonne.

Three others—Donald Duncan, Wethered Woodworth, and John Minnis—had fallen while in command, but here was Cliff Cates. Still kicking.

One man who had learned to admire and rely on Cates was the 6th Regiment's adjutant and former 2nd Battalion commander, Thomas Holcomb. He'd seen Cates's work at Bouresches, Belleau Wood, Soissons, Blanc Mont, and in those flu-ridden rainy days in the Argonne, and now told him he was going to try to get him the Medal of Honor.

"I would love to have the medal of honor [sic] more than anything in the world," Cates wrote to his sister on December 16. "If I do get that medal of honor, then you had better prepare to see me all puffed up and with the swell head."

Holcomb wrote "an extra good recommendation" for Cates, which was approved and sent through channels by John Lejeune. He cited his bravery in reorganizing the company at Bouresches; praised his "courage, resolution and judgment" in holding the town; retold how though badly burned by mustard gas himself, Cates had entered Belleau Wood and served "at a time when his services were badly needed."

He also recounted how Cates had taken over for Woodworth at Soissons, had refused to be evacuated after being wounded himself, and had also displayed "brilliant leadership and exceptional coolness and bravery" during the attack at Blanc Mont.

"In every attack made by his battalion he charged at the head of his men and by his gallantry contributed largely to the success of the operations," Holcomb summed up. "His example of fearlessness and devotion to duty have always been an inspiration to his men. . . . I believe that this officer has contributed to a greater extent than any other officer, to the efficient performance of duty by the battalion in which he serves."

Heady words, and the truth. Unfortunately, they weren't enough to get Cliff Cates a Medal of Honor. Where was the moment when he by himself captured eighty-eight prisoners and twenty-five machine guns? Or when he swam the Meuse to reconnoiter the German positions . . . and died? Or, a knife in one hand and a grenade in the other, subdued three machine-gun nests that were wreaking havoc on his men . . .

Or . . .

In the end, Cates got some chest salad for his uniform: the navy Distinguished Service Medal and the army Distinguished Service Cross with oak-leaf cluster. There were also a Silver Star . . . the French Legion of Honor . . . a Purple Heart (eventually) . . . the Navy Cross . . . the French Croix de Guerre . . .

And the biggest award of all: his life.

With the war at least temporarily over and the long march into Germany in the rearview mirror, Cates allowed his men to rest and reorganize for several weeks. He was optimistic that their "little guard duty" on the Rhine would not last long, at least for the 2nd Division.

"I believe that this division will be the first to be sent home as it has seen more fighting than any other," Cates wrote. "I'll be coming in by spring anyway."

Those were his thoughts on November 27; by December 16, he wasn't so sure about his plans.

"When are we coming home? I haven't the slightest idea," he

allowed. "I hope it will be soon, but I have my doubts. They will probably keep us here until the very last. Well, there is one thing certain:
it will not be a living hell all of the time, but I do not care how nice it
is, I want to get home."

Cates spent the last weeks of 1918 recuperating, and undertaking as
well the unpleasant task of answering for the fates and whereabouts of
the company's dead.

"Every mail that comes in brings lots of letters from boys' parents
that have lost their sons in this war," he would write solemnly. "It is
the hardest job that I have to answer those letters, but I always try to
give them all of the information that I can."

Many asked for their sons' personal effects, but there were none to
be had, "as they always have it on their person when they are killed and
it is either taken off by the burying detail or buried with them."

Christmas passed without a mention from Cates. His men, many
billeted with German townspeople, made it a day of feasting.

"For breakfast we had rice, bacon, bread and butter and coffee," the
96th Company's Private Everett Williams of Iowa City, Iowa, would
write. "For dinner we had meat balls, mashed potatoes, gravy, apple
sauce, bread, butter and coffee, with ½ lb of Lowneys [sic] assorted
chocolates, also a whole bar of chocolate.

"That evening, or Xmas night, four of us ate with a family. We had
roast pig, potatoes, gravy, jelly, bread, coffee and apple pie. Last but
not least we got some real Rhine wine."

Cates would allow that he wasn't suffering. "Since getting here, I am
getting fat as a pig, as we have three good meals a day. We have our
officers['] cook and mess-men, so we have some grand dinners; of course,
they cannot compare with the good old home dinners," he would write
with a measure of homesickness.

The life of relative ease ended with the dawn of 1919, when a new
schedule of training was instituted, this time aimed more at keeping

the marines fit and occupied, and maintaining discipline, than at preparing for another battle—although the possibility of renewed hostilities hovered over the Rhine that winter and into spring.

"We trained very, very hard," Cates would recall. "You know how
if you ease up on people after a war, they soon go to pieces."

"No doubt you people in the States think we have got it pretty soft
since the fighting has ceased, but such is not the case," the 96th Company's Private Edward O. Norman would write home that winter. "We
drill every day with the exception of Saturday and Sunday. It is worse
than going through the boot camp again."

Here, belatedly, the marines learned fire and movement, squads of
riflemen working together to attack and subdue the enemy. It was a
step forward from the so-called tactics employed in the war.

Simply standing up and going forward into the maws of a hundred
machine guns had worked for Lucky Cliff Cates at Bouresches and
Blanc Mont; not so much for many other marines whose graves lay
scattered from the Bois de Belleau to the Meuse River.

But the training around Rheinbrohl was certainly not war again;
though patrols walked the Rhine, entrenchments were dug around the
bridgehead, and a strict drill schedule was adhered to, the men also
received passes to towns within the American occupation zone—and
some lucky souls were allowed leave to travel to France, England, and
Italy.

Boxing matches and football games were also organized, and perhaps most important, the 6th Regiment's history would note, after
months of sleeping in mud and filth and often eating iron rations if they
got anything at all, "The men are well billeted, practically all sleeping
in beds, and food is plentiful and good."

For Cliff Cates, there was also an extra duty. He and Captain Gilder
Jackson of the 5th Regiment's 20th Company were chosen as candidates
to lead a composite company of marines, one of twelve chosen from men
of each brigade of the 1st through 6th Divisions. They would have the

honor of parading behind John Pershing in fetes from Paris to Washington.

About twenty men were handpicked from each company, well-decorated men who had been through the worst and proved their mettle. From a pool of about four hundred men and twelve to fourteen lieutenants, some two hundred fifty would make up a company after some whittling down.

Cates in the end edged out Jackson for command of the company.

"I was lucky," he would say.

Lucky Cates . . .

Cates's friend John West, recovered from his wounding at Blanc Mont, took over the 96th Company. Cates continued to train and drill and weed the composite company to two hundred fifty men—thirteen of them from the 96th Company—after which the regiment paraded through Coblenz.

Then it was on to Paris on July 19—and what a difference that was from the previous July 19 for the men of the 6th Regiment—and London, where four million lined the route. The regiment then spent six more weeks in Paris, where, despite the temptations, there were few incidents to report among the men.

"You can't believe how good it was because we never gave a court-martial during the entire time," Cates recalled. "If the man got out of line, we just sent him back to his outfit and that was punishment enough because they were all so anxious to stay."

They were anxious to stay in Paris . . . but impatient to be leaving Europe. By March, thirty lucky men from the 96th Company were sent home, the unit having swelled with the return of those wounded at Blanc Mont or sickened in the Argonne.

While the weeks dragged on, and rumblings of German intransigence regarding the peace talks surfaced, men from all six occupying divisions began to worry they might have to once more take up arms and push to Berlin.

In the end, the Germans reluctantly signed off on the Treaty of Versailles on June 23. Soon enough it was time to leave, and the men of the 96th Company entrained for France, where on July 25 they boarded the USS *George Washington* at Brest, arriving in New York on August 3.

The 96th Company paraded in New York with the 2nd Division on August 8, and then in Washington, DC, on August 12. On August 13, the company's enlisted men were mustered out of the service at the place it had all begun—Quantico.

One week later, every officer in the 96th was given leave; on that same day, Cliff Cates's beloved 96th Company "ceased to exist," the unit's history says.

Cates had watched his company be enveloped in gas and dissipate on June 14, 1918, only to rise from the ashes with new blood, new recruits, to fight again and again and again . . . and once more.

Now he watched as his men spread to the corners of America, some old-timers who stayed in the Corps going to the four corners of the world.

La guerre now was truly *finie*; Cliff Cates's company was truly "defunct."

WHAT IS A MARINE, PART TWO

ANOTHER SHIP, ANOTHER war now, but still the faces; the faces of young men, young marines, these barely twenty years old but already strained with worry over what was to come, what might await them, as the convoy steamed almost due north toward the island of Guadalcanal and, he was certain, another battle.

"There is a noticeable strain on everyone—which I do not remember seeing in France in the last war—as very few of them have been in an engagement before," the now forty-eight-year-old Colonel Cliff Cates would write on August 4, 1942, just three days before his 1st Marine Regiment landed on the island.

"It is just like a football game; that awful tension just before the kick-off which will disappear once the game gets underway [sic]."

Cates by then was of course well-acquainted with jumping into war, though it had been almost twenty-four years since he last saw action. He had also changed during those years; this Cliff Cates was a father and a husband now, and though still a marine, he had lost some of his carefree nonchalance about war; he had more at stake as the war in the Pacific opened than he had at Bouresches or Blanc Mont.

He worried now, more than he had during his first war; it did not make him less courageous, just more circumspect. He, too, was under a noticeable strain.

"It is very hard to try to describe my feelings upon embarking on an expedition to God only knows where," he had written earlier as he sailed across the Pacific. "It is fairly easy when a person is young and filled with the spirit of adventure to pick up and shove off to war, but it is an entirely different matter when you are older and have the responsibility of a family."

Thinking perhaps of Thomas Holcomb, his former battalion commander, who even at that moment was serving as the commandant of the Marine Corps, Cates had a new appreciation of war, of putting oneself in harm's way, of leading young men into battle when there was so much now to return home to.

"I used to marvel at the determination and guts of the old officers that had families—their's [sic] was a hard task and I realize it more now that I am in that class."

But he accepted that it was his time also to shoulder more of the burden of war, and apply all that he had learned in France to this new crusade. He knew, as always, that he was ready, that he was fit, and that he was a natural leader who would do all he could to see his young charges through the coming campaign against the Japanese.

"It is only natural that the ones who had actual battle experience in the last war should be selected as leaders of larger units in this one," he would write. "A person can be the best parade-ground soldier in the world, but he is a novice until he has experienced actual warfare under heavy fire.

"A leader has got to be able to stand up under the strain, be able to think fast and correctly. I have seen seemingly good soldiers fail completely, due to the fact that they became tired and addled and couldn't arrive at a decision when the going got tough."

The going had been tough at Bouresches, in dank, gas-laden Belleau Wood; the going had been even tougher at Soissons and Blanc

Mont, but Cliff Cates had always kept his head, always led by example, always pulled through, if miraculously on occasion.

His abilities had of course not gone unnoticed, but twenty-three years before, and despite his love for the Marine Corps and being in the thick of battle, he had been uncertain what course his life would take.

In the end, the decision—and there could be no other path—was virtually made for him during a chance encounter as he was about to clear out from Quantico in August 1919.

The day after the 96th Company had been dissolved, and his men and officers scattered, Cates himself had submitted his resignation. "I had never thought about staying in the Marine Corps," he would say.

He was walking the grounds when he saw George Barnett, Corps commandant, approaching. "I looked for some place to duck, but I couldn't," Cates would say with a laugh. "So I saluted and he returned the salute and he said, 'Young man, I understand you are resigning.'

"And I gulped a few times and said, 'Yes sir.'

"He said, 'How would you like to have two months' leave and then make your mind up?'"

Cates told him he thought it was a fair offer; Barnett told him to withdraw his resignation and put in for leave.

And with that stroke, Lucky Cliff Cates put aside all thoughts of a cushy and lucrative career as an attorney, pushed aside thoughts of bar exams and quiet hours and a pipe and slippers and a life of peace; let go of any future as a normal civilian, albeit one who had certainly paid his dues in wartime and had earned more than most the simple right to try to reach a normal life expectancy.

With that stroke, Cliff Cates became a lifer, like but not quite like the old salts such as Dan Daly who had held the young officers enthralled on those warm evenings at Quantico in the late summer of 1917.

He became Barnett's aide, and also served as a liaison to President Woodrow Wilson. In 1920, John Lejeune became Marine Corps commandant. After working with Lejeune for several weeks of transition,

Barnett asked Cates if he would like to serve again as his aide in a new posting in the Department of the Pacific in San Francisco.

In the meantime, Cates had met and wooed pretty twenty-three-year-old Jane Virginia McIlhenny, and they planned to wed. Though it was not customary for high-level aides to be married at the time, Barnett told Cates he had no problem with his getting hitched.

"I want you to get married and come out with me," he told Cates.

But Cates had had to put off plans for marriage because he didn't have the money to spring for a wedding and reception. Barnett told him, "Hell, I'll lend you the money."

When Cates and his bride did get married on October 7, 1920, it was almost an all-marine affair. Former 2nd Battalion intelligence officer Lucian Vandoren was Cates's best man, and among the ushers at Washington's St. Thomas Church were Wethered Woodworth and John Bowling, late of the 96th Company, and John West, late of the 79th Company.

Then Cliff Cates brought his bride west, and when he did, she traveled "in a smart suit of navy blue duvetyn, with a small hat of henna and Kolinsky fur," the *Washington Times* reported.

Children duly arrived: A son, Clifton, Jr., was born in 1921. In June 1923, the elder Cliff Cates left his small family behind to command the marine detachment on the USS *California*. He spent almost two years sailing the world before beginning a stint with the 4th Marine Regiment in San Diego; after doing a tour as a Marine Corps recruiter in the Northwest and Midwest, Cates was dispatched to Shanghai for three years with the 4th Marines.

By 1940 he had done two tours of duty in Shanghai—where his daughter, Ann, was born in 1931—as well as stints with the American Battle Monuments Commission and schooling in the Marine Corps Schools and Army Industrial College.

Clearly marked for advancement, Cates soon found himself a colonel, and when war was declared on Japan, he was the director of the Marine

Officers' Basic School in Philadelphia. In May 1942, his old pal Thomas Holcomb gave Cliff Cates the command of the 1st Marine Regiment.

By early August, Cates and his marines had sailed from Wellington, New Zealand, and were off the shore of Guadalcanal, at the southernmost end of the Solomon Islands chain in the southwest Pacific—and the first step in an island-hopping strategy that would mark the war in the Pacific.

On August 7, the 1st and 5th Marine Regiments began disembarking on the north shore of the fetid, steaming, miserable, and malarial island, which was held by about three hundred Japanese soldiers and eight hundred laborers.

For the first time since November 10, 1918, Cliff Cates would lead marines into mortal combat.

Appropriately, he would be in the vanguard of a three-year effort to push back the Japanese in the Pacific, a costly, grueling struggle that began with that first toehold on Guadalcanal.

By August 21, the marines had taken the vital Japanese airstrip they renamed Henderson Field. "It was kind of them to build the airfield and then let us take it with little opposition," Cates wrote. Soon enough, Americans would be engaging with Japanese Zeros and flying bombing sorties.

The marines pushed on to their objective of Grassy Knoll, four miles inland. A beachhead was established and consolidated, bombardments by Japanese planes and ships were endured day and night, and numerous attempts at infiltration of the marine lines were beaten back.

There was also the regular appearance of a Japanese submarine to contend with. "It was a Jap submarine that surfaced almost every afternoon and fired a few shots into our beachhead from about 5,000 yards," Cates would write. "We knicknamed him 'Oscar.'"

The sub proved irritating enough that Cates finally ordered the captain of his artillery to undertake a "fire mission," William Richard White and Ben Wofford would write in their book, *The Marine*.

"When he asked what target, the colonel took the captain's ear off," they wrote of Cates.

Yelling into the phone, Cates told the captain, "God dammit, man, shoot at the fucking submarine!" Not a single artilleryman believed their 75 mm howitzers could reach a target nearly three miles offshore. The captain "very politely" explained that to Cates. But the man who had had a penchant for attempting to bring down German planes with just a pistol back in the First World War now insisted on trying to sink a Japanese submarine with a piece of field artillery.

"The colonel, pretending infinite patience, told the captain he knew this, but his troops did not," White and Wofford wrote. "The troops only knew they were being shot at, and, God help us, somebody was gonna shoot back. With no further ado, our batteries fired a few rounds.

"The first shot they fired seemed to hit on his fantail and Oscar disappeared suddenly, leaving a cloud of black smoke—whether we got him or not is not known, but he left us alone after that lucky shot," Cates wrote.

It had taken him a short time on Guadalcanal to regain some of the dashing, decisive bravado of his younger days. Now that he was a middle-aged family man, and no longer a devil-may-care, twenty-something second lieutenant, it would take the heat of battle to bring him around to his old self.

"When I had first met him he had seemed nervous and fidgety and apt to imagine snipers in every tree; when the heat was on, however, he was really at home, and quite a different man," Martin Clemens, an Australian coast-watcher on the island, would recall.

Clemens found Cates "very direct but easy to talk to. Cates had the air of an experienced soldier, cool, calm, and collected; he wore breeches and knee-length campaign boots and nonchalantly smoked cigarettes from a long black holder. There was no doubt he was a bonny fighter."

Cates's clear and decisive military instincts would show themselves intact when at three ten a.m. on August 21, the thousand-man Ichiki

Battalion, which had been unloaded twenty miles up the coast east of Cates's beachhead on the Tenaru River, came calling.

The leading elements, prowling west along the coast, hit tripwires set out as warnings by the marines, and the night immediately erupted into a cacophony of banzai screams and fire from mortars, machine guns, and rifles as Colonel Kiyono Ichiki's men attacked across a small spit of land at the mouth of the river.

Several marine positions, just one hundred feet from the wire, were overrun in the black night, and others desperately poured it on as the Japanese streamed toward them. Cates, to the west and quickly getting reports, ordered the artillery to open up on the spit, which was so close to the marines "that we hesitated to fire."

The battle continued through the night. Dawn brought the grisly sight of dead and wounded Japanese soldiers piled before the marine positions, while others took refuge behind a sand embankment near the shore and others in a coconut grove. Some played dead while others continued to fire at the marines.

Cates huddled at his headquarters with Colonel Gerald Thomas, an old 1st Battalion, 6th Regiment man and operations officer for 1st Marine Division commander Alexander Vandegrift.

"Colonel Cates unfolded a map and pointed to it with a pencil," Richard Tregaskis would write in his book *Guadalcanal Diary*. "The scene was very calm, considering that a battle for Guadalcanal was going on only a short distance away."

Cates sent his 1st Battalion on a sweep to the east and below the Japanese positions. Then moving north, the marines soon blocked any escape routes for the Japanese trapped on the beach and east of the Tenaru.

Cates then sent in B Company of the 1st Tank Battalion. "With guns blazing, they roared across, right into the middle of the enemy positions and knocked out gun after gun," Cates wrote.

The Japanese now panicked, and about 250 of them raced for the beach to try to swim to safety. Between the tanks and the marines' heavy fire, "they were caught like a rat in a trap," Cates wrote.

Cates now hopped into a jeep and moved to the front, where "the Jap fire was still ricocheting thru the cocoanuts [sic] and it was plenty hot." Cates and a small group of officers took sniper fire; the captain of his weapons company was hit in the chest. "What we thought was only a fairly serious wound later proved fatal to him," Cates would relate.

Surveying the heaps of Japanese, Cates reflected on his experiences in another war, where he certainly had seen his share of dead. But, he would write, this was worse than Belleau Wood, even Soissons.

"Never, at any time in France during World War I, did I ever see such a congestion of the dead," he would write.

Even Ichiki was dead. Surrounded by trigger-happy marines, he had burned his colors and codes and shot himself in the head.

Cliff Cates learned a lot at the Tenaru. Going into Guadalcanal, he, and certainly his men, had worried that the Japanese would prove to be superior fighters, one of the benefits of experience they had gained in a ten-year war with the Chinese.

But the marines' modern weapons, as well as their steady aims, had played a large role in decimating Ichiki and his men. Cates was no longer intimidated by the Japanese; as the few prisoners undertook the gruesome task of burying their comrades, Cates's confidence swelled like the bodies of the dead Japanese that littered the Tenaru.

"They may claim to be the Sons of Heaven," Cates wrote, "but the marines certainly shot them to the wrong address the 21st day of August, 1942."

HE LIKED THE WORK

ABOUT THIRTY OF them made it that year. Old men now, they took over the motels of Tiptonville, Tennessee—the Blue Bank, Cypress Point, and Gooch's—on the first weekend in June 1971 to pay homage to the man who'd led them across a wheat field and into hell exactly fifty-three years before at Bouresches, and then did the same at Belleau Wood, Soissons, Blanc Mont, and the Argonne.

They held a memorial service for him at the Methodist church on June 4; on the fifth, they were guests at a parade that included twenty marines, the high school band, the local Boy and Girl Scout troops, and a marine firing squad.

Ruskin Bunnell . . . Sam Babcock . . . Tom Orgo . . . Ray Hanson . . . Willard Morrey. All of them had followed Cliff Cates into war and survived; they survived still.

None would ever forget Clifton Bledsoe Cates, nor their comrades, some dead these fifty-plus years, some still alive and white haired now, some in failing health, some needing canes and walkers due to the still-lingering effects of old war wounds.

They remained, though, a true band of brothers.

And Cliff Cates would always be their leader.

Cates himself had done as much as any of them to keep the flame and memory of the 96th Company alive, attending annual reunions whenever he was in-country, and keeping in contact with many of those who revered him, and whom he revered for their stamina, their pluck, and their willingness to sacrifice all in the Great War.

For someone who in April 1917 had never even heard of the United States Marine Corps, Lucky Cliff Cates made quite the career of serving in it.

He and his 1st Marine Regiment spent more than four months in the jungles of Guadalcanal, where every night they were bombed from overhead by a Japanese aviator they not quite lovingly called "Louis the Louse," and they were shelled by a Japanese naval gun they referred to as "Whistling Willie."

They turned back the Japanese at the Tenaru, Bloody Ridge, the Matanikau River, and killed hundreds of the enemy during patrols deep into the jungle. When, on December 21, 1942, they were relieved, their appearance no doubt conjured images of July 19, 1918, when Cates—his pants blown off, his helmet dented—had led the 96th Company into the hell of Soissons.

"I wish that I could paint a vivid word picture of the men as they loaded into the boats," he would write of his regiment's men as they finally disembarked from Guadalcanal.

"The phrase, 'The raggedy-ass marines are on parade,' comes as near describing them as possible. Hats and caps of every description, tattered and worn shirts (some bareback), trousers of every kind, (some cut off so short that they looked like 'G' strings), badly worn shoes of all kind (a few Japanese sneakers), and very few had underwear and socks.

"Surprisingly enough, almost everyone had his weapon and gas mask, and, most remarkable of all, they were all in very good condition. A good marine—and they were excellent marines—always takes good care of his arms, even if everything else goes to pot."

Each had lost an average of twenty pounds during the Guadalcanal campaign, and Cates was as proud of them as he had always been of his beloved 96th Company—and he was even more proud that relatively few had become casualties, at least compared to his experience in his first war.

The 1st Marine Regiment lost 106 dead, and 200 were wounded. Cates would compare those numbers to the enormous casualties his single company had endured in World War I and say it was by design.

"I have always regretted that it was so high," he would write of the 96th's casualty rate. "I try to think that it was because we had unusually difficult missions, but still I feel that it could have been reduced with better training.

"Upon being ordered to Guadalcanal, I resolved that I would do everything within my power to hold the casualties of the Regiment to a minimum and still do the job assigned."

Cates had insisted on better training, better security, better tactics. His men didn't simply "get up and go" in the face of the enemy as they had in the First World War. At the Tenaru, at Bloody Ridge, he let the Japanese come to them, where they were annihilated by superior firepower and always deadly marine verve.

Following Guadalcanal, Cates was ordered back to the States, where he became the commandant of the Marine Corps Schools at Quantico. And what better person was there for that job but one who had learned the lessons now of two world wars?

In June 1944, Cates was given command of the 4th Marine Division, which, by the time he reached it, was mopping up the final resistance on the island of Saipan.

Twelve days after taking over for Major General Harry Schmidt, Cates was with the division as it disembarked in tank landing ships (LSTs) from Saipan, made the quick trip southwest to Tinian, and landed not at the Japanese strongpoint of Tinian Town at the southern end of the island, but far to the north.

Within hours, 15,614 marines had landed, at a cost of just 77 dead and 470 wounded. Once again, Cates's desire to spare his men from the unimaginable toll of the First World War had succeeded. On the night of July 24–25, the Japanese moved north and ran up against the perimeter Cates had established.

The carnage, to the Japanese, was worse than at the Tenaru. Three times the Japanese attacked in wild *banzai* charges; three times they were met by artillery and rifle fire.

In the morning, 1,241 Japanese dead lay splayed before the marine lines, and another 700 moaned and groaned from wounds they'd incurred, or were blowing themselves fifteen feet into the air with magnetic mines—"an end at once more powerful and spectacular than the customary hand-grenade suicide," Robert Leckie, marine and author, would write.

Within a week, the island was secure, a timetable no doubt hastened by the promise of recuperation on the island of Maui.

"I spurred the men on," Cates would say later. "I said, 'Now, look here, men, the island of Maui is waiting for us. See those ships out there? The quicker you get this over with, the quicker we'll get back there.'"

Following Tinian, Cates and the 4th Division indeed went to Maui to train and receive replacements. After months of practicing amphibious landings and enjoying at least some of what the famed Hawaiian island had to offer, the 4th Marine Division on February 19, 1945, found itself offshore of Iwo Jima.

This would be no Tinian.

Defended by twenty-two thousand Japanese, Iwo Jima would hold out for exactly one month under the onslaught of three marine divisions—then 3rd, 4th, and 5th, which was under the command of Graves Erskine, Cates's old crony.

Routing out almost singly Japanese who hid in crevices, caves, and deep tunnels, the 4th Division lost 1,731 marines, and 7,359 were wounded.

Cates could do little to limit the casualties this time. He fought not only the terrain but the stubbornness of an enemy who was more than prepared to die; almost all of the Japanese died on the island.

Cates and his surviving marines now limped back to Maui, and after several months, he received the order to take Wake Island with his division. Before he could even get under way, the Japanese surrendered.

Another world war had ended with Lucky Cates still alive and well.

Cates and his marines returned to the United States, where Cates eventually took over command of the Marine Barracks back at his old stomping grounds at Quantico.

In late 1947, Secretary of the Navy John Lawrence Sullivan called him and told him to meet him in his office "at four o'clock on a certain date," Cates would recall.

When he arrived, he was surprised to find his old friend Lemuel Shepherd waiting to see Sullivan. Neither knew what was up, although the four-year term of the current Marine Corps commandant, Alexander Vandegrift, was just expiring.

Sullivan appeared, and told them, "We're going over to see President Truman and we're late now. He's going to decide who's going to be commandant. One of you is going to be commandant."

"That's the first we knew of it," Cates would say.

They traveled to the White House, where President Harry S. Truman saw Cates first. "I really don't know anything about either of you[,] but your records are practically identically the same," Truman told him. "You both have been in World War I and World War II.

"It's up to me to make a decision."

That Cates and Shepherd had the same record was not quite true. Shepherd, with the 5th Regiment's 55th Company, had been wounded early on at Belleau Wood and didn't leave the hospital until mid-August

1918 and so missed the fun at Soissons. He had, however, proved his stuff in leading marines at St. Mihiel and Blanc Mont, and in the Second World War in the invasions of Guam and Okinawa.

After a short chat, Shepherd—who had attained the rank of brigadier general—talked with Truman. When he came out of Truman's office, Cates told him with characteristic bluntness and acuity, "Lem, this is like a dog show. We're waiting to see who's going to get the prize."

A few minutes later, they were called back in to see Truman. "The President looked over at Lem and he said, 'General'—and I was just ready to reach out and shake Lem's hand, really I thought he was going to say, 'You're going to be commandant,'" Cates recalled.

Instead, Truman told Shepherd that Cates had seniority, and so would be commandant. "You'll have your chance later," Truman told Shepherd.

Cates left Truman's office, "wondering if I really wanted it."

Cates would inherit some of the same troubles that had in the end worn down Vandegrift, chiefly the efforts by Truman and his allies in Congress and in the other service branches to whittle the postwar Corps to the bone.

Many, Cates noted, had their "thumbs down on us and . . . made all kinds of plans to absorb us."

In Cates's mind, and in those of many marines, the whole issue with the army stemmed back to Belleau Wood, and the glory the Corps had somewhat accidentally bathed in.

Among the Corps's detractors were two old but influential doughboys—former artillery captain Harry Truman and General Douglas MacArthur.

The two were adamant that the Marines have no presence alongside the army, navy, and air force among the Joint Chiefs of Staff, and in fact were perfectly happy to see the Corps absorbed into another branch of service.

"The army had never forgiven the publicity that the Marines got at Belleau Woods," Cates said. "And I think there's been a certain amount of jealousy."

But there were other detractors as well who threatened the Corps's existence. One, Brigadier General Frank Armstrong, in 1948 called the Corps "a small, fouled-up army talking navy lingo. We are going to put those marines in the regular army and make efficient soldiers out of them."

Despite the glory won by marines at Belleau Wood, Blanc Mont, and from Guadalcanal to Tarawa to Saipan and Iwo Jima, some felt the Corps was "unnecessary, that it duplicates functions of other armed services," as the writer Richard Tregaskis, who had spent time with Cates on Guadalcanal, would say.

Cates—"quick-talking, alert, vigorous," in Tregaskis's words—would admit that his biggest worry as commandant "is to keep the Marine Corps alive, to keep the potent element of national security it has been in the past."

As for those who claimed the marines' role was redundant, Cates added, "We don't want to supplant land troops. We have our certain job, amphibious operations. We are shock troops. We can get in and take a beachhead and get out. And we are trained to be always in readiness for action."

Still, as Cates stood guard against "some legislative or administrative blitz" that might again threaten the Corps's very existence, a new conflict served to exacerbate tensions between Truman and his allies and the Marines.

On June 25, 1950, North Korean troops began pouring south and across the thirty-eighth parallel, an almost arbitrary divide between the Communist north and democratic south. As Seoul fell and the North's tide appeared unstoppable, Cates, as had George Barnett thirty-three years earlier, offered his marines to Truman and Douglas MacArthur.

By August, the 1st Marine Division was in South Korea; just six weeks later, proving yet again its abilities at amphibious operations, the marines on September 15 would take the port of Inchon in a surprise landing behind the main North Korean force and, at least for the moment, tilt the momentum to the South and the Americans.

In between the marines' landing and Inchon, a subtler conflict would come to a head—and leave Cliff Cates standing tall and Harry Truman groveling for his forgiveness.

On August 29, Truman, while answering an inquiry from California Republican Representative Gordon L. McDonough regarding a marine place on the Chief of Staff, referred to the Marine Corps as "the navy's police force" and added that "as long as I am President, that is what it will remain."

In words that would cause an uproar when made public by McDonough the next day, Truman added that the Corps has "a propaganda machine that is almost equal to Stalin's. Nobody desires to belittle the efforts of the Marine Corps, but when the Marine Corps goes into the army, it works with and for the army and that is the way it should be."

Truman had stepped in it. While Cates remained circumspect, Truman's Republican opponents in Congress and the newspapers had a field day, with one commentator noting Truman's horrible timing, with the marines and army fighting in Korea and "carrying out a merger essential for both efficiency and economy."

After trying to ride out the gale of criticism for several days, Truman, in what one newspaperman would call "the greatest display of presidential word-eating in recent American history," wrote a letter of apology, and on September 6 personally handed it to Cliff Cates.

Among other things, Truman said in the letter that he was "profoundly aware of the magnificent history of the United States Marine Corps," adding that he "personally learned of the splendid combat spirit of the Marines" while he himself was fighting with the 35th Division in France in World War I.

Somewhat cheesily, given his earlier stance regarding keeping the Marines as an independent fighting force, Truman avowed that the Corps "has a vital role in our organization for national security and I will continue to support and maintain its identity."

With that, Cates, and the Corps, had won.

Ironically, Cates would later say, "I think that maybe his statements really did us more good than any one thing. . . . The former marines and friends that had served with the Marine Corps—correspondents and things—they poured it on Congress and on the White House, letters and telegrams."

The man who in 1917 had never even heard of the Marine Corps became, in effect, its savior . . . with a little help from the man from the "Show Me" state of Missouri.

Cates would make several trips to the Korean front before his tenure as commandant ended in 1952. Afterward, he again took over the Marine Corps Schools before retiring from his beloved Corps on June 30, 1954. *Time* magazine would note that while Cates described his service as "a life of hardship and hazard," he wanted no other.

"He liked the work: fighting," the magazine's July 5, 1954, issue would report.

A summer home in Maine, being built on land once owned by the estate of the painter Winslow Homer, awaited, as did new digs in Edgewater, Maryland; for once, Cates and his bride would find themselves outside of a military reservation.

At both places, Cates would spend many an hour fishing or hunting. There was also time for two-week summer trips to Reelfoot Lake back in the familiar surroundings of Tennessee, and tarpon fishing in the winter in Florida.

But there was plenty of time for simple idling as well, and with an ever-present Pall Mall cigarette stuck in its holder, Cliff Cates would sit and smoke and sip and fish on his dock in Chesapeake Bay, pouring himself two fingers of Old Parr Scotch over ice at ten a.m., to be followed with the same dose hourly until dinner at six p.m.

There, he experienced the first real peace he'd had since the fall of 1917, and as many aging men will, wondered aloud sometimes whether he'd made the right call with his career, and his life. The evidence was preponderant that he had, but still, men sometimes wonder.

If he needed more evidence of a life well spent, there were the annual gatherings of the Society of the 96th Company, whose ever-dwindling ranks continued to revere Cliff Cates and appreciate the things—small and large—he'd done for them all those years before.

They would have followed him to hell in war; now they followed him to Edgewater, the site of many a reception for the company's survivors through the 1960s. Old men now, they could only marvel at the exploits they'd performed and the hardships they'd endured in a farago and nearly forgotten war, and toast those who'd perished in 1918 or in the many years in between.

And, of course, each of those old men marveled the most at Cliff Cates, who'd led them into Bouresches and through the deadly wheat below Soissons and up that hill in Champagne—and would have led them across that last river as well, had fate not finally turned a kind eye toward the 6th Regiment of U.S. Marines.

Still, there remained one more river that this time had to be crossed. As the 1960s approached the 1970s, fifty years of chain-smoking began to take their toll, and he encountered an enemy he couldn't beat—emphysema. After a two-year battle, Lucky Cates breathed his last on June 4, 1970, at the U.S. Naval Hospital in Annapolis. He was buried with full honors on June 8 at Arlington National Cemetery.

Almost exactly one year later, thirty-two former members of the 96th Company and their wives made a pilgrimage to Tiptonville and Cates Landing in honor of their former company leader.

They dedicated a flagpole in his name at the local courthouse and laid a wreath at its base. Guests of honor, they gathered around the pole and saluted Cliff Cates one last time as his personal colors were raised and a marine honor guard volleyed into the humid morning air, the sounds of the shots echoing along the riverbanks and woods that had been Cliff Cates's boyhood playground.

JULY 29, 1943

Dear General:

Congratulations upon your recent promotion. It was with a great deal of pride that I read the article in the August Leatherneck.

I will never forget what an efficient officer you were in France and how the men of the 96th Co respected you, and what confidence we had in your ability.

I remember that old helmet of yours with the machine gun bullet in it—your uniform with one shoulder bar shot off—how you always held up for your men by refusing to send us out on unnecessary dangerous missions—how when you were left behind at St Mihiel, rustled up the best feed we ever had in France, and you were waiting for us when we came out—how you brought in a barrel of vin rouge when we ran out of coffee—how you divided your money up with the boys who got to go to Paris July 14th 1918, and I remember the last time I ever saw you.

It was Oct 3rd 1918 on the Champagne front. You a 2nd Lieut. was in command of the 96th and led us over the top.

That was the only time I ever saw you in a uniform

that would pass inspection, but you led us over shell holes and up Mt Blanc. I was wounded for the second time and never went back and never saw you again.

All these years when I ran across a Marine, I always asked him about Lieut Cates. I learned about your promotion to Capt. then in the 2nd Division paper that you were a Major, then I read in Guadalcanal Diary that you were a Colonel and now you are back home a Brig-General.

My happiness for you will be complete if some day I read in the papers that Congress has confirmed the President's appointment of Lieut-General C.B. Cates as Commandant of the U.S. Marine Corps.

> *Sincerely yours*
> *Homer B. Osborn*
> *a former buck private*

BIBLIOGRAPHY

American Battle Monuments Commission. *American Armies and Battlefields in Europe*. Washington, DC: Government Printing Office, 1938.

_____. *2nd Division, Summary of Operations in the World War*. Washington, DC: Government Printing Office, 1944.

Anderson, Joseph R. *Record of Service in the World War of V.M.I. Alumni and Their Alma Mater*. Richmond: The Richmond Press, 1920.

Berry, Henry. *Make the Kaiser Dance: The American Experience in World War I*. Garden City, NY: Doubleday, 1978.

Boyd, Thomas. *Through the Wheat: A Novel of the World War I Marines*. New York and London: C. Scribner's Sons, 1923.

Brannen, Carl Andrew. *Over There: A Marine in the Great War*. College Station, TX: Texas A&M University Press, 1996.

Camp, Dick. *Leatherneck Legends: Conversations with the Marine Corps' Old Breed*. St. Paul, MN: Zenith Press, 2006.

Cates, Clifton B. *History of the 96th Company, 2nd Battalion, 6th Regiment United States Marine Corps, 4th Brigade, 2nd Division, A.E.F.* United States Marine Corps Historical Section: Washington, DC, 1935.

Catlin, Albertus W. *With the Help of God and a Few Marines*. Yardley, PA: Westholme Publishing, 2013.

Clark, George B. *Devil Dogs: Fighting Marines of World War I*. Novato, CA: Presidio Press, 1999.

Clark, George B., ed. *Devil Dogs Chronicle: Voices of the 4th Marine Brigade in World War I*. Lawrence, KS: University Press of Kansas, 2013.

Clemens, Martin. *Alone on Guadalcanal: A Coastwatcher's Story*. Annapolis, MD: Naval Institute Press, 1998.

Coffman, Edward M. *The War to End All Wars: The American Military Experience in World War I*. Oxford: Oxford University Press, 1968.

Cooke, Elliott D., et al. *Americans vs. Germans: The First AEF in Action*. New York: Penguin Books: Washington, DC: Infantry Journal, 1942.

Cowing, Kemper F., comp., and Courtney Ryley Cooper, eds. *"Dear Folks at Home": The Glorious Story of the United States Marines in France as Told by Their Letters from the Battlefield*. Boston and New York: Houghton Mifflin, 1919.

Donaldson, G. H. *History of the Seventy-Eighth Company, Sixth Marines*. Neuwied, Germany: W. Jenkins, 1919.

Eisenhower, John S. D., and Joanne Thompson Eisenhower. *Yanks: The Epic Story of the American Army in World War I*. New York: Free Press, 2001.

Fox, Henry L., and N. L. Forrestal, eds. *"What the Boys Did Over There."* New York: Allied Overseas Veterans' Stories Co., 1918, 1919.

Gilbert, Martin. *The First World War: A Complete History*. New York: Henry Holt, 1994.

Hamilton, Craig, and Louise Corbin, eds. *Echoes from Over There*. New York: Soldiers' Publishing, 1919.

Harbord, James G. *The American Army in France 1917–1919*. Boston: Little, Brown, 1936.

Harries, Meirion and Susie. *The Last Days of Innocence: America at War 1917–1918*. New York: Vintage Books, 1997.

Heinl, Robert Debs, Jr. *Soldiers of the Sea: The United States Marine Corps, 1775–1962*. Annapolis, MD: United States Naval Institute, 1962.

Hemrick, Levi E. *Once a Marine*. Staunton, VA: Clarion Publishing, 2013.

Hopper, James. *Medals of Honor*. New York: John Day, 1929.

Johnson, Douglas V. II, and Rolfe L. Hillna, Jr. *Soissons 1918*. College Station, TX: Texas A&M University Press, 1999.

Krulewitch, Melvin L. *Now That You Mention It*. New York: Quadrangle, 1973.

Leckie, Robert. *Strong Men Armed: The United States Marines Against Japan*. Cambridge, MA: Da Capo Press, 1962.

Lengel, Edward G., ed. *A Companion to the Meuse-Argonne Campaign*. Malden, MA: Wiley Blackwell, 2014.

Lewis, Charles Lee. *Famous American Marines*. Boston: L. C. Page, 1950.

Lindsey, Alfred J. *Rock Hanson: The Life of a Hero*. Macomb: Cedar Street Press, 1991.

Mackin, Elton E. *Suddenly We Didn't Want to Die: Memoirs of a World War I Marine.* Novato, CA: Presidio Press, 1993.

March, William K. *Company K.* New York: American Mercury, 1931.

McPherson, James. *Battle Cry of Freedom: The Civil War Era.* Oxford: Oxford University Press, 1988.

Metcalf, Clyde H., ed. *The Marine Corps Reader.* New York: G. P. Putnam's Sons, 1944.

Otto, Ernst. *The Battle at Blanc Mont.* Translated by Martin Lichtenburg. Annapolis, MD: United States Naval Institute, 1930.

Owen, Peter F. *To the Limit of Endurance: A Battalion of Marines in the Great War.* College Station, TX: Texas A&M University Press, 2007.

Paradis, Don V., and Peter F. Owen, eds. *The World War I Memoirs of Don V. Paradis, Gunnery Sergeant, USMC.* Self-published, n.d.

Persico, Joseph E. *Eleventh Month, Eleventh Day, Eleventh Hour: Armistice Day, 1918, World War I and Its Violent Climax.* New York: Random House, 2004.

Pottle, Frederick A. *Stretchers: The Story of a Hospital Unit on the Western Front.* New Haven, CT: Yale University Press, 1929.

Sellers, William W., and George B. Clark, eds. *World War I Memoirs of Lt. Col. James McBrayer Sellers.* Pike, NH: Brass Hat, 1997.

Simmons, Edwin Howard. *The United States Marines: A History.* Annapolis, MD: Naval Institute Press, 1974.

Simmons, Edwin Howard, and Joseph H. Alexander. *Through the Wheat: The U.S. Marines in World War I.* Annapolis, MD: Naval Institute Press, 2008.

Smythe, Donald. *Pershing: General of the Armies.* Bloomington, IN: Indiana University Press, 1986.

Spaulding, Oliver Lyman, and John Womack Wright. *The Second Division American Expeditionary Force in France, 1917–1919.* New York: Hillman Press, 1937.

Thomas, Shipley. *The History of the A.E.F.* New York: George H. Doran, 1920.

Thomason, John W., Jr. *Fix Bayonets!* New York and London: C. Scribner's, 1926.

Thomason, John W., Jr., and George B. Clark, eds. *The United States Army Second Division Northwest of Château-Thierry in World War I.* Jefferson, NC, and London: McFarland, 2006.

Toland, John. *No Man's Land.* Garden City, NY: Doubleday, 1980.

Tregaskis, Richard. *Guadalcanal Diary.* New York: Random House, 1955.

Ulbrich, David J. *Preparing for Victory: Thomas Holcomb and the Making of the Modern Marine Corps, 1936–1943.* Annapolis, MD: Naval Institute Press, 2011.

_____. *Records of the Second Division (Regular).* 9 vols. Washington, DC: Army War College, 1927.

United States Marine Corps. *History of the 96th Company, 6th Marine Regiment in World War I.* Washington, DC: U.S. Marine Corps, 1967.

_____. *A Brief History of the Sixth Regiment, United States Marine Corps.* N.d.

White, William Richard, and Ben Wofford. *The Marine: A Guadalcanal Survivor's Final Battle.* Annapolis, MD: Naval Institute Press, 2002.

SOURCES

Bowling, John D. Biographical information comes from the *Baltimore Sun*, June 19, 1919.

Brailsford, Thomas Reed. Biographical material and accounts of Brailsford's going missing at Belleau Wood from his burial file in Record Group 92, Records of the Quartermaster General, Cemeterial Division, 1915–1939, U.S. National Archives, College Park, MD (hereafter notated as ROQG). Also see Robert Asprey's notes of his interview, June 25, 1963, with Clifton Cates for his book *At Belleau Wood* (see bibliography), found in Folder 9a, Box 1, Asprey Notes, Records, and Correspondence, Marine Corps Personal Papers Collection, Archives and Special Collections, U.S. Marine Corps University, Quantico, VA. Hereafter known as Asprey Notes.

Brannen, Carl. See *Over There* in bibliography.

Butler, Smedley. *Devil Dogs: Fighting Marines of World War I* in bibliography. Excerpt from Butler's 1933 speech on interventionism found online at http://fas .org/man/smedley.html.

Cale, Harrison. Description of marine life and Belleau Wood from "The American Marines at Verdun, Château-Thierry, Bouresches and Belleau Wood," *Indiana Magazine of History*, Volume XV, 1919. Biographical information comes from the *Indianapolis News*, November 22, 1907.

Carter, James. His description of France is from the *Bridgeton* (NJ) *Evening News*, June 29, 1918.

Cates, Anderson. Biographical information comes from *History and Families, Lake County, Tennessee*. Paducah, KY: Turner Publishing, 1993.

Cates, Clifton Bledsoe. Cates's prewar and 1917–1919 letters were found in "Some Personal Letters and Notes of General Clifton B. Cates, USMC," and are part of the Clifton B. Cates Papers (COLL/3157) at the Marine Corps Archives and Special Collections Branch, Library of the Marine Corps, Gray Research Center, Quantico, VA. The author also made extensive use of the Oral History Transcript of Cates's interview with Benis M. Frank, found in the Marine Corps Oral History Collection, History Division, Quantico, VA. The anecdote about his college football career comes from an undated newspaper article titled "Brilliant Military Career for Tiptonville's Gen. Cates" found in his papers; the vignette of Cates's playing baseball from "Between Battles with Our Fighting Men" by George H. Seldes, *Atlanta Constitution*, October 6, 1918. See also Cates's correspondence with the American Battle Monuments Commission, RG 117, Entry 31—his account of June 14, 1918, gassing in Box 190, "Description of the attack of the 2nd Batt. 6th Marines" in Box 191; his "Personal Observations of the Taking of Bouresches" found in his papers and in RG 127, Entry 240, Box 49, and his brief account of Blanc Mont, "Memo Battalion Commander," found in RG 127, Entry 240, Box 36, both at the National Archives in Washington, DC. Cates also penned an extensive recollection of the Guadalcanal campaign titled, simply, *Guadalcanal*, which can also be found in his papers. Also see Asprey Notes for Cates's account of Belleau Wood.

Cates, Willis. His obituary found in the *Lake County Historical Yearbook*. Lake County Historical Society, 1985. Graciously provided by Dr. Winifred Smith.

Catlin, Albertus. See *With the Help of God and a Few Marines* in bibliography.

Cooke, Elliott D. His accounts of Belleau Wood and Soissons found in *Americans vs. Germans* in bibliography.

Cowen, Oren. The November 29, 1918, letter to his mother is from the *Altoona* (PA) *Tribune*, December 24, 1918.

Denig, Robert L. His account of Soissons from "Diary of a Marine Officer During the World War," Marine Corps Personal Papers Collection, Archives and Special Collections, U.S. Marine Corps University, Quantico, VA.

Dunlavy, Herbert. Biographical information from the *Pueblo* (CO) *Chieftain*, August 26, 1918.

Dunton, Orley M. His account of Belleau Wood from "Mussing Up the Prussian Guard," *Hearst's Magazine*, December 1918.

Erskine, Graves B. His account of Belleau Wood found in RG 117, Entry 39, Correspondence with the American Battle Monuments Commission, National Archives, College Park, MD. His account of the St. Mihiel operation from the Graves B. Erskine Oral History Transcript, Marine Corps Oral History Collection, History Division, Quantico, VA.

Finn, James M. Account of Finn's death comes from Harold D. Powell's letter in the *Neosho* (MO) *News*, August 10, 1918.

Fischbach, John. His account of St. Mihiel was found in the *Aberdeen* (SD) *American*, November 12, 1918.

Grober, Edward A. Information on his death comes from the 96th Company muster roll, April 1918, accessed via www.ancestry.com. Further biographical information comes from the 1910 federal census.

Hamilton, George. His account of the attack on June 6, 1918, is found in Cowing and Cooper, eds., *"Dear Folks at Home"* (see bibliography).

Hanson, Raymond. See Lindsey, *Rock Hanson: The Life of a Hero* in bibliography.

Holcomb, Thomas. See Ulbrich, *Preparing for Victory* in bibliography.

Hughes, Johnny "The Hard." Account of Hughes's lingering wounds from *Leatherneck* magazine, November 2001, and *Fortitudine: Bulletin of the Marine Corps Historical Program*, Volume 23, Number 2, Fall 1993.

Iotte, Charles V. The account of his criminal past comes from the *Duluth* (MN) *News-Tribune*, July 22, 1914.

Jackson, Gilder. See Gilder's monograph *Operations of the 20th Company 5th Marines (2nd Division) at Blanc Mont in the Champagne Offensive, October 1–4, 1918*, Donovan Research Library, Fort Benning, GA.

Kelly, John J. The account of his actions at St. Mihiel and Blanc Mont are found in James Hopper's *Medals of Honor*. See bibliography.

Krulewitch, Melvin L. His account of the last days of the war was found in *Now That You Mention It* (see Hamilton and Corbin, eds., bibliography).

Lapine, Meyer J. Account of patrols from "The First to Fight: The Stories of the Marines" in *Echoes from Over There* (see bibliography).

Lockhart, George B. Biographical information comes from Anderson, *Record of Service in the World War of V.M.I. Alumni and their Alma Mater* (see bibliography). Account of wounds from 96th Company muster roll, June 1918.

Mabbott, Douglas. See Cowing and Cooper, eds., *"Dear Folks at Home"* in bibliography.

McQuain, Thomas. See Owen, *To the Limit of Endurance* in bibliography.

Meek, Samuel. His account of Johnny Overton's death and the shelling he and Clifton Cates endured on September 15, 1918, can be found in Berry, *Make the Kaiser Dance* (see bibliography).

Metcalfe, James Hartford. Account of death from 96th Company muster roll, April 1918. Letter from Donald Duncan found in an undated newspaper clipping in ROQG.

Miller, John T. His account of his service is from "Why I Hate a German" in Fox and Forrestal, eds., *What the Boys Did Over There* (see bibliography).

Nelson, Havelock D. Account of Soissons from *Leatherneck* magazine: "Soissons," April 1940; "We Go In," May 1940; "In Action," June 1940; "Under Fire," July 1940. His account of the action at the Meuse River comes from "Armistice," *Leatherneck* magazine, January 1941.

Norman, Edward O. Norman's account of training at Rheinbrohl comes from the *Lead* (SD) *Daily Call*, February 21, 1919.

Osborn, Homer. Osborn's July 29, 1943, letter to Cates found in Cates's papers.

Paradis, Don V. See *The World War I Memoirs of Don V. Paradis* in bibliography.

Pike, Lloyd. See "A Marine at Belleau Wood: Recollections of WWI Action" in the July 1979 issue of *Historical Wyoming*, Vol. XXVI, no. 1.

Pottle, Frederick A. His account of gas effects from his book *Stretchers* (see bibliography).

Powell, Harold D. His description of France comes from the *Galena* (KS) *Weekly Republican*, March 15, 1918. Powell's description of the end of the war was found in the December 27, 1918, edition of the same newspaper. See also the source listing for *Finn, James M.*

Rhodes, Robert. Account of Rhodes's actions at Soissons from "Between Battles with Our Fighting Men" by George H. Seldes, Atlanta, October 6, 1918. The account of Rhodes being wounded is in Clifton Cates's December 16, 1918, letter to Cates's family.

Sachs, William L. Sachs's description of the fighting at Soissons was found in the *Brooklyn Daily Eagle*, November 15, 1918.

Sellers, James McBrayer. Most of his material comes from Sellers and Clarke, eds., *World War I Memoirs* (see bibliography). Also, "Memoirs of James McBrayer Sellers" from World War I Veterans Survey, Military History Institute, and Sellers's July 29, 1986, letter to Edward M. Coffman describing his service, also from the World War I Survey.

Shanley, Walter A. His account of the June 14, 1918, gas attack is found in Cowing and Cooper, eds., *"Dear Folks at Home"* (see bibliography).

Shepherd, Lemuel. Anecdote about taking a physical comes from Camp, *Leatherneck Legends* (see bibliography); anecdote about Cates's shooting a German officer comes from Berry, *Make the Kaiser Dance* (see bibliography).

Sheridan, Aloysius. His account of the attack on Bouresches and Donald Duncan's death can be found in Cowing and Cooper, eds., *"Dear Folks at Home"* (see bibliography).

Short, Lloyd. Letters and biographical information come from the World War I Survey, Military History Institute, and ROQG.

Silverthorn, Merwin. See Cowing and Cooper, eds., *"Dear Folks at Home"* in bibliography.

Smyser, Lynn. Account of Blanc Mont found in *Cook County* (IL) *Herald*, November 15, 1918.

Steinberg, Julius. Account of wounding and biographical information comes from *Omaha* (NE) *World Herald*, June 19, 1918; also his draft-registration card.

Stewart, Thomas. Letter from Stewart found in *Wellington* (KS) *Daily News*, July 24, 1918.

Stites, Joseph. Stites's letters found in *Hopkinsville* (KY) *Kentuckian*, August 7, 1918. See also his December 1, 1964, interview with author Edward M. Coffman in Coffman's papers at the George C. Marshall Foundation, Lexington, VA, recording transcribed by the author.

Stockham, Fred. Biographical information comes from *Leatherneck* magazine, June 2008. Also see Clifton Cates's article, "Bravest Man I Ever Knew," in the March 1952 issue of *Saga* magazine.

Turner, Bernola. Account of Turner's death is from *Beaver* (OK) *Herald*, September 4, 1919.

Turngren, Gus. Account of his death from gassing found in his file in ROQG.

Waples, Gerald. His account of the attack on Bouresches comes from *Omaha* (NE) *World Herald*, October 17, 1918.

West, John A. His account of Blanc Mont is found in RG 117, Entry 39, Box 193, Correspondence with the American Battle Monuments Commission, National Archives, College Park, MD. Biographical material is from Owen, *To the Limit of Endurance* in bibliography.

Williams, Ernest C. His account of St. Mihiel from "Operation Report Covering Period from September 12 to September 15, 1918"; account of Blanc Mont from "Operation Report Covering Period from September 29 to October 10, 1918"; account of Meuse-Argonne from "Operation Report (Covering Period Nov. 1 to 11, 1918)," all found in RG 127, Box 36, National Archives, Washington, DC. The account of his being relieved of command is from Clifton Cates's Oral History Transcript.

Williams, Everett. His account of Blanc Mont was found in *Iowa City Press-Citizen*, February 6, 1919. His account of Christmas 1918 comes from the December 26 issue of the same newspaper.

Williams, Stanley. Williams's account of Soissons was found in *Osawatomie* (KS) *Graphic*, August 22, 1918, and *Wellington* (KS) *Daily News*, November 15, 1918.

Worton, William A. His anecdotes about training at Quantico come from the William A. Worton Oral History Transcript, Marine Corps Oral History Collection, History Division, Quantico, VA.

INDEX

Adams, James P., 212
Aire River, 261, 262
Aisne-Marne American Cemetery, 121n, 255
Aisne River, 66, 220, 257, 258
Allen, T. S., 122
Alpine Chausseurs, 55
American Battle Monuments Commission, 302
American Civil War, 12, 126, 163
Amiens, 63
Anamites, 58, 69
Anderson, Earl, 53
Ansauville, 217
Argonne Forest, 197, 260
Arlington National Cemetery, 316
Armistice, 269, 279–81, 282, 285–89
Armstrong, Frank, 313
Arras, 63
Asprey, Robert B., 142
Atlanta Constitution, 193
Ayers, Brown, 13
Ayers, John, 13

Babcock, Sam, 307
Balaklava, 186
Ballard, Arthur Roland, 239
Barbed wire, 64, 206, 253
Barnett, George, 19–20, 22, 289, 301, 302, 313
Barricourt Ridge, 267, 272
Bates, George Cleveland, 239
Bayonet theory, 39
Bayonville, 270
Bayonville–Fosse road, 273
Bearss, "Hiking Hiram," 17, 207
Beaumont, 274, 275
Beaurepaire Farm, 148, 156, 162, 186
Beauvais, 67
Belfry, Earl, 99
Belgium, 289

Bellamy, David, 91
Belleau village, 74, 118
Belleau Wood (*see* Bois de Belleau)
Belval–Beaumont road, 274
Berg, Clara, 190
Berg, Gustave, 190
Berry, Benjamin, 81, 83, 86–90, 92, 93, 105, 111, 136
Berzy-le-Sec, 148, 184
Bézu-le-Guéry, 146
Blanc Mont (Blanc Mont Ridge), 6, 15, 216–17,
    220–50, 254, 254n, 256, 257, 264, 265, 271,
    283, 284, 294, 296, 299–301, 307, 312,
    313, 319
Blevaincourt, 47–51
Blodnitz Hill, 245, 247
Bloody Ridge, Guadalcanal, 308, 309
Boehm, Max von, 136
Bois de Belleau (Belleau Wood), 2, 6, 15, 68,
    72–74, 77, 79–93, 95, 101, 103, 104, 110,
    115–19, 121, 127, 129–42, 146, 150, 158, 165,
    180, 188, 189, 193, 202, 217, 221, 248, 256n,
    283, 284, 291, 293, 300, 306, 307, 311–13
Bois de Belval, 274, 275
Bois de Bouresches, 73, 77
Bois de Clerembauts, 85, 92
Bois de Four, 275
Bois de Gros Jean, 133, 137
Bois de Hazois, 267, 270
Bois de la Brigade de Marine, 135
Bois de la Folie, 272–74
Bois de la Vipère, 226
Bois de Lechelle, 157, 179
Bois de l'Hospice, 277
Bois de la Montagne, 208, 212
Bois de Montrebeau, 261, 262, 265
Bois de Quesnoy, 155
Bois de Romagne, 263
Bois de Tigny, 182

Bois du Fond du Limon, 276, 278, 280, 283
Bois du Port Gerache, 274
Bois l'Evêque, 201
Bolshevik Revolution, 61
Bouresches village, 73, 74, 77, 79, 85, 89–101,
    103–11, 115, 117, 120, 133, 137, 141, 144, 167,
    186, 193, 195, 203, 265, 284, 293, 296, 299,
    300, 307, 316
Bowers, Perry Franklin, 239
Bowling, John Dominic, 34, 101, 121n, 200, 204,
    239, 289, 302
Boxer Rebellion, 17, 19
Boyau de Bromberg, 222
Boyd, Thomas, 188–89
Boylan, James F., 239
Brailsford, Thomas Reed, 34, 95, 101–02, 121,
    121n, 137, 200, 289
Branham & Hughes School for Boys, 10
Brannen, Carl, 133, 170, 171, 173, 176–78, 182,
    186, 211, 212, 224, 228
Brest-Litovsk, Treaty of, 61
British 5th Army, 62
Brown, Preston, 73, 80
Bundy, Omar, 67, 73, 149
Bunnell, Ruskin, 307
Butler, Smedley Darlington, 17–19
Buzancy, 148, 273

Cale, Harrison, 35, 46, 47, 52–55, 71, 75, 96, 100,
    105, 124–25, 127, 129
Camp Bon Champ, 45
Canal Zone, 33, 34
Cantigny, 63, 65, 67, 87, 112, 149, 196, 262
Capps, Lieutenant, 289
Carter, James W., 51
Casualties, 6, 44–45, 53–55, 61, 62, 79, 83–85, 89,
    90, 94, 96, 101, 103, 105, 108, 117–19, 123–26,
    129, 130, 135, 137, 147, 157, 159, 161, 162,
    168–73, 176, 180, 183–87, 194, 210, 214, 223,
    225, 242, 244, 246–47, 254, 254n, 263, 271,
    272, 277, 284, 285, 309–11
Cates, Alice Jane Emily Peacock, 7
Cates, Anderson, 7
Cates, Ann, 302
Cates, Clifton Bledsoe, 4–5, 72, 79, 119, 150, 195,
    205, 207, 208, 254, 257–60, 296–98
    armistice and, 286–87
    assigned to 96th Company, 32–36
    assigned to 4th Platoon, 134
    Atlantic crossing and, 46
    awards of, 294
    barbed wire, entanglement in, 64
    as Barnett's aide, 301, 302
    at Belleau Wood, 2, 6, 84, 121, 127, 131–34, 137,
        140–41, 193, 293, 300, 306, 307
    birth of, 8
    at Blanc Mont, 216–17, 221–29, 232–36, 238,
        239, 241, 246–51, 256, 292–94, 296, 299,
        300–01, 307, 319
    at Blevaincourt, 48, 49
    at Bouresches village, 93, 95–101, 103, 105–06,
        108, 109, 111, 120, 133, 137, 144, 193, 293, 296,
        299, 300, 307, 316
    boyhood of, 7–9, 13, 317
    burial of, 316
    children of, 302
    on civilian misery, 60
    command of 1st Marine Regiment, 299,
        303–06, 308–09
    command of 4th Marine Division, 309
    as commandant of Marine Corps, 6, 78,
        311–15, 319
    as commandant of Marine Corps Schools,
        309, 315
    courage of, 6, 133, 190, 294
    death of, 316
    death of father of, 11
    on departure from Quantico, 42–43
    dugout of, 53
    education of, 9–11, 13
    enlists in Marine Corps, 15, 22, 25
    farewell party and, 41
    feelings on war, 1–3, 10, 94, 164, 172, 189–91,
        252–53, 299–300
    finances of, 25, 142–43
    firing at German planes by, 146, 159,
        178, 304
    first taste of shellfire, 52
    food and, 138, 295
    forming and equipping 96th, 32–33
    French language and, 46–47
    full pack, description of, 65
    on gas masks, 115, 123
    at Guadalcanal, 299, 303–06, 308–09, 313
    Harbord and, 70
    hatred of Germans and, 133
    health of, 256, 270, 289–90, 316
    helmet hit by bullet, 97–98
    Holcomb and, 31–32, 293–94
    as husband and father, 299
    "I will hold" said by, 181
    at Iwo Jima, 311
    lack of sleep and, 55–56, 111, 239
    ladies, interest in, 11, 40
    law degree of, 11
    leadership abilities of, 15, 23, 142, 145
    on leave, 203, 301
    luck of, 6, 31, 57, 64, 100, 109, 128, 131, 132,
        140, 141, 144, 165, 170, 181, 187, 192–94,
        213–14, 253, 257, 269, 272, 278, 287, 297, 311
    march to Germany and, 289–94
    marriage to Jane, 302
    in Meuse-Argonne, 264–65, 267–75, 278,
        283–84, 286–87, 293, 307
    on morale of men, 112–13
    mustard-gas attacks and, 40, 121–24, 127–29
    nominated for Medal of Honor, 256n, 293–94
    as officer candidate, 25

origins of, 6
outfitting of, 25
in Paris, 135, 136, 141–43
at Parris Island, 26, 29
personality of, 6, 9–10, 133, 190
physical examination of, 23–24
at Pont-à-Mousson, 197–201
postwar history of company, 45, 101
promotions of, 293, 302, 319
at Quantico, Virginia, 29, 30–31
retirement from Marine Corps, 315
Robertson and, 98–99, 99n
near St. Mihiel Salient, 213–15
selflessness of, 112
sense of humor of, 32
at Soissons, 2, 6, 160, 164–67, 170–72,
    175–77, 180–82, 184–85, 191, 193, 293,
    300, 306–08, 316
sports and, 10
Stockham and, 33
on tanks, 173
at Tinian, 309–10
training of men and, 36, 39, 45, 49–50, 296
trench feet and, 50
on weather, 64, 275, 283–84
wilderness and, 9
will of, 41
on Williams, 199, 291
wounded, 165, 170, 176, 177, 187, 193, 289
Cates, Clifton Jr., 302
Cates, Jane Virginia McIlhenny, 302, 315
Cates, Martha "Mattie" Darnall Bledsoe, 8, 10,
    11, 26, 40, 41, 53, 256
Cates, Susan Box, 7
Cates, Willis Jones, 7–11, 41
Cates Landing, Tennessee, 6, 7, 10, 11, 13, 22, 26,
    316, 317
Catlin, Albertus Wright, 17, 19, 21, 51, 67, 69,
    74, 76, 78, 86–90, 92, 110
Châlons, 219, 220, 257
Champagne, 147, 219, 257, 316, 318
Champillon, 81
Chancellorsville, Battle of, 12
Charantigny, 165
Charlesfort, South Carolina, 26–27
Charmes-la-Côte, 217–18
Charpentry, 261
Château-Thierry, 67, 72, 74, 112
Chaudon, 155, 156
Chaumont-en-Vexin, 67
Chavigny, 193, 194
Chazelle, 158
Chemin des Dames, 66
Cheppy, 261
Chicago Tribune, 87–88
China, 17, 18, 31, 33
Chlorine, 115
Churchill, Winston, 292
Clark, George B., 17, 18, 280

Clemens, Martin, 304
Clignon brook, 74
Close-order drill, 39–40
Coblenz, 289, 297
Coffenburg, Bailey, 86, 130
Cold Harbor, Battle of, 163
Colford, Sydney, 31
Company K (March aka Campbell), 189
Compiègne forest, 63
Cooke, Elliott D., 118, 119, 151, 158
Côte Dame Marie, 263
Côte de Châtillon, 255, 263, 264, 266
Crandall, Jesse L., 200
Creed, Carlos, 210
Crockett, Davy, 8
Croix de Guerre, 256n, 294
Cuba, 17–19
Cukela, Louis, 153
Cunningham, Leslie, 35, 108
Cunningham, Robert, 35, 108
Cutry, 152

Daly, Dan, 18–19, 75, 88, 301
Darnall, Henry McKinney, 8
Denig, Robert L., 162, 164, 166–68, 170–72,
    176–79, 183–85
Dessez, "Bobo," 24–25
Devareaux, Margaret, 11
Dieulouard, 196
Distinguished Service Cross, 99n, 110, 203, 211,
    231, 256n, 294
Dominican Republic, 18, 37
Dommartin-lès-Toul, 195
Dorrell, John Lee, 239
Doyen, Charles A., 70
Draft, 20
Drum, Hugh, 266
Duane, Robert, 138, 145, 167, 200, 289
Duncan, Donald Francis "Napoleon," 33–35, 41,
    44, 92–95, 97, 101, 288, 293
Dunlavy, Herbert Dillard "Tex," 34–35, 49, 79,
    100, 109–10
Dunton, Orley M., 71, 78

Eddy, William, 80
Edgewater, Maryland, 315, 316
80th Marine Corps Company, 246, 271–72,
    273, 281
Eisenhower, Dwight D., 7
Elbe trench, 222
Ellis, Michael "Mad Dog," 5
Erlandson, Alfred, 239
Erskine, Graves B., 104–08, 145, 198, 208–12,
    214, 229, 310
Essen Hook, 221, 222, 224, 228, 232, 235, 236,
    242, 245
Essen trench, 221, 224, 225, 236
Ettelbruck, 290–91
Exermont, 260, 262, 263, 265

Feland, Logan, 237
Ferguson, Louis, 21
5th Marine Corps Regiment, 20, 21, 49,
    81–83, 85, 87, 112, 116, 117, 119, 120, 124n,
    128, 136, 138, 152–57, 167, 185, 205, 207,
    221, 226, 229, 236–37, 241, 242, 246–48,
    267, 272, 274, 275, 278, 279, 284–85,
    303, 311
Finn, James M., 125, 130
1st Marine Corps Division, 20, 63, 65, 67, 87,
    148, 149, 152–53, 155, 204, 207, 262, 314
1st Marine Corps Regiment, 299, 303–06,
    308–09
1st Moroccan Division, 148, 152, 153, 155, 157,
    162, 163, 173, 183
Fischbach, John, 206
Foch, Ferdinand, 63, 147–48, 153, 197
Fort Dugny, 51
"Forty and eights" rail cars, 47
Fosse, 274
4th Marine Corps Division, 309–11
Foxholes, 76
French forces
    4th Army, 219, 220, 257, 258
    5th Army, 220
    6th Army, 67, 72
    10th Army, 148
    21st Division, 221, 232, 235, 237, 245
    22nd Division, 245, 246, 249
    38th Division, 163
    43rd Division, 74–75
    58th Division, 183, 184
    61st Division, 221, 226
    73rd Division, 257, 258
    167th Division, 81
    cavalry, 160
    French Foreign Legion, 148
    Legion of Honor, 294
French Revolution, 17
Freya Line, 267, 272
Frillman, Lewis, 211
Fritz, Bernard L., 145, 167, 200, 289

Garrett, Franklin, 292
Garrison, Russell, 168
Gas, 40, 51, 54, 114–15, 121–30, 195
Gas masks, 115, 122, 123
German forces
    14th Reserve Division, 149, 164
    28th Division, 119, 158, 164–65
    40th Regiment, 117
    47th Reserve Division, 149
    49th Reserve Infantry, 164
    74th Reserve Infantry Regiment, 233, 234
    109th Regiment, 120
    200th Division, 235
    218th Reserve Infantry, 152
    219th Reserve Infantry, 152
    237th Division, 119

398th Regiment, 93
461st Regiment, 87, 110
aircraft, 154, 159, 162–63, 177–79, 242
Gettysburg, Battle of, 66
Gibbons, Floyd, 88, 89, 111–12, 142, 291
Goering, Hermann, 154, 177
Gondrecourt, 20, 104
Gouraud, Henri, 220
Gragard, Thomas, 106
Graham, Charles D., 55
Grant, Ulysses S., 7, 163
Grauer, Earl, 179–80
Grayson, Lieutenant, 289
Greeks, 12
Green, Kirt, 271–72
Greenburg, Joseph, 77, 125, 126
Greene, Captain, 288
Grober, Edward Adolph, 44, 45, 53
Grober, Rose, 44
Guadalcanal, 299, 303–06, 308–09, 313
Guadalcanal Diary (Tregaskis), 305
Guam, 34, 312
Guantanamo Bay, 19
Guerry, John B., 126
Guerry, Theodore LeGrande, 126

Haig, Sir Douglas, 197
Haiti, 16, 18, 19
Hall, Virgil A., 124
Hamilton, George, 81–83, 242–44
Hanson, Raymond, 179–80, 307
Harbord, James, 70–72, 74, 80, 85–87, 119, 120,
    136, 149, 162, 219
Hartzell, Oscar, 89
Hattonchâtel, 207
Hayden, David, 210
Hehl, Lambert, 53
Helenen Hill, 221
Hemrick, Levi, 28, 29, 59
Henderson Field, Guadalcanal, 303
Hill 142, 74, 78, 80, 81, 119
Hill 181, 90, 91, 116
Hill 204, 73
Hill 231.5, 212
Hill 253, 270
Hindenburg Flying Circus, 177, 198, 262
Hindenburg Line, 61, 208, 255, 261, 263, 264,
    266, 267
Hines, John, 291–92
Hoadley, William T., 30
Holcomb, Beatrice Clover, 31, 94
Holcomb, Frank, 39
Holcomb, Thomas, 31–33, 39, 46, 73, 76, 92, 94,
    99, 120, 121, 130–31, 139, 140, 163–65, 167,
    168, 170, 176, 177, 180, 184, 198, 213, 247,
    256n, 293–94, 300, 303
Huebner, Clarence, 7
Hughes, Johnny "the Hard," 17, 37, 39, 74, 116,
    117, 163, 165, 168, 183

Ichiki, Kiyono, 305, 306
Ichiki Battalion, 304–05
Influenza, 218, 256, 278
Iotte, Charles V., 35
Iwo Jima, 310–11, 313

Jackson, Gilder D. Jr., 229, 237, 240, 242, 296–97
Jackson, Stonewall, 12
Jaulny, 207
Johanningsmeier, Ollie Henry, 79
Johnson, Lieutenant, 289
Joint Chiefs of Staff, 312
Juilly, 129

Kane, Barney J., 225, 289
Kelly, John Joseph, 5, 211–12, 223, 230, 231, 256n
Keyser, Ralph, 151
Kilduff, David, 209, 288
King, Mary F., 190
Korean War, 313–14
Krefeld trench, 221, 222
Kriemehild Stellung, 255
Krulewitch, Melvin L., 280, 282

La Cense Farm, 85
La Cense ravine, 93
La Ferté, 290
La Tuilerie Farm, 274
Landres-et-St. Georges, 263, 264, 270
Landreville, 270
Langston, Irby F., 36
Lapine, Meyer J., 56–57
Larsen, Harry, 242
Le Gore, Harry, 21
Le Thiolet, 73
Lechelle, 148
Leckie, Robert, 310
Lee, Harry, 110, 163, 180, 181, 183, 193, 198, 225, 247, 249
Lee, Robert E., 12
Leffincourt, 257, 258
Lejeune, John Archer, 17, 30, 219–21, 249n, 254n, 257, 258, 266, 278–79, 281, 293, 301
Lenert, Henry, 138
Lenihan, Michael, 263–64
Les Mares Farm, 74, 78, 81
Letanne, 276, 279
Limey, 205
Liverdun, 195
Lloyd, Egbert, 181
Lockhart, George B., 34, 94, 130, 200, 203, 289
Loire River, 46
Lorraine, 63
"Lost Battalion," 5
Lucy-le-Bocage, 72–74, 86, 89, 90, 115, 120, 130, 137
Lucy-le-Bocage ravine, 92
Ludendorff, Erich, 61–63, 66, 146, 147

Ludwigs-Rucken, 243
Luxembourg, 290

Mabbott, Douglas, 142
MacArthur, Douglas, 255, 263–64, 266, 312, 313
Mack, Thomas, 239
Mackin, Elton, 156–57, 243, 244, 277, 284, 285
Mahon, Eddie, 21
Maison Blanche, 120
Maison Neuve Farm, 155
Manassas, Second Battle of, 126
Mangin, Charles "the Butcher," 148
Manning, Harry, 180
Manonville, 205
Marbache sector, 197
March, William (aka Campbell, William Edward), 189
Marine, The: A Guadalcanal Survivor's Final Battle (White and Wofford), 303–04
Marine Corps Schools, Quantico, 309, 315
Marne River, 60, 67, 112, 146, 147, 185, 203
Marshall, George C., 197
Marshall, Winslow Belton, 16
Marshall Plan, 197
Masmes Farm, 273
Massed attack concept, 38–39
Massed drill, 39–40
Matanikau River, 308
May-en-Multien, 72, 73
Mazereeuw, Richard, 107
McClelland, Edward N., 152
McClelland, James C., 145
McCreary, Charles, 190
McCreary, Donald, 190
McDonough, Gordon L., 314
McIntosh, Sidney, 97
McPherson, James, 7
McQuain, Thomas, 281
Meaux, 71
Medal of Honor, 18, 19, 75, 88, 99n, 127, 153, 199, 231, 256n, 293–94
Meek, Samuel, 144, 166, 171, 171n, 192, 213–14
Messersmith, Robert, 41, 86, 126, 129, 243
Metcalf, Clyde, 278, 290
Metcalfe, Eva, 44
Metcalfe, James Hartford, 44, 45, 53
Metz, 196, 197, 219, 262
Meuse-Argonne offensive, 6, 197, 218–20, 255, 257, 260–87, 291, 293, 307
Meuse River, 51, 197, 261, 266, 269, 270, 274–85, 288
Mexico, 12, 18
Mexico, Missouri, 10
Mézières, 219, 261
Michael (offensive), 61
Miller, John T., 53–54, 75, 79, 97, 100
Miller, Roy M., 55
Minnis, John Andrew, 203–05, 212–14, 289, 293
Mississippi River, 6, 11, 26

Missouri Military Academy, 10
Missy Ravine, 153
Mon Plaisir Farm, 210
Mont Sec, 196
Mont-sous-les-Côtes, 52
Montdidier, 63, 65
Montreuil-aux-Lions, 71–72
Moreland, Oscar, 231
Moros, 16
Morrey, Willard, 99, 101, 307
Moselle River, 195, 197, 201, 218
Mouzon, 275, 276, 279, 280, 282
Mustard gas, 40, 114–15, 121–30, 195
Myers, John Twiggs, 17

Nancy, 194–95
Nanteuil-sur-Marne, 146
Nantivet Barracks, 257
Navarin Farm, 237n, 255
Navy Cross, 99n, 180, 211, 231, 294
Nelson, Havelock D., 161–64, 169–70, 172, 176, 178, 186, 188, 283, 286
Neville, Wendell, 163
New Madrid, Missouri, 6, 11
New York Herald, 111, 112
Nguyen That Thanh (Ho Chi Minh), 150
Nicaragua, 17, 18, 33, 34
9th Marine Corps Regiment, 154, 155, 157, 158, 245, 274
96th Marine Corps Company, 6, 32–36, 39, 44–57, 71–79, 85–91, 92–101, 103–12, 115, 119–29, 136–39, 141, 145, 146, 167, 170, 175–86, 190, 197, 200–04, 207–14, 221–41, 247, 254–59, 265, 267–73, 284, 288–98, 301, 308, 309, 316–19
No Man's Land, 56–57, 62, 206, 208–09, 252
Norman, Edward O., 296
Norris, Ravee, 264
Nouart, 273, 274
Nutting, Lester, 210–11

O'Bannon, Presley Neville, 17
Obion County, Tennessee, 8
Observation balloons, 120, 146, 164
Ogden, Paul J., 200–01
Oise River, 62
Okinawa, 312
Open-warfare theory, 38, 62, 65, 149
Orgo, Tom, 98, 307
Osborn, Homer B., 214, 318–19
Osborne, Weedon, 94
Otto, Ernst, 218, 249–50n
Overton, Johnny, 21, 140, 165–66, 171, 171n
Owen, Peter F., 282

Page, Lieutenant, 289
Paradis, Don V., 66, 99, 130, 166, 167, 174, 199, 234, 272
Parcy-Tigny, 164, 165, 177

Paris, 63, 65, 67, 69, 86, 135–36, 140–43, 146, 203, 297, 301
Paris–Metz highway, 58–60, 70–74, 120, 135, 141, 144
Paris–Soissons highway, 153, 184
Parris Island, 26–30, 32, 35, 175
Pendleton, Joseph Henderson, 17
Pershing, John J., 37–38, 51, 62, 65, 70, 149, 196, 197, 219, 257, 261, 297
Pétain, Henri-Philippe, 219
Petway, Helen, 11, 40
Philippines, 16, 17, 33
Picardy, 63, 65, 68
Pickett, George, 66
Pike, Lloyd, 103–04, 110–11
Pont-à-Mousson, 196–201, 204
Port Royal, South Carolina, 26
Pottle, Frederick A., 129
Powell, Harold D., 46, 48–49, 125, 286
Powers, Walter, 271
Prisoners, 62, 82, 104–05, 108, 118, 119, 138, 147, 153, 154, 156, 158, 161, 185, 196, 198, 203, 207, 214, 216, 229–31, 234, 235, 238, 246, 254n, 274, 306
Prothro, Katherine Cates, 8, 11, 40, 41, 53, 65, 293
Prothro, Tommy "Doc," 11
Pruitt, John H., 230–31, 256n
Purple Heart, 294

Quantico, Virginia, 29–32, 35, 37–43, 112, 175, 284, 298, 301, 311
Quick, John, 19, 99n

Rankin, Oscar, 106, 107
Raperie, 181
Rayner, Joan, 11
Reeves, Roy W., 231
Reims, 67, 146, 147, 219, 220
Remenauville, 205
Retz Forest, 148, 150, 158, 160, 185, 194
Rheinbrohl, 292–96
Rhine River, 289, 292, 294, 296
Rhodes, Robert M., 179, 265, 267–68
Richthofen, Baron von, 154, 177
Robertson, James F., 34, 84, 95, 98–99, 99n, 104, 120, 121, 129, 130, 145, 170, 193, 200, 289
Robidoux, Joseph, 34
Robinson, Lieutenant, 289
Romagne Hills, 255, 260
Rose, Elizabeth, 11, 40
Royaumeix, 217
Rupt de Mad, 208–09
Russia, 61

Sachs, William L., 185–86
St. Étienne, 220, 235–37, 241–43, 245–47, 249–50n, 254, 255, 257, 258, 262

St. Georges, 263, 264, 270
St. John, Alcide, 35–36, 130
St. Menehould, 258, 260
St. Mihiel Salient, 196, 197, 204–14, 217, 219,
    221, 227, 262, 283, 284, 312, 318
St. Mihiel village, 204, 261
St. Nazaire, 46
Saipan, 309, 313
Santo Domingo, 18
Saratoga, Battle of, 12
Schmidt, Harry, 309
Schneider, John G. Jr., 272
Schrank, John, 166
Scottish Troops, 55
Secession, 8
2nd Marine Corps Division, 49, 61, 65, 67, 69,
    70, 72, 73, 80, 87, 112, 146, 148–51, 153, 158,
    160, 204–07, 214, 217–21, 226, 232, 234, 250,
    254n, 255, 257–59, 262, 265–66, 273, 279,
    289, 291, 292
Sedan, 219, 261
Seicheprey, 63, 196, 204
Seldes, George H., 193
Sellers, James McBrayer, 30, 31, 36, 145–46, 159,
    217, 223, 229–31, 234, 236, 238, 242, 250, 256,
    256n, 266, 271–74, 282, 291
Senegalese troops, 149, 154–56, 161
Sensee River, 62
Serans, 65
78th Marine Corps Company, 36, 145, 217, 223,
    231, 234, 246, 250, 266, 271, 275, 282
79th Marine Corps Company, 246–48, 273
Shanley, Walter A., 126
Shearer, Maurice, 74, 136, 138
Shepherd, Lemuel, 24–25, 78, 235n, 311–12
Sheridan, Aloysius Patrick, 35, 94, 95, 98
Shinkle, Amos, 234
Short, Caroline, 190
Short, Lloyd, 175, 186–87, 190
Shuler, George K., 246, 249, 281–83
Shunk, Samuel Henry, 239
Sibley, Berton, 39, 74, 85, 89, 90, 92, 93, 110, 119,
    163, 168, 183, 205
Silver Star, 99n, 256n, 294
Silverthorn, Merwin, 88–89
Sissler, Joseph (aka Steele), 36, 94
Sisson, Mildred, 11
6th Marine Corps Regiment, 4–6, 21, 27, 29,
    32–39, 44–57, 45–46, 49, 51, 65, 71–79,
    85–101, 103–12, 115, 116, 119–29, 136–41, 145,
    146, 151–52, 160–63, 166, 167, 170, 175–86,
    190, 191, 197, 198, 200–05, 207–14, 221–41,
    245–47, 250, 254–59, 265–73, 275, 278–85,
    288–98, 301, 308, 309, 316–19
Smith, Frederick, 34
Smyser, Lynn, 232
Society of the 96th Company, 316
Soissons, 2, 6, 67, 147–49, 160, 164–67, 170–72,
    175–86, 188, 190, 191, 193, 196, 202, 203, 214,

215, 218, 219, 221, 248, 262, 265, 283, 284,
    291, 293, 300, 306–08, 312, 316
Soissons–Château-Thierry highway, 148, 157,
    162, 164, 180, 182, 185
Soissons–Meaux road, 72
Somme-Py, 220–22, 237n, 255
Somme-Py–St. Étienne road, 237, 242, 244, 245
Somme River, 61, 114
Soto, Hernando de, 8
Spalding, Evans, 34
Spanish-American War, 19
Spark, Victor D., 189
Standard Oil Company, 18
Stanton, Joseph Aloysius, 239
State, U.S. Department of, 18
Steinberg, Julius "the Count," 35, 79
Stewart, Thomas L., 59–60, 95, 109, 131
Stiles, Ruth, 11
Stites, Joseph, 101, 128
Stockham, Fred W., 33, 36, 125–27, 130, 256n
Stone, E. R., 249
Strand, Walter, 239, 289
Submarine warfare, 12, 46, 61
Suippes, 220, 221, 256–59
Summerall, Charles P., 263–64, 266, 269, 273,
    278–79
Sumner, Allen, 164, 168, 183

Tanks, 62, 149, 151, 154, 157, 160, 163, 165–67, 173,
    226, 236, 271
Tarawa, 83, 313
Taylor, Lieutenant, 289
Tenaru River, 305, 306, 308, 309, 310
Thermopylae, Battle of, 12
Thiaucourt, 206, 207, 217
3rd Marine Corps Division, 112, 147
36th Marine Corps Division, 219, 250, 254, 255,
    256, 258
Thomas, Gerald, 305
Thomason, John W. Jr., 17, 69, 81, 117, 138–39,
    153–56, 229, 243–44
Through the Wheat: A Novel of the World War I
    Marines (Boyd), 188–89
Tigny, 164, 165, 172, 176, 177, 178, 180, 182
Time magazine, 315
Tinian, 309–10
Tintigny, 290
Tonquinese, 58
Torcy, 82, 140
Toul, 217, 219
Tregaskis, Richard, 305, 313
Trench feet, 50
Trench warfare, 38, 39, 51–53, 63
Triangle Farm, 73, 75
Triangle Woods, 93, 94
Truman, Harry S., 311–15
Turner, Bernola, 228–29
Turngren, Gus Andrew "Bullet Head," 35, 125
Turrill, Julius, 81, 156

23rd Marine Corps Regiment, 245, 247, 249,
    270, 273, 274, 275
26th Marine Corps Division, 204, 207

Uhlrich, Bill, 210
United States forces. (*see also* United States
    Marine Corps)
    1st Army, 196, 218, 258, 261, 262
    1st Division, 255, 260, 263, 266
    28th Division, 262
    32nd Division, 262, 263
    35th Division, 260, 261, 262, 266, 315
    42nd Division, 255, 263–65, 266, 270
    77th Division, 279
    82nd Division, 262
    89th Division, 266, 279, 284, 285
    90th Division, 279
United States Marine Corps. (*see also* specific
    Divisions and Regiments)
    creation of, 16
    foreign operations of, 15–18
    motto of, 19
    publicity and, 111–12
    qualifications of applicants, 21
    recruitment by, 20–21
    size of, 19, 20
    stirring words spoken, 75, 88
    training and, 27–31, 36, 49–50
    Truman and, 314–15
University of Minnesota, 21
University of Tennessee, 10–11
USS *California*, 302
USS *George Washington*, 298
USS *Henderson*, 4–5, 14–15, 42, 45–46

Vale, Archie, 212, 229
Valley Forge, 12
Valmy, 258
Van Cleve, Andrew Jackson, 225, 239
Vandegrift, Alexander, 305, 311, 312
Vandoren, Lucian, 183–84, 203, 205, 217, 224,
    291, 302
Varennes, 261
Vauxcastle Ravine, 156–57
Vera Cruz, 18, 34
Verdun sector, 45, 51, 63, 64, 186
Versailles, Treaty of, 298
Verte Feuille Farm, 154, 161–62
Vierzy, 148, 156–58, 162–66, 180, 184, 189, 194
Villemontoire, 165, 172, 173, 179, 182, 183

Villemontry, 276, 277
Vimy, 186
Vosges Mountains, 47
Vosges region, 61, 63

Wake Island, 311
Walker, Phoebe, 11
Waller, Littleton Waller Tazewell, 17
Waples, Gerald, 96–97
War Is a Racket (Butler), 18
Ward, Peter, 94
Washington, George, 12
Washington Times, 16
Wass, Lester, 157
Waterloo, Battle of, 12
Weaver, William, 179–80
Weismantel, Clarence, 78
Wellington, Duke of, 12
West, John, 109, 233–34, 247–48, 297
White, William Richard, 303–04
Whittlesey, Charles, 5
Wilhelm II, Kaiser, 254
Williams, Dick "Terrible Terry," 24
Williams, Ernest C. "Bull," 199, 201, 208–09,
    213, 214, 217, 221, 225, 226, 235–37, 245,
    246, 248, 249, 257, 270–73, 278, 282,
    291–92
Williams, Everett, 255, 295
Williams, Lloyd, 75, 117
Williams, Red, 170
Williams, Stanley, 160–61, 171–72, 180
Wilmer, Pere, 168, 177, 193, 203
Wilson, Woodrow, 20, 301
Wise, Frederic "Fritz," 74, 75, 116–19, 121, 130
Woëvre plain, 196
Wofford, Ben, 303–04
Wolf, Ernest, 101–02
Woodfill, Sam, 5
Woodworth, Wethered, 138, 140, 145, 170, 180,
    200, 204, 211, 289, 293, 302
Worton, William A., 30, 34, 41–42, 48

Xammes, 207, 208
Xammes–Charey road, 208, 212

York, Alvin C., 5, 262–63
York, Holcomb, 21
Ypres salient, 66, 115

Zane, Randolph, 86, 93, 103–05, 145